Housing Privatization in Eastern Europe

Recent Titles in
Contributions in Sociology

Cultural Conflict and the Swedish Sexual Myth: The Male Immigrant's Encounter with
Swedish Sexual and Cohabitation Culture
  Sven-Axel Månsson

For Democracy: The Noble Character and Tragic Flaws of the Middle Class
  Ronald M. Glassman, William H. Swatos, Jr., and Peter Kivisto

Social Oppression
  Adam Podgórecki

Eastern Europe in Transition: The Impact of Sociology
  Mike Forrest Keen and Janusz Mucha, editors

Stepparenting: Issues in Theory, Research, and Practice
  Kay Pasley and Marilyn Ihinger-Tallman, editors

The Temptation to Forget: Racism, Anti-Semitism, Neo-Nazism
  Franco Ferrarotti

Critical Theory and Political Possibilities: Conceptions of Emancipatory Politics in the
Works of Horkheimer, Adorno, Marcuse, and Habermas
  Joan Alway

Demographic and Structural Change: The Effects of the 1980s on American Society
  Dennis L. Peck and J. Selwyn Hollingsworth, editors

Family, Women, and Employment in Central–Eastern Europe
  Barbara Lobodzinska, editor

Constructing the Nation–State: International Organization and Prescriptive Action
  Connie L. McNeely

New Poverty: Families for Postmodern Society
  David Cheal

Housing Privatization
in
Eastern Europe

Edited by
David Clapham, József Hegedüs,
Keith Kintrea, and Iván Tosics,
with Helen Kay

Contributions in Sociology,
Number 117

GREENWOOD PRESS
Westport, Connecticut • London

Every reasonable effort has been made to trace Jörg Köhli and Stoicho Motev, who are contributors to this book, but this has proven impossible. The editors and publisher will be glad to receive information leading to more up-to-date acknowledgments in subsequent printings of the book and, in the meantime, extend their apologies for any omissions.

Library of Congress Cataloging-in-Publication Data

Housing privatization in Eastern Europe / edited by David Clapham . . .
   [et al.].
      p.   cm. — (Contributions in sociology, ISSN 0084–9278 ; no.
   117)
      Includes bibliographical references and index.
      ISBN 0–313–27214–X (alk. paper)
      1. Housing—Europe, Eastern.   2. Privatization—Europe, Eastern.
   I. Clapham, David.   II. Series.
HD7332.9.A3H68   1996
363.5'0947—dc20   96–10740

British Library Cataloguing in Publication Data is available.

Library of Congress Catalog Card Number: 96–10740
ISBN: 0–313–27214–X
ISSN: 0084–9278

First published in 1996

Greenwood Press, 88 Post Road West, Westport, CT 06881
An imprint of Greenwood Publishing Group, Inc.

Printed in the United States of America

The paper used in this book complies with the
Permanent Paper Standard issued by the National
Information Standards Organization (Z39.48–1984).

10 9 8 7 6 5 4 3 2 1

Contents

Figures and Tables   vii

Acknowledgments   ix

Introduction   xi

1   Analyzing Housing Privatization   1
     David Clapham and Keith Kintrea

2   The Disintegration of the East European Housing Model   15
     József Hegedüs and Iván Tosics

3   The New *Länder* of Germany   41
     Jörg Köhli and Keith Kintrea

4   Hungary   57
     József Hegedüs, Katharine Mark, Csilla Sárkány, and Iván Tosics

5   The Russian Federation   79
     Mikhail Berezin, Olga Kaganova, Nodezdha Kosareva,
     Andrey Pritkov, and Raymond Struyk

6   Bulgaria   97
     Sasha Tsenkova, George Georgiev, Stoicho Motev,
     and Dimitar Dimitrov

7   Poland   119
     Edward Kozlowski

8   Czechoslovakia   135
     Peter Michalovic

9   Slovenia   151
     Srna Mandič

10   The Patterns of Housing Privatization in Eastern Europe   169
     David Clapham and Keith Kintrea

Selected Bibliography   191

Index   195

About the Editors and Contributors   203

Figures and Tables

FIGURES

4.1 Privatization of Budapest public rental stock 71

4.2 Characteristics of the public rental stock in Budapest
by privatization status 72

4.3 Characteristics of occupants of the public rental stock
in Budapest by privatization status 73

6.1 Output of new housing in Bulgaria, 1965–88 101

6.2 Housing tenure in Bulgaria, 1975–91 103

6.3 Privatization of public housing: The gap between state
and market price, in Bulgarian Leva per square meter 111

6.4 The output of new housing in Bulgaria, 1988–92 113

TABLES

1.1 Public and Private Characteristics of Housing 4

2.1 State and Cooperative Housing Construction in the Year
of Greatest Output and in 1988 33

4.1 The Percentage of Inhabited Dwellings in Hungary
and Budapest, by Tenure 59

4.2 The Structure of Housing Revenues and Costs in Budapest 61

4.3 The Changes in Tenure Form in Inner Budapest, 1990–93 65

4.4 The Number of Firms in Construction Industry 69

4.5 Housing Construction in 1981, 1989–92 69

4.6 Number of Construction Companies by Type
of Organization, 1989–92 70

4.7 Privatization Process and the Equity Issue
in the Budapest Public Rental Sector 74

5.1 Ownership of Housing in the Russian Federation,
by Size of Total Floor Area, 1990 84

5.2 Housing Construction in the Russian Federation
by Types of Property, 1990 85

5.3 Sales of Apartments to Individuals in the Russian Federation, 1990 89

5.4 Sales of Apartments to Individuals in the Russian Federation,
January–October, 1991 89

6.1 Market Prices for Housing and Urban Land, in Bulgaria 110

7.1 Selected Indicators of the Housing Situation in Poland, 1988 120

7.2 Occupied Dwellings by Sector, Poland, 1988 121

7.3 Number of Households and Number of Available Dwellings, 1988 122

7.4 Number of New Dwellings Completed in 1992 and 1993,
by Type of Investor 122

7.5 Total Usable Floor Area of New Dwellings Completed
in 1992 and 1993 by Type of Investor 123

7.6 Changes in the Profile of Investors in Housing Construction
by Sector in 1952, 1978, and 1993 123

7.7 Changes in Terms of Construction Credits in Poland, 1983–90 124

7.8 Proportion of Housing Stock by Sector, Showing Proportion
Purchased by Tenants 127

8.1 Housing Stock in Czechoslovakia, 1989 139

8.2 Proportion of Housing in Each Sector in Czechoslovakia
in 1980 and 1992 142

8.3 Housing Stock in Czechoslovak Federal Republic, 1970–91 143

8.4 Dwellings Completed by the KBV System, 1987–91 146

8.5 Average Rent for Public Sector Tenants as a Proportion
of Household Income 147

9.1 Percentage of Housing Stock in Different Tenures:
Past, Present, and Future 160

Acknowledgments

The editors' thanks go to:

- The Economic and Social Research Council of Great Britain, which provided some funding to assist the conference around which this book is based.
- Betty Johnstone of the Centre for Housing Research and Urban Studies, University of Glasgow, who made an excellent job of producing the final script, as well as the many drafts of the chapters.

Introduction

This book aims to describe and analyze the processes of housing privatization in Eastern Europe in the time since the political changes of the late 1980s and early 1990s. We use the term "Eastern Europe" to denote those countries that were formerly part of the Eastern Bloc, together with the European part of the Soviet Union. We would also include Albania and the former Yugoslavia within the definition. We acknowledge the use of the term "Central Europe" to cover much of this territory but have chosen to use the more commonly used term.

The origin of the book was a seminar organized in Budapest in spring 1992, under the auspices of the East European Working Group of the European Network for Housing Research. The expenses of the seminar were underwritten by the Economic and Social Research Council in Britain and USAID. The aim of the seminar was to share the experiences of different countries in moving toward a market-based housing system. Participants were asked to look at the mechanics of privatization in their country, but also to step back from the process itself to examine its aims and the impact it was having, and was likely to have in the longer term.

Following the seminar, participants were asked to produce chapters on their countries, wherever possible adopting a similar framework of issues; a number of other chapters were also commissioned. Revision of the chapters took place up to early 1994, and authors were asked to update their contributions wherever possible. Therefore, the chapters largely show the position in these countries at the end of 1993. Inevitably, much will have happened since then, but the chapters provide a fascinating picture of attempts at a fundamental restructuring of housing systems by inventing new policy mechanisms and institutional structures as well as copying and adapting those of other—particularly Western—countries. The collection offers interesting insights into the difficulties of far-reaching reform and into the relationships between housing change and changing political, economic, and social systems.

The book starts by offering a framework for analyzing privatization. It examines the definition of privatization, arguing that it involves more than the sale of housing and also incorporates the commercialization of public organizations. Therefore, in Eastern Europe privatization has included the restructuring of public housing organizations in an attempt to make them more private sector-oriented, as well as the sale of public housing stock to tenants.

This is followed by a discussion of the aims of privatization, focusing on three major areas: (1) the reduction of public expenditure; (2) the promotion of a more efficient housing system; and (3) the symbolic importance of privatization. It is argued that all three have been important in privatization in Western countries and deserve consideration in the analysis of experience in Eastern Europe. The final part of the chapter outlines the key issues that should be borne in mind in assessing the impact of privatization.

Chapter 2 discusses the development of housing systems in Eastern Europe. It argues for the concept of an East European housing model that encapsulates the fundamental principles and the political, economic, and social pressures that have shaped the housing systems considered in this book. It is argued that the ideal model of a socialist housing system was never fully implemented, and cracks have been appearing in it for a number of years. These are discussed in relation to periods in the development of the housing systems, culminating in the economic difficulties from the 1980s onward, which created a crisis in the housing sector and led to precursors of the later housing privatization reforms.

Chapter 3 is the first of the chapters analyzing the privatization of housing in individual countries. It examines a unique case: the integration of what have been called the "new *Länder*" into a reunified Germany. This has meant that a coherent structure of legislation and institutions existed on which the reformed East German system could be based; it has also meant that public finance from the old *Länder* in the West has been used to overcome the lack of funds for investment that have hindered reform efforts in other countries. Alone of all the countries, Germany has adopted a high-cost strategy for the sale of existing public sector stock, reflecting policy in the old *Länder*. As a consequence, the chapter focuses on government attempts to encourage tenants to buy through pilot programs, which, among other things, have provided help with rehabilitation and repair.

Chapter 4 covers Hungary, which is more advanced in privatization than any of the other countries, largely because it started reform in the 1980s, under the Communist regime. There is also more empirical evidence from Hungary than elsewhere on the impact of privatization on the spatial and equity consequences of public sector sales to tenants and on the impact on tenants of the privatization of housing management.

Chapter 5 focuses on the Russian Federation, where housing reform has been slow and uneven. Although a national policy has been slow to develop, some cities such as Moscow and St. Petersburg have adopted their own programs of reform.

The experience of Bulgaria is covered in chapter 6. Bulgaria is unique among East European countries in that it had a very small state-rented sector, even under the Communist system. Although the authors argue that the fundamental principles of the housing system were similar to those in other East European countries, only 10 percent of the stock was in the state rented sector. As a consequence, issues concerning privatization are seen in sharp focus. The authors report that half of the already small public sector was sold in the first years of reform, fueling speculation over the future consequences of such a change.

Poland is considered in chapter 7. The picture here has some parallels with that in the Russian Federation, as reform has been very slow and economic problems have been pressing. Poland has also suffered from political paralysis caused by the large number of political parties.

Chapter 8 shows the speed of events in Eastern Europe as it concentrates on the former Czechoslovakia, which has now split into two separate countries. The chapter reviews the housing system before the split and draws out differences between the Czech Republic and Slovakia. Although both countries were in their infancy when the chapter was written, it looks at some privatization measures since the split.

Slovenia, which is the subject of chapter 9, only became an independent country in June 1991, following a short war with Serbia. The chapter reviews the Slovenian housing system when it was part of Yugoslavia and the privatization measures that have followed independence.

Finally, chapter 10 reviews the aims of privatization in the different countries and highlights the major mechanisms that have been used. It also examines the impact of privatization, reviewing the little systematic research available and making some judgements about the probable medium-term implications. The chapter also considers the effect of privatization on the housing systems of East European countries. It builds on the analysis in chapter 1 by arguing that the transitional problems experienced by the East European countries and the solutions adopted to meet them justify the typology of a transitional model as a useful tool to encapsulate the fundamental features of their current position. However, it is argued that governments are adopting reforms designed to produce Western-style housing systems. Therefore, the uniqueness of their present circumstances could soon disappear if these reforms continue.

The chapters in this book present a picture of attempts at a fundamental reform of housing systems as a consequence of economic and political change. At one level they provide an interesting historical record of events that are still unfolding, but at another they offer insights into the nature of housing systems and their relationship to political and economic forces.

Housing Privatization
in
Eastern Europe

1

Analyzing Housing Privatization

David Clapham and Keith Kintrea

INTRODUCTION

The aim of this chapter is to raise three key issues concerning the privatization of housing: (1) What is it? (2) What are its objectives? (3) How can it be evaluated? The chapter draws upon the experience of, and the debate about, privatization in Western countries in the 1980s, particularly in Britain, where privatization has been a consistent aim of government policy for 15 years and where the housing system has been subject to extensive change. Privatization in the West has led to far-reaching and profound changes in housing systems in terms of their efficiency, their distributional impact, and the extent to which housing can be influenced by public policy. Obviously, there are major differences between privatization in Western, capitalist countries and East European countries formerly dominated by a socialist model of a housing system. In the West, governments intent on transforming social rented housing into market provision had the advantage of an existing parallel private market of buyers and sellers and landlords and tenants, as well as a strong banking system to provide financial services. In the East, none of this existed; it has all had to be created anew. Nevertheless, there are sufficient parallels between Western governments privatizing the assets and machinery of a welfare state and Eastern countries attempting to shake off the socialist housing model to allow the experience of the former to inform the analysis of the latter.

With respect to the three key issues, the answer to the first question is not simple. The label "privatization" has been attached to many different policies and programs that have different aims and vary in their impact. It is also the case that what is called privatization varies, sometimes considerably, between countries. Therefore, it is important to develop a common language about the term "privatization" and to be clear about what is meant by it.

The second question reflects the considerable variation in the objectives of privatization. For example, the objective may be to reduce public expenditure or to divest central or local government of financial or administrative problems. Alternatively, privatization may be seen as a way of moving toward the creation of a more market-oriented housing system, which may be desired either on the grounds that it is supposedly more efficient or as a way of legitimizing markets as a means of producing and distributing other kinds of products and services. Privatization in housing may not necessarily be aimed at purely housing objectives; it may also have wider social or economic goals, such as liberating private capital for investment. Privatization may be the product of any one of these aims or a complex mixture of several of them. Also, different aims for privatization may be held by different political groups or by different sections within government or society.

Third, the varying aims of privatization make evaluation of its impact difficult. What criteria of evaluation should be used? Should the aims of those pursuing privatization be the touchstone of evaluation, or is there a set of objective criteria that is relevant? It is important to make explicit the criteria that are used in evaluation and to open up a debate about the appropriate measures.

These three issues recur throughout the following chapters, which concentrate on the privatization of housing in individual East European countries. The concluding chapter returns to these issues, draws out the general lessons to be learnt, and attempts to answer the challenging questions posed here. The objective of this chapter is to provide a framework for the rest of the book, which can be applied to the experience in different countries. The short experience of the privatization of housing in East European countries inevitably means that, as an initial step at least, questions and concepts have to be drawn largely from countries such as Britain, which has a much longer experience of privatization measures. Nevertheless, in the following discussion of the three issues, the East European context is constantly referred to.

WHAT IS PRIVATIZATION?

At first glance, this question may seem to be superfluous. Surely privatization is about replacing the public sector with the private sector. However, this definition becomes problematic if an attempt is made to draw a line between the public and private housing sectors. For example, "social housing" in (West) Germany is often funded through state loans and subject to state regulation but may be owned by privately owned companies. In Britain, council housing is planned and managed by local authorities and, for most of its history, has been subsidized by central government, but it was built mostly by private companies and financed by loans from the private sector. To take another example, owner-occupied housing in most Western countries is developed and built by private companies or individuals and is owned by individual households, who fund the purchase usually by means of loans from private sector financial institutions. Nevertheless, development of new housing for sale is publicly controlled through the land-use planning system, and both central government and local authorities, from time to time, act to support and stimulate production for private consumption. For example, successive U.S. governments have been involved in supporting private lending for home ownership since the 1930s and have operated several loan subsidy programs. The central government usually also provides income-tax relief on mortgage interest payments. The extent of these tax breaks in Britain has led to the owner-occupied sector being described by some as the "true public sector."

In many East European countries, there has also been a mix of public and private attributes within housing tenures. In Hungary, for example, it has been possible for a number of years, even before recent political reforms, to buy and sell the "right-to-reside" in a state-owned apartment through private transactions. This has given the tenure some characteristics of the private sector, because households have a tradeable asset in the "right-to-reside," although the state owns the land and buildings. In principle, private transactions were controlled by the state, which could set the price and determine who the buyer was, although these powers were not always used in practice. Also, in many East European countries cooperative housing involved a mixture of state and private financing, with individual households having to make a down payment on "buying" a cooperative apartment. In addition, cooperative members sometimes had a say in the construction and management of their homes, although the primary role was usually taken by state enterprises.

As these examples illustrate, it is often difficult to distinguish between what may be called the public and the private sectors. A more detailed analysis of the components of private and public sector characteristics is necessary to start to make sense of what constitutes privatization. Three main categories of characteristics can be identified—provision, subsidy and taxation, and regulation—and within each there are a number of individual components. Table 1.1 attempts to distinguish between these and to indicate how they apply to the public and private housing sectors.

Privatization implies a deliberate attempt to make particular activities or services conform to the ideal private sector model. However, privatization measures may also involve important changes between the three main categories of characteristics. For example, the sale of state-owned houses to individual owners changes state provision to private provision. However, in this case, in Britain the amount of subsidy is increased considerably by means of a discount on market price to buyers and, if applicable, tax relief on mortgage interest payments. After the sale of council houses, substantial state involvement is maintained, as state provision has been replaced by state subsidy for those buyers with mortgages.

Table 1.1. Public and Private Characteristics of Housing

	Public	*Private*
1. PROVISION		
i. Ownership (of housing or other assets)	by state (central or local) or state institutions	by private individuals, private institutions or collectives of individuals
ii. Main source of investment strategy	state (from taxes, revenues borrowing)	private (from individuals or institutional sources
iii. Implementation and management	by state bureaucracy	by autonomous private companies and individuals
iv. Objectives	to meet socially or politically defined needs and demands	private profit or private consumption
v. Accountability	to state officials or elected representatives	to investors and customers
2. SUBSIDY & TAXATION		
i. Subsidy	usually present	largely absent
ii. Type of subsidy	to production (e.g. direct capital subsidies to house building)	to consumption (e.g. housing allowances or tax relief)
iii. Taxation	institutions not taxed	institutions taxed
3. REGULATION		
i. Regulation by state	present, direct	present, by use of law
ii. Control of output levels by state	present	largely absent

Another example of privatization is provided by the increasing extent to which public services in Britain are contracted out by the state (particularly by local government). By law there is a compulsory process of competitive tendering for services such as refuse collection, street cleaning, and the running of swimming pools and other leisure services. The process has been extended to council housing maintenance and will apply to the management of council housing in the near future. Similar proposals have been made for "troubled" public housing agencies in the United States. In general, the process involves the preparation of a detailed brief by the local authority (or other state agency), which stipulates the quality and frequency of the service to be provided. Agencies, which may include private companies, voluntary agencies, and the council's own staff, then bid the price for which they are willing to provide this level of service. The lowest bid must be accepted, subject to certain conditions being met. Once the successful bidder has gained the contract, the local authority regulates the service and can hold the contractor to the levels of service laid down in the contract.

If the contract is won by a private agency, competitive tendering represents a move from state provision to state regulation, particularly in respect of the implementation and management of the service. However, if the contract is won by an existing department or by another public agency, the service is still state-provided. Nevertheless, the relationship between the department and the state institution has changed and been put on a more commercial footing, because the department acts as contractor and the state as employer. Therefore, the department may begin to act more as though it is a private company rather than part of the state bureaucracy.

In East European countries, there may be substantial scope for this form of privatization, as under socialism most state housing was managed and maintained by (usually large) state monopoly enterprises, and there was much dissatisfaction with the standard of service provided.

Another view of privatization, which includes the commercialization of state institutions, is as follows: "In very broad terms 'privatization' can be seen as a term used to describe the set of policies which aim to limit the role of the public sector and increase the role of the private sector, *while improving the performance of the remaining public sector*" (Young, 1986, p. 236; italics added).

An example of this approach in Britain is the reorientation of housing associations to make them more commercially oriented. (Housing associations are nonprofit organizations managed by volunteers but subsidized and regulated by the state.) Recent measures have forced housing associations to raise loans from private financial institutions to fund part of their developments. The proportion of capital funding from the state has been reduced, and the method of funding has been changed to place the financial risk of new housing development firmly on the shoulders of the housing association rather than on central government agencies, where it had rested previously. The system of rent setting has also been changed from a state-controlled system to one that requires associations to set their own rents to cover costs on individual schemes. Therefore, if the costs of development are greater than planned, or if the level of empty properties and rent arrears is higher and, consequently, rental income is lower than planned, the housing association itself is responsible for making up the shortfall by raising rents, increasing borrowing, or using its reserves. In (West) Germany, the attempt to create private institutions in the housing field has gone even further. At the end of the 1980s, the tax privileges of most voluntary housing organizations were abolished, leaving them to compete on identical terms with private, profit-oriented companies.

In East European countries, this form of privatization could be extended to state-owned maintenance or construction enterprises. They could be forced to compete with each other or with new private companies and encouraged to operate in a businesslike manner by, for example, adopting commercial pricing criteria and private sector working practices. Commercialization may be seen as an alternative to the sale of the enterprises to the private sector or, alternatively, as a prelude to sale.

Other definitions of privatization have attempted to sidestep the public/private distinction by emphasizing instead a distinction between the state and the market. For example, privatization has been defined as "an umbrella term for very many different policies loosely linked by the way in which they are taken to mean a strengthening of the market at the expense of the state" (Heald, 1983, p. 398).

However, there are problems within this definition in determining the boundary between market and state. For example, in the U.K. National Health Service, the Conservative government has attempted to create competition between different state agencies. Individual hospitals have been encouraged to opt out of local health authority control and to compete with each other for contracts with the health authority for the provision of services. In addition, some general practitioners have been given budgets that can be used to buy services for their patients from competing hospitals. The question here is whether or not the system that has thus been created is a market. Le Grand (1991) has characterized these types of arrangements as "quasi-markets." Certainly they at least replicate some of the features of a market in that there are buyers and sellers, although they are clearly not free markets in the accepted sense. The problems in defining the criteria for constituting a market are as difficult as those involved in defining a term such as "private."

Stoker (1991) has suggested that the only way out of definitional problems is to describe privatization in terms of the specific programs and policies pursued at a particular point in time in a particular country, rather than to look for a watertight overarching definition. For Britain in the 1980s and early 1990s, he suggests that privatization has three elements:

1. the sale of public (local authority) assets;
2. initiatives aimed at introducing "market discipline" into service delivery;
3. encouragement of private sector provision and investment.

He then provides a list of policies and programs in Britain that fit into one or more of these categories. There may still be problems in deciding on definitions of "private sector" or "market discipline," but these terms are easier to define in relation to specific policies and programs than in abstract terms. Therefore, in looking at the privatization of housing in East European countries, Stoker's three elements should be borne in mind. However, it must be emphasized that the scheme is not exhaustive and is only a starting point, as the East European experience differs substantially from that of Britain.

WHAT ARE THE AIMS OF PRIVATIZATION?

There are large numbers of possible reasons why privatization measures may be proposed and supported by politicians, political parties, and interest groups. The objective of this section is to outline some of the aims that have been important in Britain and to make a preliminary assessment of their relevance to the position in East European countries. Some of the aims included here have been explicitly stated in policy documents of political parties or in government statements or circulars; others, which have not been explicitly stated, have been ascribed to privatization programs on the basis of their impact, or the judgements of academics, professionals, or opposition politicians about what the government was trying to achieve. The main aims are: to reduce public sector borrowing and expenditure; to promote a more efficient housing system; and to provide a symbol of the legitimacy of private ownership in society. These are now considered in turn.

Reducing Public Expenditure

Concern about high levels of public expenditure has been a key motive behind privatization in many Western countries, including the Netherlands, Germany, and Britain. In the British context, successive Conservative governments have used the receipts from the sale of public assets to bolster government revenues and so to keep taxes down at a given level of public expenditure. A key objective of government economic policy since 1979 has been to control public sector borrowing as a means of holding down inflation. In this respect, the sale of council houses has been particularly important. Although local authorities have faced restrictions on their ability to spend the proceeds, a considerable proportion of new capital spending on housing by local authorities has come from the revenue from sale of council houses, with a consequent reduction in borrowing. Forrest and Murie (1988) estimated that council house sales raised £13 billion between 1980 and 1990, which represented half the total proceeds from all privatization programs.

In the East European context, the aim of raising revenue from the sale of assets is clearly an important one. In many countries, the economic problems of the 1980s have left governments with major problems of debt. In addition, the transition to a market economy creates a need for government financial support to cushion changes, for example, by providing unemployment benefit to alleviate the impact of growing unemployment, and to support the modernization of the industrial base.

In addition, in many East European countries the past 45 years have seen a lack of investment in repairs and improvements, which has led to very poor physical conditions, with much property in urgent need of repair and modernization. There is therefore a strong incentive for the state to dispose of its stock in order to avoid responsibility for ongoing maintenance costs and, in some cases, for extensive rehabilitation. There is a widespread belief that selling state housing will encourage residents to spend their savings on housing improvements.

The success of asset sales as a means of saving public expenditure and generating income is, however, dependent on the willingness and ability of existing occupiers or others to buy the property. The economic problems of the last few years have left many people with low disposable incomes and small savings. In addition, low rents and the disrepair of the stock provide a disincentive to purchase in many cases.

Promoting a More Efficient Housing System

Privatization is often held to lead to a more efficient housing system in two main respects. First, the socialist model provided cheap housing to all its consumers, regardless of their needs; subsidy was heavy, but it was deliberately not targeted. Greater private ownership of housing through owner occupation and market renting opens up the possibilities of targeting any subsidies more efficiently to those judged to need or deserve them. Thus, in Britain, in (West) Germany, and in France, there has been an increasing reliance since the 1980s on means-tested housing allowances rather than the provision of social rented housing. In the Netherlands, at present, there is considerable policy concern about the "maldistribution" of social housing—that is, good-quality, subsidized apartments being let to better-off people.

Second, and more generally, privatization is most often pursued by governments that have an ideological belief in the superior functioning of markets over state provision. The belief usually is that markets lead to more efficient production of goods through competition between producers. Markets are also said to increase consumer choice and power, thus making producers more responsive to consumer demand. The result is supposed to be superior products or services at lower prices than the state can produce.

The superiority of markets is strongly disputed by opposition political forces, who have argued that strong state intervention in the housing system is required to achieve efficiency and to empower consumers, particularly those on low incomes. But the political debate about privatization is often an ideological one, which reflects the beliefs of politicians and political parties. The important point here is that privatization may be promoted or opposed as an end in itself rather than as a means of achieving particular housing objectives.

Since the introduction of electoral democracy, most of the countries in Eastern Europe have governments with a strong belief in private markets. Nevertheless, as the following chapters show, there are big differences in the speed and determination with which reforms have been pursued, in both the economic and the housing spheres. However, the belief in the efficacy of markets has been almost universal, and most political debate has focused on the speed and appropriateness of particular mechanisms rather than on the desirability of privatization.

Kemeny (1993) has claimed that the overwhelming belief in private markets in housing derives from what he sees as the hegemony of the "Anglo-Saxon" housing model. By this he means the housing system of the United States, Australia, Canada, and, to a lesser degree, Britain, which rely heavily on private provision. He argues that an alternative "European" model based on unitary rental sectors, such as those in Sweden and the Netherlands, which allow a greater share for state and voluntary activity, has been relatively neglected, and that East European politicians and policymakers are unaware of this model. Clearly, organizations such as the World Bank and USAID have been very active in Eastern Europe and have promulgated the "Anglo-Saxon" (market) model. It is likely that many politicians in the East are aware of the "European" alternative but choose to reject it on pragmatic and political grounds. The pragmatic reasons relate to the difficulties of retaining a strong state role and responsibility when government finances are in such a poor state. Even Sweden has rolled back social expenditure in an attempt to cut its budget deficit. The political reasons stem from a decisive rejection of collective solutions to social problems stemming from the experience of the past 40 years.

Privatization as a Symbol

A development of the previous point is the idea that policy measures often have a symbolic importance, which outweighs their practical impact. This was obviously the case under socialism in Eastern Europe, where cheap state housing was meant to signify the state's responsibility for its citizens' lives, even if there was a perpetual shortage of housing in most countries and the quality of what was produced was often low. Similarly, the privatization of housing may be used as a symbol of a belief in markets as a general political philosophy.

In Britain, the privatization of housing is seen by its advocates as a way of changing public perceptions by encouraging an "enterprise culture" in which working-class people identify more strongly with a capitalist economic system. Privatization is also intended to change what is seen as a "culture of dependency" on the state and, instead, encourage individuals to take more responsibility for themselves and their families. It is also intended by the government to introduce many working-class people to the experience of property ownership and give them a common interest with well-established home-owning social groups from the middle class. The aim is to change their political allegiance away from the Labour Party and to alter their attitude to private ownership in other spheres as well, thereby lending added legitimacy to the private ownership of industry.

In East European countries, there is an additional necessity to legitimize the new regime by quickly illustrating that it has material advantages for "ordinary" citizens. The privatization of industry and services has not always proceeded quickly. Where it has occurred, enterprises have often been sold to Western companies or to existing top managers. Although there have been a number of voucher programs designed to give everyone a stake in privatization, these have not been widespread and have not always captured the public imagination to any great extent. More often than not, formerly successful enterprises have closed down, and their workers have been laid off. Altogether, there is considerable social and economic upheaval, with rising unemployment creating economic insecurity. Rising prices have led to hardship in some cases, and high inflation in some countries has wiped out many people's personal savings. Therefore, the privatization of housing offers a way for people to be given a stake in the new system. The ownership of a house may be viewed as offering a degree of security to people at a time of considerable instability and uncertainty, and it may be seen as an important symbol of the advantages of a market economy when other material gains may be slow to materialize.

Restructuring the Economy

Privatization of housing in Britain was intended to help a process of economic restructuring by increasing labor mobility. Council housing is said to discourage mobility by making it difficult for households to move from one part of the country to another for employment reasons because access to housing was controlled by bureaucratic rationing, not by consumer demand. In the mid-1980s, expansion of market provision was seen as a way of making it easier for people to move within Britain, particularly from the North to the South, in order to take up employment in the booming areas.

The restructuring of the economies in East European countries may make such objectives important, particularly in a situation where much housing is owned by state enterprises and there are few well-developed housing exchange mechanisms.

HOW CAN PRIVATIZATION BE EVALUATED?

The aims of housing privatization can offer a starting point for an evaluation. The simple question that can be posed is, "has the privatization of housing achieved the aims set out for it?" There are, however, three problems with this approach. (1) Some of the aims—particularly the political ones—outlined in the previous section were imputed to policymakers, but not explicitly stated. Therefore, it is not always clear which aims should be taken into account. (2) Some of the aims—for example, the symbolic importance of privatization in housing—are very difficult to evaluate in practice. Any evaluation would need to involve the measurement of changes in public attitudes over a wide range of issues over time, and it might also be influenced by many factors other than housing privatization. (3) A sole concentration on objectives would mean that many of the unintended impacts of privatization would be ignored completely.

Therefore, the way forward adopted here is to identify a number of dimensions that could form the basis of an evaluation. The balance between them may be decided on the basis of their relevance in particular countries, or on the practical grounds of the availability of information on which a judgement can be made. The list of evaluation criteria is based on the list of objectives outlined in the previous section, but is not confined to it.

Reducing Public Expenditure

This is perhaps the easiest of the objectives to measure. It should be possible to identify the receipts from the sale of housing and the savings made by the change of ownership in, for example, reducing the costs of management and maintenance falling on state institutions. However, two problems emerge. (1) Some privatization measures may be aimed at improving efficiency, which may result in reductions in public expenditure but may be very difficult to measure. This point is considered later. (2) Reduction in public expenditure may be achieved at the expense of private individuals or agencies; for example, the state may shift responsibility for management and maintenance costs onto individual home owners. Therefore, it is important to chart the financial costs and benefits accruing to all parties, not just to government agencies.

Efficiency of Housing Production and Management

Efficiency gains from privatization are more difficult to measure than are single savings. Nevertheless, some broad-brush measures may be possible. For example, measures of the cost of producing a given quality of newly built housing unit may be available. It may be possible to compare the costs of private and public agencies, or to chart changes in public agencies over time. For example, do efficiency gains mean that similar dwellings can be produced more cheaply after privatization measures than before, allowing for changes in the overall price level? The same kind of exercise could, in theory, be carried out for management and maintenance expenditure.

However, it must be recognized that privatization measures in Eastern Europe are relatively recent and that efficiency gains may take some time to have an impact. It must also be considered that privatization may bring about efficiency losses as well as gains. For example, private agencies or individuals may lose economies of scale, or levels of profit may be high if a monopoly situation is created.

Promotion of Market Provision

The impact of privatization can be assessed in terms of the growth of market provision. In simple terms, this can mean measuring the increase in the proportion of owner-occupation and private rental, compared with state tenants. However, many privatization proposals are more subtle than a simple change of tenure and may aim to make market processes more effective or to introduce some market processes into a state system, as discussed earlier. These forms of privatization are more difficult to evaluate because judgements have to be made about what markets entail.

The position is also very difficult in East European countries, where there are few longstanding market processes to be expanded. Rather, privatization measures are aimed, at least in part, at creating a market where none had existed before. Thus an important element in any evaluation of privatization in housing is the extent to which an effectively functioning private market is brought into existence. This is not a simple matter, because there is little agreement over what constitutes an effective private market. Nevertheless, it should be possible to evaluate whether or not essential elements of a market exist. For example, is there an appropriate set of legal structures for the private ownership of property? Is there a system for the buying and selling of private dwellings? Does a private construction industry exist?

Consumers

Many—but not all—of the aims of privatization concern the position of consumers of housing. Therefore, finally, and perhaps most importantly, there are issues about the impact of privatization on households as consumers of housing. Does privatization mean that households have more choice? Has it resulted in better or worse housing conditions? What is the redistributive impact of privatization? Does it have a differential impact on social, economic, or ethnic groups in terms of the costs they face and their physical housing conditions? One of the major criticisms of housing privatization policies in Britain has been that their redistribution effect has been unequal. Privatization has, on the whole, brought benefits to skilled working-class people, but it has led to a deterioration in the housing circumstances of the poorest in society, particularly those unable to achieve owner occupation.

Finally, if the information is available, it is important to assess the attitudes toward privatization held by the population at large and by different groups within it. Are the privatization reforms popular? How do households judge the impact of privatization on their own housing circumstances?

CONCLUSION

The aim of this chapter has been to highlight some factors that are important to an understanding of why privatization policies are being pursued and what impact they will have. The issues raised here are based on the experience of privatization of housing in West European countries and particularly in Britain, where it has been most extensive. The intention is to provide a framework for understanding the current experience of privatization in East European countries. Clearly these countries are starting from a different position from that of the West, and their experience may be very different. Nevertheless, it is important that such questions about the nature, objectives, and impact are asked now, to ensure that policymakers are aware of the possible outcomes. It is a key objective of this book not only to describe what is happening in East European countries, but also to understand why it is happening and what impact it is likely to have. The questions set here are a step toward this objective, even if the early stage of the development of privatizing and research gaps prevent the presentation of definitive conclusions.

REFERENCES

Forrest, R., and Murie, A. 1988. *Selling the Welfare State*. London: Routledge.

Heald, D. 1983. *Public Expenditure*. Oxford: Martin Robertson.

Kemeny, J. 1993. *Comparative Rental Systems: From Implicit Anglo-Saxon Model to a Theory of Change*. Working Paper. Gävle: Swedish Institute for Building Research.

Le Grand, J. 1991. Quasi-markets and social policy. *Economic Journal* 101, 1256–1267.

Stoker, G. 1991. *The Politics of Local Government*. Basingstoke: Macmillan.

Young, S. 1986. The nature of privatisation in Britain 1979–85. *Western European Politics* 9 (2), 235–252.

2

The Disintegration of the East European Housing Model

József Hegedüs and Iván Tosics

INTRODUCTION

This chapter deals with the development of the East European housing systems, with their internal contradictions, and, consequently, with the failure of these models. It concentrates on the development and disintegration of the East European housing model and does not discuss in detail the developments of the 1990s. The first question to address is in what respect may we speak about an East European model. Leaving aside Albania and the former Yugoslavia, which, for historical reasons, have followed other routes, in a political and economic sense, the post-Second-World-War history of this region has its origin in one common feature—the extension of the area of influence of the Soviet Union. Similarly, in 1989 or 1990 common forces led to the disintegration of the Eastern Bloc. Our hypothesis is that within this common frame, a common housing model developed. Although each country had its own housing system, all showed the same signs of crisis arising from the East European path of development. We believe that behind the very different East European housing systems there existed a common logic of housing policy, which has established the "rules" of behavior of the state and private sector, the state institutions, and the various social and economic groups.

The first part of this chapter deals with the rules and institutional framework, giving some basic theoretical hypotheses on the way the model worked. In the second part we give an overview of the development of the East European housing model. In the last part of the chapter we formulate an evaluation of the achievements of the model with respect to its social and economic performance.

STRUCTURAL TENSIONS
OF THE EAST EUROPEAN HOUSING MODEL

The Centrally Planned Economy

After the Second World War, East European countries were brought into the sphere of influence of the Soviet Union, and, under the reign of Communist parties, an economic development system was introduced that had the aim of rapidly restructuring the economy, increasing economic development, and strengthening the economic and military potential of the region. In this economic model, the primary aim was to increase investment in the production sphere, even at the expense of holding back internal consumption (Fehér, Heller, and Márkus, 1983). In general, the so-called nonproductive sector, which included housing, was pushed into the background, behind other economic and political priorities.

Originally, the successful realization of these economic and political aims was taken for granted because of the supposed superiority of the centrally planned economy. At the beginning of the 1950s, in almost all East European countries, a model was imported from the Soviet Union according to which the most important economic decisions were made by a narrow political elite within the framework of the so-called planning system. In addition to centralized decision making on questions of economic development, one of the most important elements of this system was income regulation. A wage system was developed that did not include the cost of housing, education, health care, and infrastructure. The costs of these services were not to be borne by individual consumers but paid for by a kind of taxation on enterprises, which was redistributed through the state budget. In this way, all market relations were intended to be replaced by central planning.

In this economic system, however, the theoretically unlimited decision-making possibilities of the central organs were, in reality, somewhat restricted. In particular, the interests and endeavors of subordinate state institutions and companies had, to a certain extent, to be recognized. The Hungarian economic sciences give a good description and explanation of the phenomena of "plan bargaining" (Bauer, 1982; Kornai, 1980; Soós, 1986). Similarly, individual and group interests could influence the economic system through a series of bargains and compromises. Although the market, in general, lost its integrating function in the economy (Polányi, 1976), and a centralized planning system took over this role, specific limited-value, segmented markets came into existence in these economies. In these limited markets, some functioning of demand and supply and of the price mechanism was allowed, but the behavior of individuals and institutions was not wholly determined by these market-type relations.

The East European Housing Model

The theoretical model of the socialist housing system can clearly be deduced from this economic model. Exclusion of the market, the omission of housing costs from incomes, and the centralization of all important investment decisions were preconditions of a system in which all important aspects of housing were meant to be under the control of state institutions. Housing was intended to be a form of public service, in which the private sector should not have a role either in production or in distribution.

The socialist housing model, however, has never been realized in this pure form. One of the reasons arises from the long-standing nature of housing as a good; "stocks" are nearly always high in comparison to "flows." Each country inherited its stock of housing from presocialist times and was not able to carry out a complete redistribution of ownership. To do so would have involved extensive administrative and political costs, which practically no system was willing to pay, except for a relatively short period of drastic redistribution mainly involving the best-quality dwellings. Where no total redistribution took place, previous social and economic relations continued to influence the housing system in the long run.

A second reason was that the control of the private transactions of citizens entailed extreme administrative costs. In the absence of effective and strict control, governments had the alternatives of either completely prohibiting private transactions or turning a blind eye to them while maintaining a formal policy of control, depending on the costs and the strength of political determination. It was almost inevitable that private transactions would play an ever greater role in the allocation process. In practice, private transactions were not limited to the exchange or sale of privately owned apartments, because in many countries cooperative or state-owned apartments could also be the subject of private transactions.

It was also difficult in practice to exercise a state monopoly in housing construction. Totally effective prohibition of private initiatives, which was introduced during certain periods and in certain countries, caused political tensions. Therefore, housing policy preferred to use indirect means of regulating housing construction—for example, control over the supply of building material, land policy, and so on. In practice, there was a part of the sphere of construction that was not centrally controlled, but remained extant while officially prohibited. Because it was an activity of the underground economy, it was missing from official statistics.

In practice, then, the East European housing model was one in which the state sphere and the private sphere were both working. In each country, however, there was a different combination and interaction of state and market. The question is how and under which conditions the roles of the state and the private sphere were interacting and changing in these housing systems.

Political Feedback and Economic Feedback

In some circumstances, the private sphere actually had predominance over the state sphere, both in the stock and in the flow. The real importance of the private sphere, however, was determined not by its ratio, but by its wider role in the housing system. The private sector within the socialist housing model had limited effects on the rest of the housing system. Private transactions were taking place, and the mechanisms of prices, supply, demand, and shortage were being formed. However, the fact that demand exceeded supply did not encourage or increase production and supply, so although there were quasi-market conditions, there was nothing like a functioning housing market. Of course, within the state sector no feedback mechanism was formed based on the interaction of price, demand, and supply, as these were all centrally planned.

This does not mean that no feedback within the housing sector existed at all. Feedback was, however, of political character—that is, it was operating through the mediation of political interests. Changes in housing policy, such as relieving controls, increasing housing construction, or increasing subsidies, were a reaction to political tensions.

Therefore, one of the most important characteristics of the East European housing model was that the private sphere, however large its relative weight, did not influence the economic mechanism. When economic feedback became predominant, the political role of the state controlling reproduction conditions was first limited and later terminated, significantly modifying the model itself.

Conflicts within the State

According to our definition, the state sector means all institutions controlled and integrated by the (Communist) Party. In practice, a wide range of organizations competed for power, and through them resources could be distributed. In the history of East European countries, this institutional system had been transformed several times. The aim of the institutions concerned with housing was to increase their influence and control over the allocation of subsidies. It was the task of the central state to establish consensus among the institutions and to ensure that the individual institutional endeavors could not threaten macroeconomic targets.

The different institutions and organization of the planned economy competed with each other, with the aim of obtaining control over the distribution of apartments and subsidies, and in this way over public goods. Their various positions were very much dependent on this capacity—for example, their position in the job market—because they used their ability to provide housing subsidies as an indirect wage. The form of control over the allocation processes varied between institutions: it could simply mean the right to assign tenants; alternatively, it might mean power over the allocation of state grants. An important characteristic of the East European economic system was that the financial cost to the companies and institutions arising from housing did not constrain their growing influence over housing markets, since such costs were incorporated into the bureaucratic prices of their goods and services. One good example of the consequences was the land-use pattern of the socialist cities, where the transactions among the state organs were determined by political power rather than economic forces (Dawson, 1984). This was legitimated by an administrative process and not by the market. The housing expenditures of companies were handled practically in the same way as wages; they were recognized in prices at the time when the company plan was approved.

An additional source of conflict was the purchase, sale, and exchange of dwellings by private individuals. These were, in principle, regarded as a kind of threat to social goals and were under state control. For example, in the Soviet Union,

transactions relating to the disposition of property . . . are handled by the Soviet notary . . . a government official . . . [whose role] enables the government to supervise private transactions. The terms of money contracts, which in other countries are ordinarily left to the determination of the parties to the agreement, are subject to mandatory regulations. (Sawicki, 1977, p. 118)

Control over "Elitist Apartments"

In the East European housing model, the state could not have complete control over moves within the housing system. In certain countries and during certain periods, this control covered only a small percentage of all of the housing construction and housing market transactions. Similarly the redistribution of the housing stock was confined mainly to high-quality, well-situated dwellings. The state was satisfied with directly reserving the best-quality new or vacated apartments only for the *nomenclatura* (the top party officials and other specially favored groups). For the other strata of society, the state was content to adopt other, less interventionist mechanisms, including state distribution incorporating some social criteria or perhaps quasi-market mechanisms.

"CRACKS" IN THE MODEL

"Voice" and "Exit"

An ideal typical East European housing model, as we have argued so far, could not be formed in practice, since it would have entailed large administrative and political costs. In the development—or, more properly, in the disintegration—of the original model, the dynamic element was not a lack of state control but, rather, the success of individual and institutional motivations and endeavors.

In the period of economic growth, housing needs played an important role. Economic restructuring combined with substantial regional mobility to induce radical increases in housing needs. This phenomenon was explained by the "underurbanization" theory (Konrád and Szelényi, 1974), which was "a spatial expression of distinctively socialist economic growth" (Szelényi, 1988, p. 11).

The state was unable to meet these demands, which caused chronic tensions on the housing model.

Individuals, intent on achieving their housing goals, had basically two theoretical possibilities. One was to work within the system and use whatever openings existed to achieve their demands, which could be described as a "voice" option; the other was "exit"—stepping out of the state sphere and searching for a solution in the private sphere.

The voice option was completely in conformity with the East European housing model and was basically the driving force of organizational and institutional changes. Experience shows that the voice option has taken an assortment of forms in the past, including various types of corruption and patronage concerned with housing applications. The exit option was heavily influenced by state housing policy and by regional policy. For example, migration was regulated in almost all countries up to the late 1980s by limitations on applications for state housing for families moving into cities. Moreover, in certain parts of the housing system, the exit option was excluded by the state—for example, in elite areas of cities, where close control was a basic state interest. This exclusion could, however, greatly differ according to countries and periods. Variants of the exit option were transactions based on agreements between private individuals and the self-help form of new construction. In these cases, the controlling role of the state was limited; it basically had only a role of approval.

Voice Options.   The institutional system of the early centrally planned economies was organized hierarchically and also divided into sectors. In the decision-making system, information and resources had to flow through the vertical hierarchy. In addition, in the original system, housing was organized partly according to sectors, which meant that individual ministries controlled different parts of new housing investment, according to their interest. One of the basic conflicts in these systems was between spatial and sectoral planning. Regional organizations—backed by the local Communist Party—tried to get more control of regional investments, since they had minimal influence on economic and political decisions. An important aim of the economic reforms was the strengthening of the regional principle against the sectoral one. For example, in Russia after 1957, "over 100 regional economic councils or *savnarkhozy* replaced all but a handful of ministries as the apparatus for central planning" (Bater, 1977). In Hungary, the planning system was changed after 1956, but in housing local councils gained influence only after the Housing Reform of 1971.

Internal conflicts surrounding the distribution system can be discovered when examining the effect of state distribution on social inequalities. Empirically, state housing distribution could not be regarded as a homogenous activity. In the history of East European housing systems, a large number of institutions (local councils, companies, ministries, etc.) distributed apartments and provided subsidies according to a wide range of principles and through many different procedures. From time to time the social groups controlling power positions have given way to pressures from middle-class and lower social groups, and policy and practice in housing allocation have changed. We have to reject the approach that considered state allocation as a "large-scale conspiracy" (Morton, 1980), but similarly we reject the standpoint of official East European documents, which consider state intervention as a manifestation of social justice.

Exit Strategies.   In the shortage economies of East European countries, systematic, forced saving characterized the consumption behavior of the population (Kornai, 1980). Economic policy aimed at economic growth, primarily rapid change in the macroeconomy, and did not aim to satisfy consumer demands (Bauer, 1982). Money accumulated by the population, since there was little to spend it on, was translated into a potential demand for housing within the quasi-market (Kansky, 1976). Thus, prices for housing began to be determined by supply and demand. Musil also pointed out that, with regard to Czechoslovakia,

Besides collective or social goals, as expressed by the state or by the regional and local authorities' decisions, there also exists a sphere of individual households preferences, decisions and acts. They are materialised in the purchases and sales of private houses and in the exchanges of flats. All these transactions are subject to the approval of local authorities and one can thus speak in this sphere of a regulated housing market, which complements the non-market allocation of housing. (1987, p. XX)

Furthermore, it is important that these quasi-market prices were often not the result of open transactions, as in many cases they were illegal or at best informal. For example, the exchange of state-owned apartments was mostly under (more or less strict) control. But in spite of the fact that private renting and private subtenancies were formally under state control, prices were much higher than in the state sector. This was actually illegal because of rent control, but nobody could check the real prices paid. The common feature was that a thriving demand faced a fixed supply, since the decisions regarding supply lay with the central planning system, which was insensitive to prices developed in the quasi-private sphere.

One of the most typical forms of exit was individual housing construction. In principle, another possible form of construction was speculative building, but this was prohibited until the middle of the 1980s and, even if it existed before, it was possible only in a totally illegitimate way. Individual self-building existed in every East European housing system; the difference between countries was only the extent to which it was tolerated or encouraged.

In the Soviet Union, "Discrimination in supplies of materials, together with administrative difficulties, is increasingly acting against private housing construction" (von Beyme, 1981, p. 342). Even in the 1980s, the building-material trade was controlled by local councils. But while the state could restrict private housing construction, it could not prevent it completely.

The informal economy could provide the conditions for individual housing construction, even if its macroeconomic importance remained restricted. Building plots could be obtained through private transactions and official site assignments, as well as by "self-reorganization"—building on plots owned by relatives or building without permission. A shortage of building materials did not mean an absolute limitation, since materials from demolition and those "leaking" from state housing construction were available. Labor could be provided through self-help, avoiding the official labor market and state intervention (Faltan, 1987; Kotacka, 1987). Financing of private housing construction could also be supplemented to a certain extent by "forced savings." Finally, administrative control of private housing construction could be avoided through construction without permission or by implementing plans different from the officially approved version.

Kansky sums up the situation prevailing in the 1960s:

The average private family house was constructed by using the family's savings, ingenuity, labour and "do-it-yourself" skills, and most of its leisure time, after purchasing, legally or illegally, the necessary construction materials. The general lack of housing materials on the market has contributed to purchases from the "black market" and from government warehouses by the spending of Western currency obtained usually from relatives or friends living in the Western world. The largest amount of work has been performed, according to a recent survey, by the family itself. About 30 percent of the less extensive family houses were built by the family itself, and about 17 percent of total were constructed almost exclusively by the family, with little help from professional builders. The services performed by professional builders were too expensive for an average income family. (1976, p. 111)

PERIODS AND TURNING POINTS IN THE DEVELOPMENT OF EAST EUROPEAN HOUSING SYSTEMS

The East European housing systems were subordinated elements of the socioeconomic developmental model, aiming at the acceleration of economic growth. A common feature of East European housing policies was a limitation of housing expenditure, both in the state and in the private spheres. Individual housing policy courses differed between counties in the extent and means of control. A very rough periodization can be established as follows:

• 1947–56: redefinition of property rights;
• 1957–68: concessions to the private sector;
• 1969–80: the new wave of centralization;
• 1980–90: decentralization as a consequence of economic crisis.

The exact timing of the periods is almost impossible to determine, even in the case of one country. In countries where the economic reforms of the 1960s had important effects, it makes sense to make further divisions. For example, Bunchak and Michalovik (1988) split the years between 1964 and 1988 into three periods: 1964–70, 1971–80, and 1980–88. Kozlowski (1988) also follows this pattern. Bessonova (1988), however, regards 1965–88 as a single period, because according to her interpretation the Soviet housing system did not change significantly during this period.

Redefining Property Rights, 1947–56

Until the mid-1950s, the housing systems of most of the East European countries were characterized by the rebuilding and redistribution of most of the housing stock. During these years very rapid—even revolutionary—changes took place. The turning point in the housing system was the reduction of individual property rights, for some years even a total elimination of them, and the extension of public control. The legal preliminaries of these changes were to be found in the war economy, with the difference that the "military economy of housing" was justified by the housing needs of the new elite and by industrialization (or preparation for the next world war).

The first issue was to change land ownership. In general, East European countries rejected total nationalization of land, and they did not follow the U.S.S.R. model, which had, through a 1917 decree, declared all land to be state property. Hoffman explains:

In the GDR, the absence of total nationalization of land ownership was explained by the specific features of the transitional period. It was promised that as they progress along the road to the complete build-up of socialism, further nationalisation is to transpire, strengthening state land ownership. At the same time, it was mentioned that the difference between the new people's democracies and the Soviet Union in the regulation of land ownership and land rights was not essential, but only formal. (1972, p. 38)

This last point hints at a kind of regulation that practically made impossible the free use of land, even if, formally, there was still private property. In fact, an Act of 1963 in the German Democratic Republic (GDR) made it compulsory to obtain the permission of the local council for any development activity, which could only be granted if the transaction served the interest of the socialist state (Hoffman, 1972).

In other countries, controls with nearly the same effectiveness were maintained, albeit through less direct means. These included the first right of refusal of the state over development sites and the possibility of introducing building prohibitions for an undetermined period of time based on master plans (Hegedüs and Tosics, 1983).

With the introduction of the socialist housing model, an important question was to create a difference between private property and personal property. While private property was considered as something the owner might keep only temporarily and which, in the long run, would turn into public property, "personal property over consumer goods by certain numbers of socialist society" (Hoffman, 1972, p. 58) was considered acceptable from an ideological point of view.

This may be the reason why the total nationalization of smaller properties, such as individual private houses, was never pursued in East European countries (e.g. in Hungary houses containing fewer than six rooms were exempt from nationalization), and why individual housing construction was not prohibited. An important consequence of the differentiation between private and personal property, however, was the regulation that introduced an upper limit of one apartment, or one family house, plus one weekend house as the maximum real estate allowed per family.

After the Second World War, a private rental sector remained in the majority of East European countries from a formal legal point of view. However, the extension of control by local authorities over the rules of renting, including rent levels, and the obligatory accumulation of reserves for maintenance meant that the sector was worthless as an investment. Nationalization of the private rental sector gradually occurred in Poland, Czechoslovakia, and the GDR. In the GDR, the owners were anxious to give up their property rights, which were a disadvantage, rather than an advantage, to them.

Hoffman (1972) reported that half of the tenements in the GDR were private property. These, except for the houses of war criminals, were left untouched. Landlords in the GDR were likened to "modern slaves," who were exploited by the state (Hoffman, 1972). Similarly, in Poland, only abandoned apartments were nationalized. Ball and Harloe reported that "There was no general policy of nationalization of residential buildings after the war so that much of the pre-1945 state housing consists of houses taken over in the pre-1939 German territories and is thus concentrated in West Poland" (1974, p. 22).

In Czechoslovakia, nationalization took place only around the end of the 1950s, but the private tenancy sector had already been placed under state control (Kansky, 1976).

Finally, with the exception of the GDR, the majority of tenement houses were taken over as state property. For example, in Hungary in 1952 the nationalization of the private rental sector was carried out in one step.

In the case of owner-occupied houses, while dwellings remained personal property, state control was extended. In certain cases, control was only formal, while in others it was substantial and real. In Bulgaria, sales and purchases were strictly controlled. Gallagher explains: "Someone wishing to sell must arrange the sale throughout the People's Council who take one percent of the sale price (however there are no legal or other costs involved). The People's Council must approve the sale agreement and nominates the new purchaser on the basis of housing need" (1982, p. 124).

Control was somewhat more moderate in Czechoslovakia. According to the rules, "The privately built family house is then owned by the family and may be sold. The transaction is, however, supervised by a local governmental agency, which also estimates the price. The official price is often modified by both private parties, and a secondary 'illegal' transaction complements that proposed by the governmental agency" (Kansky, 1976, p. 112).

Private property rights, however, were not totally eliminated by the authorities. As a consequence, later it was difficult to prevent the development of a secondary market, even in the case of exchange of state rental apartments.

In the first period of the socialist housing model, the huge social changes generated significant population mobility, which had to be accommodated in the housing system with a minimal level of new housing construction. The new elites and the lowest strata of society were the most mobile groups, but they had very different kinds of housing problems. To supply the new elite with housing, dwellings vacated by people who had left the country after the war were commandeered, but apartments were also vacated by pushing families out of larger cities. By solving the most severe housing problems in this way, the new political system wanted to demonstrate its own authority, and it meant open actions against social groups who enjoyed good housing conditions.

To accommodate those in housing need, new rules were introduced defining minimum space standards; surplus quantities of living space could be expropriated by the authorities, in a manner very similar to war-time regulations. As a consequence of this, a mass volume of cotenancies—previously an almost unknown form of housing—was formed in the large East European cities in the late 1940s and early 1950s (Kozlowski, 1988; Kansky, 1976).

The distribution of the very limited number of state rental apartments was also regulated by the artificial narrowing of the demand for these apartments. Most bigger cities became "closed" in the sense that applications for apartments could only be submitted with certain conditions. The logic behind this was to limit demand, but this certainly could not prevent population flow into the cities.

In the 1950s, state expenditure on new housing construction was set at a minimal level, and an increase in the number of state-built apartments was achieved by specifying minimalist standards. In Poland, for example, standards limited the size of new apartments to between 22 and 58 square meters, with the upper limit reduced to 44 square meters in 1959. There was a rule that only 20 percent might have four or five rooms. In 1959, the percentage of one-room and four-room apartments was raised (Cegielski, 1969). In Hungary after 1955, a so-called "reduced-quality" housing program was introduced for four years, the aim of which was to limit the housing standards in order to increase the number of newly built apartments.

Concessions to the Private Sector, 1957–68

The East European socialist countries first pledged themselves to solve the housing problems at the end of the 1950s, after the loosening of the Stalinist model and some decentralization of political power. The uprisings in 1953 in

Germany and in 1956 in Hungary were serious warnings that the economic policy, which was holding back consumption, was flawed, and they drew attention to the housing situation, which was one of the most important factors of the standard of living. During the 1950s in the East European countries there was an absolute deterioration in the housing situation as population growth outstripped housing supply and migration to the cities accelerated. In Czechoslovakia, the number of apartments per 100 inhabitants decreased from 193 to 280 (Kansky, 1976). In Poland, the number of inhabitants per room increased from 1.6 to 1.7 between 1950 and 1956 (Cegielski, 1969). The situation deteriorated in other East European countries as well.

These circumstances caused political leaders to start making promises with a view to solving the housing problem. Under the leadership of Khrushchev in the Soviet Union a decision was made to eliminate the housing shortage, and large-scale programs were adopted. At the Ninth Congress of the Czechoslovakian Communist Party, a program for constructing 1.2 million apartments was announced. In Hungary, the 15-year housing construction program started in 1958, with the aim of building a million apartments by 1975.

Such promises were considered to be feasible because in the early 1960s, optimistic economic forecasts were published. Behind them, there was a belief that the liquidation of the Stalinist political structure would automatically lead to economic growth and to an affluent society within a short time. However, decentralization within the political leadership did not lead to the restructuring of the institutional system of the economy. Investment policy continued to be subordinated to industrialization, and housing investment was given only a low priority. Housing policy then tried to compensate for the contradictions of ideology and the economic sphere in two ways: by a more liberal regulation of private housing construction and by the revival of housing cooperatives.

Part of the reason for allowing private house building in the 1950s was to give vent to accumulated political tensions, as the example of Hungary demonstrates. A private housing construction campaign was started in 1954, the result of which was mainly the distribution of building sites and not construction itself. Between 1954 and 1957, nearly 4,000 building plots were given to those planning to build a house of their own, but in the meantime there was a building materials shortage that completely paralyzed the campaign.

The change in political atmosphere and the consolidation and stabilization after 1956 brought about the greatest changes in the housing system in Hungary. The real estate market began to gather strength, prices were increasing, and transactions were no longer conditioned by fear produced by the political atmosphere. Government decisions struck a balance between the needs of industrial investment and the demand to reduce restrictions on housing consumption. The most important reforms included giving back legal guarantees, the revision of certain exaggerations of nationalization, and the improvement of the supply of building materials for private housing construction.

One of the most important innovations in the housing sector during this period was the introduction of housing cooperatives or, rather, in the majority of East European countries, their revival. The introduction of housing cooperatives raised important questions of ideology. Housing cooperatives operate on the basis that the consumers participate in financing new developments by making a down payment on an apartment. This clearly means a departure from the original logic of the socialist housing model: the state takes into account the savings of the private sector in solving housing problems. Most forms of cooperative housing remain within the state sphere in the sense that development, construction, and allocation of new apartments are under the control of state institutions. Even so, cooperatives can be seen as a compromise with the private sphere, because of the financial participation of the population.

The price of a new cooperative unit, sold by state organizations such as savings banks or local councils, was the same and did not vary according to location or developer. For example, in Bulgaria the price was set for a five-year period (apparently to make planning easier), which clearly shows that the price was not driven by the market in any sense.

The financial contribution by consumers could be considered as a kind of allocation criterion on the basis of income and savings. However, most people could afford a cooperative apartment, and this criterion lost its importance very quickly and only excluded a very narrow low-income layer of the population. Cooperative apartments were in practice allocated on the basis of waiting lists: there was no feedback between housing demand and construction. In Poland and Hungary, in the 1960s, more people were waiting for cooperative apartments than for state-rented ones since many middle-income people were above the income limits for state-rented housing.

Supply was restricted by the availability of finance from state banks to the developers of cooperative apartment houses. The amount of credit granted was limited by economic policy priorities, and surplus demand had no influence on credit policy. "Credit facilities are treated as a cost to the state rather than individual expenditure financed by loans. . . . Not all loans are repaid so that some of the credit allowance will, in fact, be state expenditure" (Ball and Harloe, 1974, p. 29). It occurred several times in Hungary that loans for cooperatives stopped in the course of the year since the National Savings Bank had run out of funds.

The other key characteristic of housing cooperatives in Eastern Europe was that the development and allocation processes were all under state control, exercised by local councils, by enterprises, or by other state institutions. In addition, there was a type of cooperative where the private sector played a more significant role, but this was an insignificant proportion of the sector.

In the case of Poland, the role of the state was characterized by Marmot in the following way:

The amount and type of output of each mode of housing provision is ultimately guided by state policies on land allocation, finance and the construction industry.

Each of the 49 provincial co-operative boards, for example, must compete for all allocations of finance through the Central Union of House Building Co-operatives under the Ministry of Building and must employ the services of the state building enterprise in the construction of their dwellings. By these means the role of housing in the national economy is kept under control to conform to the national plan. (1981, p. 180)

The Czechoslovakian case was not very different:

From the very beginning of the program the co-op construction was directly controlled by various levels of the governmental hierarchy. Not only the volumes of the co-op apartments to be constructed during a year in a city, district, or county but also the daily participation of the members of the co-op in work assignments were regulated by one or another agency of the local government, by the council of the co-op, or by local unit of the Communist Party. . . . Since March 1969 executive branches were put in charge of their territorially subordinated co-operatives. These branches were, together with the Czechoslovak State Bank (which was involved in providing and controlling governmental subsidies and credits) responsible for all the activities of housing co-operatives. (Kansky, 1976, pp. 113–115)

In Czechoslovakia in the 1960s, cooperative housing construction, exclusively in the form of apartments, became the dominant form of new housing, and the principles of housing distribution were the same as for state-owned apartments (Franek, 1967).

Leaving aside the small privately organized cooperatives, two basic types of housing cooperatives were developed. One of them was the cooperative of the tenants, where the apartments were in the collective ownership of the cooperative and private households rented the apartments. This is similar to the usual form of housing cooperative in Western countries. The other was the building cooperative, which worked only in the period of the construction. After completion it was either transformed into an operating cooperative or it was terminated, and the apartments became individually owned. Both types were in existence in Czechoslovakia, Poland, and the GDR. However, in Hungary, Romania, and Bulgaria, only building cooperatives existed.

The introduction of cooperative housing changed the distribution of political control by state organizations over housing allocation. Among East European countries, however, there were great differences in the extent to which cooperatives meant local initiative and control.

Overall, the 1960s were characterized by a contradiction in the East European countries. On the one hand, decisive political steps were made toward the improvement of the housing situation; however, on the other these decisions were not followed by sufficient investment. The reason was that in the economic sphere there was no interest group that lobbied in favor of the housing construction sector. This explains the fact that, in spite of the liberal character of housing policy, new construction declined, and there was heavy reliance on private housing construction.

The New Wave of Centralization, 1969–80

The roots of the third period were in the weak housing construction output of the 1960s. In the late 1960s, decisions were made to start large-scale housing investment programs using prefabricated techniques. This was assisted in part by loans, as East European countries opened toward the West. In consequence, the volume of housing construction started to grow radically in almost all East European countries.

In Czechoslovakia, the industrialization program for the building industry was accepted as early as 1955, and the proportion of prefabricated housing units among the new construction reached 55 percent in 1965 (Franek, 1967). In Hungary the decision was taken later, and prefabricated housing became dominant in the 1970s. The new housing policy based on panel technology necessarily led to a centralization of direction and planning that was completely consistent with the "rationalization" programs affecting the institutional system of East European countries. The rationalization included the reorganization of public administration, the growth in the scale of local government units, and the merger of industrial enterprises. Housing policy gradually became part of this centralized state decision-making power apparatus, mainly because the majority of central housing investments and subventions were distributed through this hierarchy.

The aim of the new housing policy was the elimination of the so-called quantitative housing shortage, which was a justification for limiting individual housing choices in order to reach the maximum housing output with a given industrial capacity. The logic of new centralization called for a housing policy that limited private construction as much as possible and restricted the demand for housing, both from the qualitative and the quantitative points of view. The more liberal regulations of the 1960s were revoked, for example, in Poland, where the recentralization of building material supply for private housing construction in fact meant a new limitation on private building.

In addition to the restrictions on private construction, the limitation of quality standards in state housing construction played an important role. In the case of Poland, Kozlowski (1988) explains that quantitative targets were achieved by decreasing costs by lowering average apartment sizes and by decreasing specifications, particularly in terms of equipment and finishes. In Hungary, the average size of the constructed unit was also in the center of the political discussions at that time.

By setting up factories to manufacture prefabricated building panels and large construction companies, new actors were brought into the housing sector. It was in the interests of these firms to influence the allocation of the budget in their favor, and, owing to their power, the levels of subsidies held up during the 1960s.

As a result, in contrast to other spheres of consumption, the financial burdens of the population did not increase within the state housing sphere.

The consequences of the dominant role of the housing industry were dramatic and lasted until the mid- or late 1980s in most countries. However, the price paid by society for the increased housing output was very high. The rate of demolition increased to make room for large-scale projects in urban areas and displaced large numbers of people (Bunchak and Michalovic, 1988; Kansky, 1976). The quality of housing decreased as a logical consequence of the permanent shortage of construction capacity and the monopoly position of the companies. Construction costs increased, and the construction sector demanded ever more from the budget.

In the 1970s, however, other tendencies could be observed, which were leading to divergences between East European countries. In countries strictly following a centralization policy—in Romania and the GDR, for example—the private sector and individual housing construction were increasingly suppressed. Hungary, on the other hand, gradually deviated from this development model through its economic policy in the second half of the 1960s, the so-called New Economic Mechanism. Because of the importance of the growing secondary economy, largely based on agriculture, a feedback mechanism developed between the performance of the private economy and housing construction, especially, but not only, in rural areas, where private house-building was buoyant. This was related to the fact that control over the income of the population loosened. Private building was less and less hindered by a central housing policy. Moreover, it was supported to some extent through government policy on the supply of building sites and building material and on building standards. At the same time, the state maintained the priority of state housing construction in the distribution of finance.

With more money being able to be spent, the quality of private housing began to improve, so that it soon far exceeded the state sector. With this, a tension was built into the system. However, a more liberal economic policy, although it alleviated budget burdens, did not bring about structural changes in the whole economy, so tensions between primary and secondary economies became permanent.

Economic Crisis and Decentralization

The fourth period was ushered in by the economic crisis, which began in the West with the oil price explosion in the mid-1970s and had spread to the socialist countries by the end of the decade. The relatively smooth period of extensive housing development in the 1960s and 1970s ended, and economic difficulties reached the housing sector in every East European country. At the beginning of the 1980s, socialist countries had to decide how they would react to the increasing economic difficulties. This was the second turning point of the housing model, since significant differences developed between the socialist countries in reaction to the crisis. The origins of selecting different routes of development, however, were not be found in the housing sphere, but in the economy and in politics.

There were three identifiable sets of reactions to the economic crisis among the East European countries: (1) In the GDR, and to a lesser extent in Bulgaria, politics did not let the crisis enter the housing sector. Output was sustained, and regulation of the sector continued unchanged. In the GDR, this approach was possible because the economy was stronger than elsewhere, and the period of growth lasted until the mid-1980s. (2) In Romania, Czechoslovakia, and Poland, the reaction was to reduce output, but to make few other reforms. (3) A third type of reaction to the economic crisis was to experiment with housing reform, with the aim of stemming the reduction in output by restructuring the housing finance system and reducing subsidies. This approach was pursued in Hungary.

While most of the East European countries reacted to the economic crisis by stricter central regulation of the economy, Hungary did just the opposite. Here, from the early 1980s on, a series of reforms were adopted, that gave increasing preferences to the private sphere of economy. As a result, the secondary economy, which was legalized in 1968, gained an increasing share and gradually turned into a private economy, having potentially the same rights as the state sector. The transition was a slow process: the share of the private sphere was less than 5 percent of the economy by the end of the 1980s. However, the direction of change was clear, and it was significant that there were no longer restrictions on private incomes for ideological reasons.

The slow transformation of the economy toward a market system took place without a significant reform of the political system. The state gave up control only over individual incomes, and, right until the end of the 1980s, it continued to restrict investment of private capital in commerce and industry. The most accepted investment for individual savings was the real estate market; this meant that the state made it possible for income differences to manifest themselves in housing, since the principle of only one house per family was maintained until 1989. There was, therefore, an acceptance of a kind of "performance principle," which at the same time made it possible for the state to reduce the volume and ratio of strongly subsidized state housing construction.

As well as these economic reasons, hidden pressure by the political–economic elite also had a role in the transformation of the housing system. These social groups had benefited significantly in the earlier period, when state housing construction was at the fore. Since they did not want to fall behind the "new-rich" groups in the secondary (private) housing system, they exerted pressure to convert their positional advantage into market advantage—that is, to convert their state-owned apartments to private ownership.

So, at the beginning of the 1980s, within the framework of the economic–political changes, which provided further allowances for the private sector, a general housing reform was introduced. The new housing policy of 1983 gave up restrictive control over the private sector, withdrew part of subsidy to the state sphere, and extended subsidy to include the private sphere.

This reallocation of resources resulted in a reduction in state housing construction, which was counterbalanced for a short time by a boom in private construction. Inflationary pressures in the economy had a larger impact on the housing sphere and involved transferring the burdens of housing construction needs to the credit sphere. This temporarily alleviated the problems of the housing sector, but since essential transformation of the economic mechanism did not take place for political reasons (support for nonprofitable companies was not terminated), by the end of the 1980s inflation gained impetus and created a bankruptcy situation as the costs of Western loans began to become substantial.

As a consequence of economic crisis during the 1980–85 period, housing construction was reduced significantly in Czechoslovakia, Poland, Hungary, and Romania, falling back to the level of the 1960s. This decline came only later, and to a less significant extent, in the GDR and in Bulgaria. The Soviet Union bucked the trend and increased its housing construction performance from the mid-1980s onwards, after having had the lowest output of all East European countries in the late 1970s.

System building also began to be challenged effectively, although the power of the companies had previously meant that analyses made no difference to policy. Research centered on prefabricated technology and was highly critical.

Results . . . show that the concrete, steel and energy input into industrialized panels could instead have yielded 70 percent more dwellings if channelled into traditional methods. Attention is now being directed to the high energy losses inherent with the cold construction materials in Poland's harsh winter, to the high cost of transport between factory and site, the underemployment of expensive machinery, such as tower cranes, and the long-term costs of the system's maintenance. (Marmot, 1981, p. 183)

The result was that the situation changed in the 1980s: the budgetary crisis was deeper, subsidies were reduced, and so housing plants had to restrict their production. Table 2.1 demonstrates the extent to which output was reduced in state and cooperative housing construction—where panel technology was generally used. In Bulgaria and the GDR, there was significant prefabricated construction even at the end of the 1980s. Prefabricated production also fell back in Czechoslovakia, Poland, and Romania, where there was no radical transformation of the housing policy. The rate of decline cannot, however, measure up to that in Hungary, where the housing reform in 1983 dissolved the special allowances given to plants producing prefabricated elements.

Another consequence of the crisis of the socialist housing system was the reduction of the support for those in severe housing need. The state housing construction boom of the 1970s was characterized by the extension of the sub-

Table 2.1. State and Cooperative Housing Construction in the Year of Greatest Output and in 1988

Country	Year of greatest output	Units (in thousands) Peak year	1988	1988 as proportion of peak year (%)
Hungary				
State	1975	50	18	36
Cooperative	1975	38	5	13
Czechoslovakia				
State	1975	105	65	62
Cooperative	1975	36	24	66
Poland				
State	1978	210	125	60
Cooperative	1975	88	40	45
Romania				
State	1980	190	97	51
Cooperative	—	—	—	—
Bulgaria				
State	1977	40	30	75
Cooperative	1977	40	30	75
GDR				
State	1985	100	95	75
Cooperative	1986	70	68	95

Source: Matras, 1989.

sidy system to the lower social classes in the cities. Modification of housing policy in the 1980s had the severest effect on the situation of the most impoverished social groups. One of the essential features of the East European housing model was that state subsidies were attached to types of housing rather than to qualitative characteristics of apartments or to the actual income of families: "Differences in household expenditures compared to net household income are more pronounced among the types of housing than among their category of quality. The dwellings' quality differences are not mirrored by the rents" (Raban, 1976, p. 15). The deterioration in the situation of the most needy is best shown by the decrease in the number and ratio of new state-owned apartments, which were the only form of new housing available to the very poor. In this respect, too, there are important differences in timing between the East European countries.

Of course, Table 2.1 does not indicate precisely the changes in the chances of lower-income social groups to obtain apartments, since other kinds of state subsidy also existed and the allocation of state-owned apartments was not based exclusively on social principles. It seems certain, however, that the reform of the socialist housing model in the 1980s worsened the chances for those in need of housing.

With respect to Czechoslovakia, Raban reports that the policy consisted of:

New formulation for housing distribution; new regulation for sale of dwellings; new adjustment of rents without any social considerations which should be handled by social subsidies; legal guarantee for temporary lease (private renting); to increase the role of co-operatives in new building; to replace the local authorities' control over temporarily empty family houses with progressive house tax and to lift any control over rents in private rental sector; to allow private landlords up to three dwellings. (Raban, 1976)

In Bulgaria, a new housing policy was introduced in 1986, with the aim of increasing further the share of private provision and replacing state construction, which was not able to solve the housing shortage in large cities and industrial centers (Koleva, 1988). As part of this shift, a number of restrictions on private provision—for example, the regulation of maximum floor space—were eliminated. A new regulation is being worked out to replace the administrative measures with economic regulators and stimulators and to introduce gradually a socially regulated market—however, with the intention of allotting some increase in the number of rental dwellings to socially weak groups (Bulgaria, 1987).

The changes in Eastern Europe in 1989 created a completely new situation in the political and economic systems, and consequently in the housing systems. One of the central elements in the East European housing model was the heavy state subsidies, although their amount and purpose varied significantly in different periods. The programs formulated to put an end to the economic crisis (and the proposals by the World Bank and the International Monetary Fund, which were also taken into account in formulating these programs) contained as a crucial element a radical reduction in state budgets. One of the most important items challenged in the budget was housing subsidy, which amounted, in the case of Hungary at least, to 15 percent of state expenditure and 5 percent of GDP in 1989. With the adoption of radical restructuring programs, it became impossible to retain subsidies to the state housing sector. At the same time it could not been seen how individual families could make up for the loss of state subsidy: only those involved in the private market were able to increase their income in real terms. Yet the number of these families was increasing only slowly.

The other important element of the East European housing model was the autocracy of the state. As one of the most important elements of the change in the political system, this autocracy was brought to an end. As a positive consequence, it became impossible to reproduce political privileges by influencing the housing system. But from the point of view of those in severe housing need, it was not at all clear what the real effect of the elimination of ideological pressure on the housing system would be. Restriction on property rights (that is, the "one family–one apartment" rule) were lifted in order to increase the capacity of the housing sector to perform and to encourage speculative housing construction. However, many doubted that the new system would contribute, even indirectly, to the improvement of the situation of those in need. The real danger was that, as market reform in the housing sector increased, the state would escape totally from the housing sector, instead of operating an effective social housing sector (Hegedüs and Tosics, 1990; Szelényi, 1990).

The process of radical change and total transformation of the economic and political socialist system has just begun. It is still not clear what kinds of new models will be introduced and how socialist economies, operating nearly exclusively with nonmarket structures, can be reformed by market means. In the housing system sharp disputes are apparent between market-oriented financial experts and those who stress the desirability of housing systems that cater for the social needs as well. The results and impact of the more radical attempts at transformation (for example, the Polish "shock strategy") are not yet visible.

THE SOCIAL AND ECONOMIC PERFORMANCE OF THE EAST EUROPEAN HOUSING SYSTEMS

Two issues form the conclusion of this theoretical and historical overview: (1) What effect did the socialist housing model have on the allocation process and on the social structure in general? (2) What was the contribution of the housing sector to economic performance—in other words, what was its role in the failure of the centrally planned economy?

The Social Effects of the East European Model

With regard to the social effect of the East European housing model, two theoretical approaches can be identified. One derives from a Western left-wing analysis and declares solidarity with the socialist housing systems, regarding them as superior to the market economies. The other approach, originating from East European authors, paradoxically has many similarities to the standpoint of Western right-wing (conservative) analysts and those critical of the East European system and denies any positive role for the socialist state.

The first approach, although to some extent it questions the effectiveness and success of the East European way of development, claims that the socialist housing model brought about positive changes in handling social problems and moderating inequalities. Empirical evidence of this is considered to be the low level of rents, the relative equity of housing consumption, and the low level of social segregation. The second approach questions the "social" character of state socialism and considers the housing problems of the East European countries to be a consequence of this social system. It emphasizes negative features, such as the continuing housing shortage, the privileges of the elites, and the distortions caused by the black market. Among the critical approaches, the most important is that of Ivan Szelényi (1978, 1983). According to his account it was the socialist state that created inequalities, and, in comparison with state allocation, even market processes had had equalizing effects.

When studying the housing system of Hungary in the 1970s, we started from Szelényi's structural theory, but we were looking for an explanation for the changes to the East European housing model. It was concluded that changes to the housing model may be explained by the conflict of the state and the private sector (Hegedüs and Tosics, 1983), which we have further developed into a theoretical explanation, described in the first part of this chapter. We did not question Szelényi's analysis of the inequalities within the housing system in the 1960s (although we tried to show that different processes were emerging in the 1970s, at least in Hungary), but we did not agree with his purely structural explanation, which attributed either a "good" or a "bad" role to the socialist state, irrespective of the given phase of development. Our conclusion is that the operation and the outcomes of the housing system are influenced within the very wide frames of economic rationality by conflicts of different interest groups within the population and of institutions with interests in housing policy and the housing market. To some extent, ideological elements are also important.

Szelényi further developed his concept, based on developments in Hungary in the 1970s, especially the introduction of market-oriented economic reforms. According to the new hypothesis, as well as inequalities caused by state redistribution, the market, as a secondary distributing mechanism, also causes inequalities (Szelényi and Manchin, 1986). These two inequality systems strengthen rather than weaken each other. This model was more similar to (and partly built on) our empirical investigations, which were carried out in the mid-1980s. We do not agree, however, with the political conclusion drawn on the basis of the theory. According to this, the introduction of a third mechanism—so-called "welfare redistribution"—is necessary to counterbalance the inequalizing effect of the state and the market. Instead, we have drawn attention to the basic definitional problems of the distribution spheres, and to the necessity of separating private and market spheres and the proposed social control of these spheres.

As a result of the developments at the end of the 1980s, with the collapse of the socialist economic system and the spread of market-oriented ideas in East European countries, Szelényi has again modified his theory (Szelényi, 1990). Criticizing endeavors aimed at the privatization of state institutions, assuming the slow breakdown of the central economic institutions, it is necessary to maintain and even strengthen the state sector in housing. Now he considers that the state primarily has welfare and social functions and is quite different from the state he analyzed in the 1960s in Hungary which was exacerbating inequalities.

Our standpoint is less optimistic regarding the internal changes of the socialist housing model and its ability to transform itself into a welfare housing model. We argue that maintaining or even strengthening the welfare role of the state seems to be unrealistic from an economic point of view. The economic problems of the central planning system have been as serious in the housing sector as elsewhere, and the process of privatization occurring in all East European countries is strengthening the role of the market and weakening the role of state regulation.

As a final remark on the equity of the socialist housing model, we cannot accept theories that arrive at a general conclusion merely from the decisive role of the state in redistribution. The rejection applies equally to those theories that regard the state as a force for great equity and those that regard it as a source of inequity. Instead, we argue that the essence of the socialist housing model was its decision-making structure, in which the planning organs—both party and state— had a decisive role in determining the conditions of informal contracts with the most important institutions and layers of the population. The socialist housing model differs from Western housing systems fundamentally in this respect. In Western systems, the formation of housing policy depends more on the citizens, with their decisions how to spend their (larger) incomes and on institutions independent of the state, including financial institutions and the construction industry, which form part of a market economy.

This does not mean, however, that in the socialist housing model citizens have no influence on the development of housing market processes at all. In our study we have suggested various voice and exit options open to citizens. Nor does it mean that the model is static from its birth. We have shown that significantly different submodels were developed as a result of the change of concepts of the socialist economy, modification by institutional forces, and political and economic circumstances within individual countries. At the beginning the socialist housing model was based on political, economic, and housing policy principles worked out and exported by one country, the Soviet Union; yet after a short while these principles were handled quite flexibly by the individual countries.

The Economic Performance of the Socialist Housing Model

The economic performance of the model is as questionable as the social character of the allocation. The basic problem of the system was that housing was separated from the economy, and the economic position of households was only very indirectly tied to their housing situation. According to the original model, housing was regarded as a social good, but no society could really afford this. The system generated its award system with the allocation of the best housing according to the "positional" principle. This was, of course, a very inefficient mediation of job performance with housing, and much less effective than in the market economies. The majority of state-controlled allocation had nothing or very little to do with the economy, and this, in turn, had an effect on both the economy and on the housing sector. The effect on the economy was that the system lost one of the most importance incentives. The effect on housing was that consumer feedback on quality was usually absent.

The cost of housing was low, because of price controls, including grants and subsidies, and control over rents, utility fees, loan repayments, and interest rates.

38   •   Housing Privatization in Eastern Europe

As a consequence of the housing shortage, a secondary market was formed, with very high access costs. Even the countries that went the furthest toward market allocation did not achieve anything like a functioning housing market; at best, there were quasi-markets, which influenced the allocation of existing houses but did not influence production, because of the lack of feedback mechanisms to the job market, and the construction and housing finance sectors.

In conclusion, the question of how to achieve equity and efficiency is the most important task during the period of transition from socialism. On the one hand it is important to ensure some control over the main housing sectors in order to achieve the social goals of housing policy; on the other hand it is important to integrate the housing sector into the emerging market economy in order to increase its efficiency.

REFERENCES

Ball, M., and Harloe, M. 1974. Housing policy in a socialist country: The case of Poland. *Research Paper No. 8.* London: Centre for Environmental Studies.
Bater, J. 1977. Soviet town planning: Theory and practice in 1970s. *Progress in Human Geography* 1 (1), 177–207.
Bauer, T. 1982. A második gazdasági reform és a tulajdonviszonyok [The second economy reform and the property relations]. *Mozgó Világ* 11, 17–42.
Bessonova, O. 1988. Reform of the Soviet housing model: Search for a concept. Paper presented to the East European Housing Working Group of the European Network for Housing Research. Budapest.
von Beyme, K. 1981. *Economics and Politics within Socialist Systems.* New York: Praeger.
Bulgaria. 1987. *National Monograph: Regional Planning, Urban Planning and Housing Policy.* Sofia: Committee for Regional and Urban Planning.
Bunchak, J., and Michalovic, P. 1988. Housing dynamics in Czechoslovakia—What brings the mass housing construction? Paper presented to the Conference on Housing Reforms in Eastern Europe. Noszvaj, Hungary.
Cegielski, J. 1969. *Stosunki mieszkaniowe w Warszawie w Latach 1864–1964* [Housing in Warsaw in the years 1864–1964]. Warsaw: Arkady.
Dawson, A. 1984. *The Land Problems in the Developed Economy.* London: Croom Helm.
Faltan, L. 1987. *Housing in Country Settlements: A Socio-Cultural Problem.* Bratislava: SPTU.
Fehér, H., Heller, A., and Márkus, G. 1983. *Dictatorship over Needs.* Oxford: Blackwell.
Franek, J. 1967. *Housing in Czechoslovakia.* Prague: Research Institute for Building and Architecture.
Gallagher, P. 1982. Housing in Bulgaria. *Housing Review* 31 (4), 124–126.
Hegedüs, J., and Tosics, I. 1983. Housing classes and housing policy: Some changes in the Budapest housing market. *International Journal of Urban and Regional Research* 7 (4), 467–494.

Hegedüs, J., and Tosics, I. 1990. Hungarian housing finance, 1983–1990: A failure of housing reform. *Housing Finance International* 4 (4), 34–41.

Hoffman, M. 1972. *Wohnungspolitik der DDR*. Düsseldorf: Verlag Wohnungwirtschaft.

Kansky, K. 1976. *Urbanisation under Socialism: The Case of Czechoslovakia*. New York: Praeger.

Koleva, M. 1988. *Housing policy trends in Bulgaria*. Mimeo.

Konrád, G., and Szelényi, I. 1974. Social Conflicts of Underurbanisation. In M. Harloe (ed.), *Captive Cities*. London: Wiley.

Kornai, J. 1980. *A Hiány* [The economy of shortage]. Budapest: KJK.

Kotacka, L. 1987. *Some socioeconomic correlates of family housing in Czechoslovakia*. Mimeo.

Kozlowski, E. 1988. Directions of housing transformations in Poland. Paper presented to the East European Housing Policy Working Group of the European Network for Housing Research, Budapest.

Marmot, A. 1981. Polish Housing. *Housing Review* 30 (6), 180–182.

Matras, H. 1989. Structure and performance of the housing sector of the centrally planned economies. *Discussion Paper* (Report INU 53). Washington DC: World Bank.

Morton, H. 1980. Who gets what, when and how? Housing in the Soviet Union. *Soviet Studies* 32 (2), 235–259.

Musil, J. 1987. Housing Policy and the sociospatial structure of cities in a socialist country—The example of Prague. *International Journal of Urban and Regional Research* 11 (1), 37–60.

Polányi, K. 1976. *Az archaikus társadalom és gazdasági szemlélet* [The archaic society and economic view]. Budapest: Gondolat.

Raban, P. 1976. *Housing Policy in Czechoslovakia*. Prague: Orbis Press Agency.

Sawicki, S. 1977. *Soviet Land and Housing Law: A Historical and Comparative Study*. New York: Praeger.

Soós, K. 1986. *Terv, Kampány, Pénz* [Plan, campaign, money]. Budapest: KJK.

Szelényi, I. 1978. Social inequalities under state redistributive economies. *International Journal of Comparative Sociology* 29 (1–2), 61–87.

Szelényi, I. 1983. *Urban Inequalities under State Socialism*. Oxford: Oxford University Press.

Szelényi, I. 1988. *East European Socialist Cities—How Different Are They?* Los Angeles: UCLA Department of Sociology.

Szelényi, I. 1990. Development in socialist economies. In W. van Vliet and J. van Weesep (eds.), *Government and Housing* (pp. 236–241). London: Sage.

Szelényi, I., and Manchin, R. 1986. Social policy under state socialism: The role of redistribution and market in the formation of social inequalities. *Medvetánc* 2–3, 69–111.

3

The New *Länder* of Germany

Jörg Köhli and Keith Kintrea

INTRODUCTION

The privatization of housing in the former East Germany (German Democratic Republic—GDR) provides a unique case within this book. Instead of pursuing an independent path to a new democratic future, in effect East Germany no longer exists. Officially, Germany was "reunified" in 1990, but the new enlarged German state is not an amalgam of East and West. The GDR has been subsumed within the Federal Republic of Germany (FRG), its territory described as the "new *Länder*," contrasted with the "old *Länder* of West Germany.

The FRG developed in the postwar era to become one of the world's most successful capitalist economies. In 1989, its per capita GDP was $19,200, compared to Britain's $14,600 and the United States' $20,600 (OECD, 1992). Economic growth was accompanied by reasonably strong social provision, including good social security and unemployment benefits, subsidies for "social housing," and, latterly, a housing allowance scheme. Since reunification there has been a massive effort to align the new *Länder* with the old by extending West German institutions to the East. That privatization has been high on the agenda is no surprise: West German governments have always believed in a strong private sector. The current government is led by a right-wing coalition, of which the Christian Democrats (CDU) are the largest group by far. Housing, however, is not at the forefront as an issue following reunification, although its importance is evident by the inclusion of housing proposals in the Unification Treaty. More political attention has been given to privatizing the former state-owned enterprises of the GDR, which were taken over by a Federal agency, the

Treuhandstalt; they have gradually been turned over to new owners or, in many cases, closed down.

The social stability of the new—and indeed the old—*Länder* is a criterion that underlies much of the strategy of privatization. East Germans lived for years in conditions of relative austerity compared to their affluent Western neighbors, and reunification was expected to bring material rewards. But most of East German industry, like much in Eastern Europe generally, when exposed to competitive markets, became an overnight failure. For many East Germans, reunification has brought unemployment, and average incomes for those still in work runs at 70 percent of those in West Germany. There is a continuing hemorrhage of the more skilled and educated out of the new *Länder* into the old, increasing housing shortages there.

Unemployment and feelings of powerlessness, despite the fall of communism, have helped to fuel unrest in East German cities, including some violent demonstrations by neo-fascists. Thus the strategy toward reunification has been to minimize the effects of changes and to avoid creating undue hardship. This chapter outlines the housing systems in both East and West Germany and then considers the major changes since reunification. The focus is then on privatization in the new *Länder,* with particular emphasis on the problems that have emerged to hinder the central government drive for privatization. Lessons are drawn from a number of projects established to explore ways of overcoming obstacles to privatization.

HOUSING IN THE FEDERAL REPUBLIC OF GERMANY

In order to understand the approach taken to privatization in the new *Länder,* it is worth sketching the key functions of the housing system of the FRG. As Ulbrich and Wullkopf (1993) explain, the dominant philosophy, shared eventually by both Christian Democrats and the Social Democrat opposition is that of a *Soziale Marktwirtschaft* [a socially responsible market economy]. Essentially, this means a reliance on the private sector, both owner-occupation and private renting, with safeguards of social housing and, more recently, *Wohngeld* [housing allowances].

In the 1980s, the West German housing system became more market-orientated; there was a cut-back in new social housing construction, thanks to declining political support, and much social housing was converted to market-rented housing as the conditions attached for loans given for its construction were relaxed as the loans were repaid. Housing costs rose, and the *Wohngeld* bill grew sharply. At the end of the 1980s the laws governing nonprofit housing organizations were changed: the tax advantages of these organizations were abolished, with the intention that they would begin to act in a more entrepreneurial fashion. West Germany, at the end of the 1980s, had an owner-occupied sector and a private rented sector, each representing 42 percent of the market, while 16 percent was social housing for rent, owned by a variety of different landlords, including profit-making companies.

HOUSING IN THE GERMAN DEMOCRATIC REPUBLIC

The GDR, of all the countries considered in this book, is perhaps the one where the socialist model of a housing system disintegrated least. There were two main reasons for this: the relative strength of the East German economy, which was able to sustain a vigorous house-building program right up to 1989; and the relative success of the authorities in suppressing potential political pressure concerning the inadequacies of the housing system.

The GDR's housing system has recently been described (in English) by Bucholz (1990), Lundqvist (1992), Marcuse and Schumann (1992), and Dienemann (1993). As usual, the state assigned itself the leading role in housing provision, intending to be the main housing developer while attempting to control private activity in the housing system. Less usually, the state met with considerable success, particularly in its role of developer. Lundqvist submits that "the scale of the GDR's efforts to 'solve the housing question as a social problem by 1990' is simply astounding" (1992, p. 20). By the end of the 1980s, 42 percent of housing in the GDR was state housing, 19 percent held by cooperatives of different types, and 41 percent privately owned.

Private ownership in the GDR requires explanation. After the Second World War, unlike many other East European countries, very little existing housing was taken into state ownership. Instead, privately owned apartment houses and tenements remained in private hands, while individual houses, if tenanted, were encouraged to be sold to their occupants.

However, rent control, which had been established by the Nazis in 1936, was continued, and rents for privately owned dwellings remained frozen at 1930s prices until after reunification. New private building for rent was discouraged and could make no economic sense in any case, given prevailing rents. Old privately rented buildings could be bought and sold, but they had no value because of the rent levels that could be charged. This privately owned rented housing was managed by the state, and most owners took no interest in the property. Some of this housing was transferred into state ownership, but according to Marcuse and Schumann (1992) the local authorities often turned down gifts of property because it was a financial liability and seen as a hangover from capitalist urban development, which was politically repellent.

By the 1980s, this kind of property represented slightly more than half of private housing in the GDR. Much of it was in a very bad condition, having had no maintenance or reinvestment since the 1930s. Uneven patterns of development and modernization (see below) meant that there were great disparities in house condition and amenities between different areas of the GDR. In Dresden, for example, only 61 percent of houses had an inside toilet in 1990, compared to

95 percent in Berlin (Dienemann, 1993). Although there is an absence of recent disaggregated data, Marcuse and Schumann (1992) report that in terms of repair, the bigger "underprivileged" cities and medium-sized towns were the worst, with the exception of Berlin, the showpiece, which was the best. Unsurprisingly, privately owned rented housing in poor condition was disproportionately occupied by older people and other disadvantaged groups.

The other component of the private sector was owner-occupation. Like other East European countries, individual owner-occupation of (mostly) detached houses was encouraged at various times for pragmatic reasons. In the period after 1953 (when there was an uprising against the government), state loans and building plots were made available to individuals, which raised output of individual houses considerably. Between the construction of the Berlin Wall in 1961 and 1973, private construction fell away, as the emphasis was on state building for rent.

After 1973, there was again a boom, so that by the 1980s individual house building accounted for about 10 percent of production in most years (Bucholz, 1990). A characteristic of the owner-occupied section of the GDR was that it was heavily controlled. A licence to build an owner-occupied house was based on household size and type, and building regulations insisted upon the use of particular techniques and materials. There seems to have been very little, if any, unauthorized self-building. By the end of the 1980s, around 20 percent of housing was owner-occupied, representing half of the privately owned housing stock.

State housing in the GDR was planned centrally, according to (perennially unfulfilled) five-year plans. The 1950s saw the rise of system building techniques and the production of huge housing estates of identical apartment buildings, built up in subunits of 5,000 residents. By the mid-1960s, 90 percent of new state housing was of prefabricated panel construction (Bucholz, 1990). Unlike other East European countries, the GDR in the 1970s and 1980s saw a renewed boom in state housing construction, with a million houses being built following Erich Honecker's election and his political determination to solve the housing problem. Mostly these state-owned apartments were small (only 16 percent had more than three rooms) and built in very high-density estates, but they were not necessarily as brutal in their scale or visual impact as, for example, Soviet housing (Dienemann, 1993). By 1989, there were 317 state housing enterprises in the GDR, managing 2.8 million apartments, or around 42 percent of the country's housing.

The 1970s also saw the start of the modernization of old housing, which had previously been ignored because of ideological opposition to capitalist housing forms, although some had also been demolished. Such housing was taken from its private owners by the state. By 1985, over four houses were being modernized for every six newly constructed, but in about half of these cases modernization seems to have been confined to the installation of plumbing and inside baths.

The final component of the housing system was various types of cooperative housing. Like individual house building, these cooperatives emerged first after

1953. The earliest ones were always connected with a particular enterprise. Later, in the 1950s, independent housing cooperatives, many of which had been in existence since before the war, were revived as housing developers. As in other East European countries, cooperatives received considerable state help, including land and cheap loans, but individual households were expected to use their savings to help finance the housing. Another feature common with other European countries was the weakness of cooperation and democratic control, made worse by mergers between cooperatives. Cooperative output rose from nothing in 1953 to over half of new housing construction by 1961. Completions fell away to about 1 percent of output by 1971, rising to over 40 percent by the end of the 1980s. By the time of reunification, there were nearly 800 cooperatives, holding about 17 percent of the housing stock.

A common feature of private rented, state, and cooperative housing was that it was extremely cheap. Rent setting was a political issue, and rents were kept low "to buttress the claim that socialist was guaranteeing basic necessities of life for all" (Marcuse and Schumann, 1992, p. 112). Although not all the reportage is consistent, on average, rents seem to have been between 2.7 and 4 percent of average incomes. Management and maintenance costs alone were estimated to be at least three times the cost of rent (Bucholz, 1990).

At the time of reunification, the problems of housing in the GDR, seen from the West, could be summarized as follows:

- very poor housing conditions, decay, and a lack of amenities in the prewar stock, with cramped apartments in bleak and mostly undermaintained modern concrete structures—preunification estimates were that 700,000 dwellings out of about 7 million were fit only for demolition;
- an overall housing shortage, despite a falling population;
- rents too low—insufficient even to cover management and maintenance costs, far less new investment;
- a total lack of market signals in production and consumption, leading to an inefficient and ineffective use of resources.

PRIVATIZATION

It was inevitable that the Federal German government would seek to create a "social market" housing system out of the state-dominated GDR, involving extensive privatization. Reunification meant turning away from state housing control. It was believed that state control should be replaced, for the most part, by private decision-makers, whose actions are guided, on a decentralized basis, by considerations of profitability. In line with its overall philosophy, the Federal government saw privatization as the decisive element for the efficient management of the housing stock and the rational behavior of investors in new housing construction. These decentralized decisions, guided by expectations of profitability, were held to lead to optimum results for the economy as a whole, provided rents were consistent with scarcity. The signaling effect of rents is, after all, intended to bring about a balance between supply and demand. In addition to relatively narrow concerns about the housing market, there was also an ideological interest in promoting housing privatization. Private property was seen as an indispensable pillar of a market-oriented society. Private ownership was held to be a prerequisite for responsible action, since the consequences of people's own actions then react directly and in an undiluted form on the people taking the action themselves (Köhli, 1993).

Another advantage of privatization, assuming a similar pattern of preferences on the part of the population of both the new and the old *Länder*, is that extensive private capital can be mobilized. This is likely to produce multiplier effects throughout the economy.

The goals for the housing sector in the new *Länder* have been set in order to capture these advantages of a private housing market. The aim of privatizing the housing stock was specifically laid down in the Unification Treaty, which the Federal Republic of Germany concluded with the GDR in 1990. However, housing "enterprises" are not being treated like the manufacturing or service sector. Instead of being structured to meet competition and privatized by the *Treuhandstalt*, state-owned enterprises in the housing sector are covered by special regulations. As a first step, state-owned housing assets have passed into the ownership of the local authorities, which have become landlords for roughly 2.8 million dwellings. However, it is intended under the Unification Treaty that the local authorities will gradually privatize this housing stock by, at first, setting up housing enterprises under private law, which will be owned by the authorities themselves. Later, as a final step to privatization, the government hopes that a substantial portion of the housing stock will be sold to private investors and, in particular, to the tenants themselves. However, while privatization is a key aim of the Federal government, it is up to the local authorities to determine their own priorities (Dienemann, 1993). The council can decide whether, and how, to dispose of its housing. Although there is a strong demand by some tenants to become owner–occupiers, there is no "right to buy" in any part of Germany.

It is notable that there seems to be little interest in transforming state housing into conventional Western forms of rented housing—either social renting or market renting. This reflects the downplaying of the role of social housing and nonprofit organizations in the FRG in the 1980s and the priority given to the growth of home ownership. The government believes that selling state housing to private households will lead to the efficient management of the housing stock. It is argued that private households pay close attention, as a rule, to how they use their income and try to obtain good value for money in housing provision, as in other fields. In view of the great need for repair and modernization work in the new *Länder*, privatization is intended to ensure that it is carried out not only at a reasonable price but also in keeping with individual needs and preferences.

The Federal government is, therefore, striving for a significant increase in the level of home ownership in the new *Länder*, not only on overall economic grounds but also on grounds of a positive view of home ownership. Home ownership not only is considered to offer security against rent increases, it also represents a manageable way of creating wealth. The purchase of an owner-occupied dwelling is seen to have proved its worth in the old *Länder*, in particular as a means of providing for old age and as a way of protecting financial assets. This is a little ironic, given that, at 42 percent, West Germany has one of the lowest rates of owner-occupation among Western nations.

A smooth transition to a new market system is complicated by the presence of property restitution. Under the provisions of the Unification Treaty, all property, except industry, nationalized by the GDR is to be given back to its former owners or their heirs. At the beginning of 1992, 1.2 million applications for restitution of private property had been made, of which only 5 percent had been resolved (OECD, 1992). In addition, the majority of housing property was never formally transferred to the state, although it was under *de facto* state control. Nevertheless, the real ownership of much of this property is difficult to trace.

RENTS AND HOUSING ALLOWANCES

A crucial prerequisite for a functioning housing market, apart from private ownership, is rents that are in conformity with the market. Since rents in the former GDR were kept at 1936 levels until reunification, there is substantial need for adjustment. The previous rents bore no relation to the real costs or value of housing. It was not possible in the GDR to finance necessary repair work to cover regular running costs or, indeed, to meet the capital costs involved.

The Federal government is authorized under the Unification Treaty gradually to bring the rents in the new *Länder* up to West German rent levels, in accordance with the growth in incomes. However, earned incomes in the new *Länder* lag behind the old *Länder,* and the restructuring of industry has meant that the East German workforce has been reduced to below 6.5 million, from nearly 10 million in 1989 (OECD, 1992). This means that rents cannot rise to equivalent levels quickly. The first stage of the rent reform came into force in October 1991, the second in January 1993. Since reunification, tenants' expenditure on heating, hot water, other running costs, and rent has increased more than five-fold. Under the old regime, no service charges were levied for heating, hot water, and water supply. At the same time, the *Wohngeld* has been introduced into the new *Länder*, which significantly reduces the burden of housing costs for lower-income households.

THE POTENTIAL FOR SALE OF STATE HOUSING
TO RESIDENTS

Since the housing stock in the new *Länder* is very varied in its type and quality, the suitability for privatization, in particular with regard to the sale of dwellings to private households, varies considerably (Köhli, 1991). The stock of prewar housing is the most suitable for privatization in terms of location. Of course, much of this housing is already privately owned, and much of the rest is subject to restitution claims. Vast numbers of individual cases of ownership need to be resolved, and it is not clear how much housing will prove to be in the ownership of the state and require to be further privatized. Whoever owns this housing, a massive amount of investment is required to bring it up to acceptable standards.

This leaves, for the most part, dwellings that were erected during the postwar period in system-built blocks. However, large sections of this housing stock are suitable only to a limited extent for sale as owner-occupied dwellings, because of the unpopularity of their location (for example, large housing estates on the urban periphery) and the building type (in some cases buildings have more than 10 floors). For the rest of the stock, an important element in determining the sale price is the extent of the repair and modernization work necessary.

There are also problems of privatization arising from the administration of the stock of state-rented housing. The basis for conversion of rented dwellings into owner-occupied dwellings is the extensive body of condominium law in Germany, which stipulates a long series of administrative steps. Even if the conversion of rented dwellings into owner-occupied dwellings could be carried out without the special problems caused by the structure of the economy and the administration in the new *Länder*, privatization would still be a long-term process. The practice of privatization shows that large sections of the local authority administration are not in a position to perform the tasks involved in creating owner-occupied property within a reasonable period of time. Even where local government staff are well motivated, their skills and qualifications are often insufficient for coping with the daily administrative work. At a practical level, six important difficulties can be listed: (1) A major difficulty with immediate, large-scale privatization stems from the large amount of preliminary survey and legal work required. Limited resources mean that there are considerable delays, though with increasing experience gained from individual projects, this process will probably accelerate steadily. (2) As a result of their lack of expertise, local authorities, their housing enterprises, and cooperatives shrink from making a determined start with tackling these tasks. As is the case in many other sectors, this has raised extensive training needs, which can only be met in the medium term. (3) An unfavorable impact is also caused by the widely held view that the state could make better decisions, particularly in the field of housing, than entrepreneurs or private households. In many local authorities, the politicians and administrators have survived from the old GDR regime. A substantial shift in attitudes is still necessary here. (4) The housing stock represents a considerable amount of capital and hence a source of economic and political power in the hands of local government decision makers. Hence considerable resistance to more rapid privatization is evident. (5) It is exceptionally difficult to determine selling prices for housing. Price calculations are taking place within property markets that are barely developed or are too narrow, so that use often has to be made of estimated values. In addition to the usual uncertainties of the value of locational attributes, there is the extra complication of debt burden. As Dienemann (1993) points out, a major problem in privatization is that not only the houses, but the debts associated with them, were handed over to the local authorities. Reunification was accompanied by monetary union between the GDR and FRG, so debts in Ostmarks were translated directly into debts in Deutschmarks. On average, these debts represent about 85 percent of the historic cost of construction and, of course, in many cases exceed the market value of the buildings. As a result of the severe problems of the new *Länder* in summer 1993, the law for part-liquidation of indebtedness for the housing economy of the new *Länder* was enacted. This means that the Federal Government has assumed half the debt burden, including accumulated interests which amounts to 35 billion DM. This part-liquidation is conditional upon the communal and cooperative authorities committing themselves to privatize at least 15 percent of their housing stock within the next ten years. This condition offers a new chance to accelerate the privatization process. (6) Finally, subsidized rents have so far prevented any great interest developing among tenants in purchasing their property. However, the attractiveness of purchase is increasing in parallel with the rise in rent levels. In spite of the high level of interest rates, the cost of a loan to buy owner-occupied property and for rent is converging in many cases.

ASSISTANCE MEASURES AND PILOT PROJECTS

Considerable legal and administrative difficulties prevented much privatization during the first year following reunification. However, with the adoption of the law to remove obstacles to the privatization of enterprises and to promote investment that came into force in 1991, important preconditions for more effective action on the privatization of housing were created.

The speed of privatization, through the sale of local authority dwellings to the tenants, is also being promoted by way of a special grant. In addition to this financial assistance being provided for the repair and modernization of the building stock, a choice between grants and low-interest loans was made available in 1991 and 1992. The Federal government is also promoting the rehabilitation of the housing stock by providing additional tax concessions.

With a view to promoting the privatization of housing, the Federal government is also carrying out 31 pilot projects (Köhli, 1992). In selecting the projects, a range of different approaches was chosen, according to: (1) the type of privatizing agency (commune, housing enterprise, or external agent); (2) the type of building and dwelling (for example, panel construction, new building, old building); (3) the size of the commune; and (4) the *Länd*. Several goals are being pursued with these pilot projects. They are intended to explore the special problems in the new *Länder* in connection with the sale of dwellings to tenants, in order to ascertain the suitability of different types of building in the housing stock for privatization and, where possible, to identify solutions.

The pilot projects open up the possibility for all those involved to gain experience of the privatization of housing in order to channel this into bigger subsequent projects. Not only the housing companies, local government decision makers, and project executors, but also construction firms, craft enterprises, notaries, credit institutions, and the administrative authorities involved are testing out practical cooperation in the course of these projects.

INTERIM FINDINGS OF THE PILOT PROJECTS

The question as to whether the dwellings would be sold before or after rehabilitation played a role in all privatization projects. On one hand, the cost of rehabilitation increases the selling price quite considerably; on the other hand, those interested in purchasing a dwelling wish to put in some work of their own after purchasing their property. However, all the experience so far advises against selling dwellings before rehabilitation work has been carried out, since under German condominium law the individual can be forced, immediately after purchase, by the association of property owners to contribute to the cost of rehabilitating the common parts of the building—including the roof, the external walls, any load-bearing building components, the stairwell, and also piping and wiring. People with little capital who purchase dwellings are then often confronted with insoluble problems. Basic rehabilitation work, at least, should be carried out prior to selling a dwelling in order to protect the purchaser from unforeseeable financial burdens. The probable costs in the near future for the owner-occupied dwelling are then already known at the time the decision to purchase is made.

There was much discussion in the pilot projects about the possibility of rehabilitating dwellings built in panel construction. On balance, the conclusion was that these dwellings are capable of being rehabilitated at a reasonable cost and, in some cases, are also suitable for privatization. The first successful sales show that there is keen interest in this area. In particular, vacant buildings in panel construction can, to a large extent, be converted into owner-occupied dwellings without any great difficulty, since there is a large pool of potential purchasers to draw on.

The scope of rehabilitation work necessary is determined in some cases by the haphazard nature of housing maintenance in the GDR. Different amounts of maintenance work were carried out by the former housing administrations on buildings of the same type and age and standing side-by-side. Also, tenants put in a considerable amount of their own work in some cases, which has resulted in higher selling prices. This work has to be adequately taken into account in selling prices, partly to promote tenants' willingness to purchase dwellings.

The pilot projects show that privatization and rehabilitation agencies should present a range of options for repair and modernization work for discussion. On the one hand, care should be taken to avoid having an unmanageable number of proposals to discuss; on the other hand, there should at least be a limited range of possibilities to choose from.

Single-family houses are obviously easier to sell to tenants than individual sections of housing blocks built in rows or terraces. The reason for this is that not only is it possible to improve the immediately neighboring environment—such as parking spaces, gardens, access road—to a greater extent, but these measures also benefit, first and foremost, the property owners, who also bear the costs, and not the neighbors in general.

Provided financing is secure, a community of tenants exists, and the property can be rehabilitated at reasonable expense, there is almost always a strong tendency to purchase, given the extensive possibilities available of receiving assistance. With intensive counselling and promotional activities removing people's hesitancy about the strange subject of home ownership, a positive change in attitudes toward owner-occupied property often occurs. The people in the age group between 35 and 45 in particular want to avail themselves of the opportunity of acquiring owner-occupied property at a reasonable price.

ISSUES IN PRIVATIZATION PRACTICE

A point raised by the pilot projects is the optimum size of communities of owner–occupiers, which are formed on the basis of condominium law. Larger groups of owner–occupiers in apartment buildings can have advantages, as the administrative costs per housing unit are lower. However, of much greater importance is the fact that in smaller groups of owner–occupiers, decisions on communal issues, which must be taken by the group as a whole, can be reached and enforced much more easily.

The provision of early and adequate information on the proposed privatization of housing is of paramount importance for the progress of privatization projects. However, the provision of adequate information requires that the questions and problems of those affected are known. The privatizing agency can only take account of individual needs if the flow of information runs in both directions— that is, also from the tenant to the selling party. Consequently, one of the primary tasks of the privatizing agency is to establish a dialogue with the tenants.

In parallel with the "open" meetings providing information, which can take place with all interested parties, individual counselling is also valuable if offered at an early stage. The talks focus on the legal position of the tenant as well as on the individual possibilities of financing available and calculation of repayment schemes.

An important criterion for determining the suitability of a property is the occupancy structure, which permits an initial assessment of the potential interest in purchasing to be made. Since buildings with higher owner–occupier ratios are simpler and cheaper to manage, efforts to privatize are being concentrated there. In addition, if nonbinding offers to buy have already been submitted, the starting position is particularly favorable. However, only in very rare cases will it be possible to sell all the dwellings in rented housing blocks to the tenants. Where it is not possible to arrange an exchange of apartments with other tenants willing to purchase, housing units that cannot be sold remain as rented dwellings in the possession of the communes. The tenants must, however, pay a higher rent after rehabilitation work has been carried out, since they also benefit from the refurbishment of, for example, the façades, the roof, the piping and wiring, and the neighborhood environment.

Apart from the price, a variety of other factors also influences the tenants' interest in purchasing property. Willingness to buy is closely associated with tenants' previous satisfaction with the housing, and this is not only focused on the dwelling and the neighborhood, but also depends on the cohesion of the previous and present community of tenants. Good relations with the neighbors and with other tenants in the housing block considerably increase the tenants' interest in home ownership.

The interests of the local authorities and would-be purchasers are usually diametrically opposed when it comes to fixing the selling price. Whereas the local authorities want to obtain a high price, the purchasers try to buy their dwellings on the most favorable terms possible. However, there are very large sections of the housing stock owned by the local authorities in the new *Länder* whose maintenance costs are rising but whose revenue from rent is not yet sufficient to finance maintenance requirements. In view of the fact that the backlog of repair work is growing all the time, losses are occurring on an increasing scale. Local authority interest should, therefore, focus not on maximizing profit by setting particularly high selling prices but on keeping losses to the minimum necessary in the short term by obtaining the highest possible privatization ratios. Even selling at a low price relieves the commune of losses that would arise if management of the dwellings continued.

Tenants in cities as well as rural areas are being offered the option of purchasing their dwellings. However, where high urban land prices are taken fully into account in the selling price, city dwellings are very difficult to sell. One reason for this is that a tenant in a city neither earns significantly more than one in the countryside, nor does he have a greater amount of capital at his disposal. On the other hand, rents are not differentiated significantly according to location, and their cheapness offers no incentive to buy at the higher prices in cities. In contrast with the situation in rural areas, the monthly repayments associated with home ownership in the city are much higher than the rent for a corresponding dwelling as a result of the high land prices in central locations. The potential for future appreciation in value is, by contrast, not yet adequately taken account in the decision-making process.

CONCLUSION

German privatization, then, relies on two distinct measures: the restitution of prewar property to their former owners and the sale of state rental apartments to tenants. At present, the outcome of restitution is not clear, but given the massive scale of private landlordism in West Germany, it is not unreasonable to suggest that restitution will eventually form the basis of a market-rented sector in the new *Länder*. Rents remain protected, although they are rising quickly, and tenants retain security unless the owner requires the property for his or her own use. However, by July 1995 it is planned that the transition to a market-related rent system based on that of West Germany will be complete.

The scale of the privatization of former state-rented apartments depends to a large extent on the existence of a positive attitude at local government level. In practice, willingness to sell is subject to substantial time lags, especially in areas governed by the smaller authorities. This often reflects the close interconnections among decision makers, their personal relationships, and, in some cases, the plurality of offices involved.

Compared with the number of people interested in purchasing property, there are still few local authorities and cooperatives willing to sell. True, the Unification Treaty specifically envisages the privatization of those sections of the housing stock owned by the local authorities, with a particular emphasis on the sale of dwellings to the tenants. However, it is not currently possible to enforce the sale of property legally against the will of the local authority. The decisions on the timing of the sale as well as on the type and number of dwellings to be offered rest with the present property owners. Tenants, therefore, still have to assert their interests in a politically effective manner. Meanwhile, the Federal governments of the *Länder* draw attention to the task of privatization again and again in their public relations work, and housing allowances are available to plug the gap between income and housing expenditure.

This situation contrasts strongly with policies elsewhere in Eastern Europe. Often tenants have been given a "right to buy" by central government over the heads of local government and regardless of any long-term concern about the condition of the houses. The FRG had a tradition of decentralized government and effective legal measures to ensure a high standard of housing. It is to its credit that these considerations remain, in spite of the pressure to privatize.

Experience so far shows that privatization of housing is possible, if the willingness to carry it out is there, both at local government level and among the decision makers in the housing administrations and companies. However, as in other areas the privatization of housing requires an efficient administration. The need for extensive administrative support from the western *Länder,* therefore, continues to exist. In order for privatization to proceed more rapidly, the acceptance of privatization by local authorities must be improved. In some cases, potential purchasers also need to be convinced about the benefits of home ownership.

With about 8,000 housing units sold in 1991 and probably a further 20,000 housing units in 1992, the initial phase of the privatization of dwellings has, however, been completed. Central to housing policy at present is the task of giving this process a greater momentum, identifying obstacles, and further improving the success of privatization measures. The government view is that even though it is clear that extensive privatization can only be achieved in the medium term, there must be no deviation from the goal of establishing a "socially responsible market economy" in housing.

The transition from the centrally planned economy of the former GDR to a social market economy is proving to be more difficult in the housing sector, as in other sectors, than it was first assumed. However, in contrast to the situation in the countries of Eastern Europe, there is a ready-made and well-tested set of legal instruments and housing policies. It is also possible in the FRG to draw on the services of a highly specialized administrative machinery that is familiar with market economy mechanisms. This helps to convey the relevant expert knowledge to the new *Länder* and to develop the necessary legal transitional arrangements and regulations for adjustment.

Unavoidable frictions during the restructuring process are made socially tolerable with the aid of transfer payments of various kinds to the new *Länder*. In 1993, these amounted to 218 billion DM, over half of which was to be spent on consumption subsidies and interest payments, not new investment. Although Germany has developed a budget deficit through excess public expenditure, and is making more welfare cuts in response, the country's economy is still massively strong compared with any of the other countries described in this volume. In the field of housing, attempts are being made using considerable amounts of financial resources to raise the standard of housing within a few years, without going beyond the financial possibilities of the population in the new *Länder*. Although needs and aspirations are still growing faster than real progress in the quality of life, important legal and economic developments in the field of housing have already been initiated.

REFERENCES

Boelhouwer, P., and van der Heijden, H. 1992. *Housing Systems in Europe. Part 1: A Comparative Studies of Housing Policy*. Delft: Delft University Press.
Bucholz, H. 1990. Housing policy in the German Democratic Republic. In J. Sillence (ed.), *Housing Policies in Eastern Europe and the Soviet Union*. London: Routledge.
Dienemann, O. 1993. Housing problems in the former German Democratic Republic and the "New German States." In G. Hallett (ed.), *The New Housing Shortage*. London: Routledge.
Köhli, J. 1991. Wohnungsprivatisierung und Wohnungseigentumsbildung [Dwelling privatization and the creation of private dwelling ownership]. *Bundesbaublatt* 10, 640–646.

Köhli, J. 1992. Neue Bundesländer—Modellvorhaben zur Wohnungsprivatisierung [The new Federal *Länder*—Pilot projects for the privatization of dwellings]. *Bundes-baublatt* 12, 914–926.

Köhli, J. 1993. Die Wohnungsprivatisierung in den neuen Ländern [Privatization of dwellings in the new *Länder*]. *Betrieb und Wirtschaft* 47 (6), 197–203.

Lundqvist, L. 1992. Germany: And what now, when the twain have met? In B. Turner, J. Hegedüs, and I. Tosics (eds.), *The Reform of Housing in Eastern Europe and the Soviet Union*. London: Routledge.

Marcuse, P., and Schumann, W. 1992. Housing in the colours of the GDR. In B. Turner, J. Hegedüs, and I. Tosics (eds.), *Reforms of Housing in Eastern Europe and the Soviet Union*. London: Routledge.

OECD. 1992. *OECD Economic Surveys: Germany*. Paris: OECD.

Ulbrich, R., and Wullkopf, U. 1993. Housing affordability in the Federal Republic of Germany. In G. Hallett, *The New Housing Shortage*. London: Routledge.

4

Hungary

József Hegedüs, Katharine Mark,
Csilla Sárkány, and Iván Tosics

The political changes of 1989 and 1990 brought to an end the East European Housing Model (see chapter 2). Substantial reforms had already taken place in Hungary before the political changes of the 1980s, but despite the longer history of reform, the transition toward a market-oriented housing system will take several more years in Hungary. Privatization is one of the crucial elements in this process, which is as important as the nationalization of the 1950s, when the East European Housing Model was introduced. Of course, privatization is not limited to the housing system: it dominates almost all spheres of the economy.

In this chapter we describe and summarize the process of privatization in the Hungarian housing system, which has led to the withdrawal of state activity and the expansion of the market. We examine housing policy and provide an overview of privatization of the public rental sector, housing management, and new construction. We pay special attention to the analysis of the changing role of privatization during the transition period within the political context at national and local level.

The first section of the chapter describes the recent changes in the political, legal, and economic environment that provides the "framework" for housing. The second section summarizes the main features of the housing system prior to the transition period. In the third section we describe the new legal regulation of central and local housing policy. The fourth section provides an analysis of the trends in privatization, and the fifth presents the research findings on the impact of privatization measures.

CHANGES IN THE BROAD FRAMEWORK FOR HOUSING

The New Political and Legal Environment

The first free parliamentary elections took place in Hungary in April 1990, and this constituted one of the most important steps in the political transition. The Conservative Christian Democratic Coalition formed from the Hungarian Democratic Forum, the Smallholders Party, and the Christian Democratic Party won the election, and the other three parties, the Alliance of Free Democrats, the Alliance of Young Democrats, and the Socialist Party were in opposition. One of the first activities of the new parliament was to pass the Act on Local Governments. This brought substantial change at the local level, where the Soviet-style council system has been replaced by a truly independent local government system. The Transfer of State Property Act of 1991 transferred the ownership of public housing and public utility companies from the central state to the local authorities. In the special case of Budapest (the only two-tier local government in Hungary), the district level was assigned as the local government authority responsible for housing. One year later, under the Capital City Act of 1992, some planning power was also given to the municipal authority.

In October 1990, six months after the national elections, in the first free local elections the liberal parties won control in almost all the larger cities. In Budapest, for example, 21 out of 22 districts elected a leader either from the Alliance of Free Democrats or the Alliance of Young Democrats, or a leader supported by these parties. The overall leadership of the Budapest municipal authority was also liberal. The difference in political color between the central government and the largest local authorities did not lead to optimal circumstances for the creation of new laws and economic regulation for the local governments. The governing coalition in Parliament did not want to make decisions that favored the larger local authorities controlled by the opposition parties.

Housing is one of the sectors of the economy in which the new institutional, financial, and legal framework has been set up very slowly. In 1990, the attempt to set up a Government Housing Office was rejected by the Parliament. This decision was considered at that time by the Parliament and the Government to be a "sign of democracy" that would avoid bureaucratic centralistic regulation of the housing sector. Since then, however, it has become clear that the chosen way was even worse: the responsibility for housing at the ministerial level was split among five ministries—those of Social Welfare, Interior, Finance, Environment, and Industry and Trade. This made the formulation of housing policy complicated and slow. Partly because of this, the very urgently needed housing and social legislation was not passed until 1993.

Trends in the Economy

The economic situation, which was already quite bad in 1989, has deteriorated over the last four years. The per capita national debt, which was accumulated in the 1970s and 1980s, is one of the largest not only in Eastern Europe, but in the whole world. Output, as measured in real GNP, declined by 17 percent between 1990 and 1992; the previously hidden unemployment rate reached 12.3 percent in 1992; annual inflation has been above 20 percent (in some years above 30 percent); the budget deficit increased to 197 billion Forints in 1992 and to 350 billion in 1993.

All these negative trends are partly due to measures undertaken by the government to restructure the economy, such as privatizing the state enterprises, cutting consumption subsidies in the budget, and giving compensation to the victims of the unlawful nationalization during the Communist years. In addition to these unavoidable measures, however, it is a common belief that the government paid much more attention to the past and to ideological questions, and not enough to the present problems of economic transition. This approach is changing with the new government established in the summer of 1994 as a coalition of the socialist and the liberal (Free Democrat) parties.

HOUSING BEFORE THE TRANSITION

Housing Stock and Ownership

The most important step toward the creation of an extensive state rental sector was the nationalization of the urban private rental stock in 1952. Unlike the situation in the Soviet Union or Yugoslavia, the urban housing stock in Hungary was not totally nationalized: only apartments in buildings with more than six rooms were transferred to state ownership, although this nationalization was carried out without compensation to the owners. More than 200,000 dwellings were nationalized in Budapest, where as a result the public sector grew from 30 percent to 75 percent of the stock. However, the state rental sector in Hungary as a whole never dominated the housing stock: its 25 percent share of the housing stock remained quite stable during the socialist period. Only in the larger cities, including Budapest, did the share of the public rental sector exceed 50 percent of the local housing stock (Table 4.1)

Table 4.1.   The Percentage of Inhabited Dwellings in Hungary and Budapest, by Tenure

		Owner-Occupied & Cooperative %	*Public Rental (%)*
1980	Budapest	43	57
	Hungary	75	25
1990	Budapest	47	53
	Hungary	77	22

Source: Housing Statistics Yearbook, 1980, 1990.

One of the most notable features of the state rental sector was that tenants had property rights to their dwelling. They were entitled to exchange the rented dwelling for another rented or owner-occupied dwelling. After 1971, a mandatory sum of "key money" had to be paid to the local council on entry to a rented dwelling, and tenants giving up their tenancy were entitled to the reimbursement of their "key money" payment. The strength of the tenants' property rights is illustrated by the fact that tenants who vacated their dwellings after 1980 received a sum of money several times greater than their initial key money payment from the council. In Budapest, the sum was ten times greater than the initial payment when an apartment with all facilities was returned to the local council. Local councils wanted to encourage tenants to return their apartments to local authority control rather than exchanging them on the free market. Even so, not many units were returned to the local council in Budapest, demonstrating that the "market value" of a public rented dwelling was even higher than the increased level of repayments.

Another critical feature of the public rental sector was the low rent level. Rents were set on the basis of square meters of floor area, with some variation according to quality, only some minimal adjustment for location within a settlement, and some insignificant variation between cities and towns of different sizes. Rents were only a fraction of the estimated market levels and have been consistently less than the amount required to cover operating costs. The state introduced a special form of cross-subsidy, allowing local councils to retain the revenue from commercial rents, which could then be used for management and maintenance of the public rented stock, undertaken by the state-owned management companies, the IKVs (Table 4.2).

The management of 90 percent of the state-owned housing stock was provided by the state-owned management companies, the IKVs, until 1991, when their ownership was transferred to the local authorities. These companies were inefficient and were blamed for the poor maintenance of the stock. IKVs were different from other East European Housing Corporations in that they were not owners of the stock but managers with some property rights, although the allocation of property to new tenants had always been the responsibility of the council. The IKVs received significant subsidies, amounting on average to 45 percent of their total budget, from the central state until 1990, when central state subsidies were completely eliminated.

The crisis in the public rental sector was steadily growing in the 1980s due to the deterioration of the stock, the dominance of private transactions, and the huge financial deficit. The Housing Act of 1983 tried to solve the problems by increasing market controls, but with only limited results. The rent increase in 1983 could not compensate for inflation, so the financial deficit in the sector increased at the end of the decade. The offer of three to ten times the face value of the key money for vacated dwellings did not increase the local authority control over the reallocation of public rental units. Only between 30 and 40 percent of tenancies were

Table 4.2.   The Structure of Housing Revenues and Costs in Budapest (in percent and in millions of Hungarian Forints)

	1987	1988	1989	1990	1991
Revenues					
Rents of flats	28.0	23.2	28.4	44.6	39.8
Other rents	26.2	23.7	28.0	55.4	60.2
Central subsidy	46.0	53.0	43.6	0.0	0.0
Total (%)	100.0	100.0	100.0	100.0	100.0
Total (million forints)	9,486	12,521	10,595	8,650	8,124
Costs					
Operation	22.5	21.7	27.0	-	-
Maintenance	28.0	33.0	37.3	3,490	3,415
Renovation	49.4	45.3	35.7	2,775	1,937
Total (%)	100.0	100.0	100.0	-	-
Total (million forints)	9,367	10,919	10,008	-	-

Source: Annual Handbook of Capital Government, 1992.

allocated by the local council, the majority of tenants obtaining their dwellings through market transactions. Moreover, attempts to restructure the IKVs were unsuccessful. In 1989, a proposal for a 100 percent increase in rent was rejected; one of the last actions of this parliament was to approve a rent increase of 35 percent.

Privatization of the Public Sector before the Transition Period

The transformation of the public rental sector began long before the political changes of 1989–90. The sale of public rental units to tenants became possible as early as 1969, but the first regulations applied only to small properties (buildings with two apartments, later those with up to twelve apartments). Substantial changes were introduced around the middle of the 1980s when the strict constraints on the privatization of bigger buildings were lifted and a system of huge financial discounts was introduced for tenants. The demand from sitting tenants to buy their dwelling was, and still is, substantial because of the uncertain future of the public rental sector and the very favorable terms of sale. Most rented dwellings were sold for 15 percent of their market value, this being the selling price of any public dwelling that had not been extensively modernized during the previous 15 years. The price was set at 30 percent of the market value if extensive modernization had been undertaken within the previous 5–15 years, and 40 percent if the modernization had been undertaken in the previous 5 years. Moreover, tenants were given a further 40 percent discount on the discounted sales price if they paid for the property in cash. The other option was to pay in installments: in this case, 10 percent of the discounted sale price had to be paid in cash, and the remainder in monthly installments over 35 years at a low fixed interest rate, which was set at 3 percent for the whole repayment period, even though annual inflation was between 20 and 30 percent by the end of the 1980s.

According to the regulations, privatized apartments could be resold or rented out by the owner immediately following the purchase without any restrictions, except for the obligation to repay the installments in the case of resold properties. Moreover, there was no restriction on turning the apartments into offices or shops, and these changes did not have to be reported to the local authority. This very liberal regulation of privatization which favored sitting tenants by giving them a huge "gift" in the form of a substantial and marketable discount, has been sharply criticized by many housing experts. The main push for this "give-away" privatization came from the main beneficiaries, the families living in the best public rental apartments, as well as from local government. Without the possibility of increasing the rents, public rental housing was considered by the local authorities to have a negative asset value (Buckley, Henderson, and Villani, 1992).

The number of units sold was insignificant until the liberalization of the privatization regulations in the middle of the 1980s, after which housing privatization speeded up. Due to the subsequent changes in privatization law, local councils were now entitled to determine the level of discount on the sale of rented dwellings, although in Budapest the city council regulated this issue, and not the district councils. Initially local authorities could only influence the volume of sales through the speed of the administrative process and their willingness to sell or not, as it was necessary to obtain a decision from the Executive Committee for each dwelling. However, around 1989/1990 not only the volume of sales but also the financial terms began to differ among local authorities.

Less than 2 percent of the public rented stock in Budapest was purchased by tenants in 1988 and 1989. In contrast, 20 percent of the stock was sold to sitting tenants between January 1990 and January 1992, and a further 5 to 7 percent of the stock was in the process of being sold (BRPS, 1992). The demand from sitting tenants to buy their units was substantial, but the bureaucratic process was slow, and most local authorities implicitly required a threshold of demand, in that no housing unit was considered for sale until 35 percent of tenants in that building had applied to buy their dwelling.

THE NEW LEGAL FRAMEWORK
FOR CENTRAL AND LOCAL HOUSING POLICY

The process of modifying the basic laws regulating housing was slowed down because there was no single ministry to take responsibility for housing. The Property Transfer Act of 1991 transferred the ownership of the state rental stock to the local authorities, and in Budapest this meant the district councils. The new local authorities were given the right to set rents, but none of the districts of Budapest and very few of the cities used this option before June 1993, when a one-year moratorium was introduced on rent increases. The real value of rents continued to decrease, and the local authorities had to increase cross-subsidization. Moreover, as a consequence of the elimination of central budget subsidy for maintenance, large-scale rehabilitation came to a complete halt, and maintenance activity was substantially reduced.

The Social Act, passed by central government in February 1993, contained a proposal to introduce a new subsidy system and ordered the preparation of new regulations to provide housing allowances by September 1993. This meant that local authorities were allowed to establish their own housing subsidy system although they received only a small amount of funding from the central budget. In May 1993, a housing policy decree was accepted by the government, which agreed to establish a National Housing Strategy. As a first step, the government set up an intergovernmental committee to coordinate the work. As this committee lacked staff and financial backing, it could not replace an effective Housing Office.

Direct political influence can be seen in the Rental Housing Act, passed in July 1993, which regulated privatization and the respective rights of landlords and tenants. This law was expected to be passed two years earlier but was postponed many times. Basic changes to the original proposals prepared by the Ministry of the Interior were made in response to the successful lobbying of the Association of Tenants, but also with an eye to political considerations related to the approaching general election of 1994. As an "election present" from the government to the tenants, the existing low rents were frozen for one year—that is, until the end of the election period. As an even more important political step, all residential and commercial tenants gained the right to buy their dwellings or commercial leases during the five-year period from January 1994. This very broad privatization effort of the government, however, was turned down by the Court of Constitution at the beginning of 1994; only residential tenants were given the right to buy, and only during a one-year period—between April 1994 and April 1995. Even so, this new regulation, which is very similar to the Right to Buy policy introduced by the Thatcher government in the United Kingdom, strengthens the rights of residential tenants vis-à-vis the local authorities and is creating a totally new situation in local housing markets.

To summarize the political and legal changes that affected housing, the new regulations imposed by the central government up to the middle of 1993 were aimed at strengthening the decision-making powers of local government. The ownership of the public rented stock was transferred to the councils, who obtained the right to set rent levels and establish a local system of housing allowances. They were also given the responsibility to make decisions on the privatization of housing management and determine some of the basic rules on housing privatization. However, the Rental Housing Act of 1993 took the opposite direction: for obvious and directly political reasons, it strengthened the rights of tenants in public rented dwellings, at the same time removing the rights of local authorities to make decisions about their housing stock. The government wanted to achieve similar measures in the case of commercial properties—the most important assets of local authorities—making possible a cross-subsidization of housing maintenance with the relatively higher commercial rents. However, the right to buy commercial property (with huge discounts on the sales price) was eliminated by the Court of Constitution.

LOCAL OPTIONS IN THE PRIVATIZATION OF THE HOUSING SECTOR IN THE 1990s

In a discussion of the main options for local housing policy we used extensive data and empirical analysis to show that the maintenance of low rents and the continuation of privatization at low "give-away" prices is not the only solution available (Hegedüs, Mark, Struyk, and Tosics, 1993). Moreover, the research showed that careful privatization close to the market price, plus increases, together with housing allowances and institutional changes in housing management could constitute a new model for the public sector. This model could lead to the elimination of the deficit in the public rented sector and provide new opportunities for low-income households. However, the analysis also demonstrated that the Rental Housing Act of 1993 made this second option impossible by limiting the power of local government to increase rents and making it compulsory for them to sell their rental property at "give-away" prices.

The new laws passed in the early 1990s favored local independence, transferring decision-making rights to local governments for almost all aspects of local housing policy. Thus, from early 1992 onwards, local authorities could decide on rent levels, the volume of sales, and the level of discount on the market price. In this situation, local governments had two options regarding their local rental housing policy: whether to preserve a substantial rental stock and try to establish new mechanisms by which prices express real value and subsidies are targeted on poorer families, or to reduce the volume of public rental stock as much as possible. The main difference between these two options was in the rent levels and in the regulation of privatization.

Local authorities who chose the first option had to increase rents, and increase the sale price of rented dwellings by reducing the level of discount on the market value of the property, and/or find other ways to slow down privatization. Rent increases, however, were almost impossible at the local level because of the absence of a comprehensive housing allowance system. To increase sales prices by reducing discounts was also difficult politically because of the previous practice of selling public stock at very low prices. Some local authorities reduced the discount level, but more of them chose indirect methods to slow down the privatization process: They maintained a high entry threshold for sales within apartment buildings by requiring that some minimum proportion of the tenants in each building made application to buy before any one sale was permitted; they also established extensive prohibition lists of buildings that were not available for privatization; some even introduced a moratorium on sales for a period of time before the Rental Housing Act was passed.

Local authorities who chose the second option took the opposite course of action and increased their rate of sales at a low price. They applied the previous central regulations on the terms of sale, which were very advantageous to sitting tenants. Furthermore, they applied a low threshold or none at all, reduced prohibition lists to a minimum, and tried to speed up the bureaucratic processes of privatization.

The outcome of these two different options can be seen in the data shown in Table 4.3. There are huge differences in the volume of sales between the various districts of Budapest. In District 5, which is the central business area and where the rent gap between current and potential rent is greatest, more than half of the public rented stock was sold within the three years between 1990 and 1993. In contrast, some districts in the transitional belt, which had a lower rent gap and a very mixed stock, had more opportunities to resist "give-away" privatization for a long time. For example, the new local authorities in Districts 7 and 8 were introducing a moratorium on sales.

Table 4.3. The Changes in Tenure Form in Inner Budapest, 1990–93 (in thousands of units)

District	Total No. of Dwellings 1990	Public Rental Units, 1990	Public Rental Units, 1994	Privatized Dwellings as a % of 1990 Public Stock
5	19,752	17,834	6,656	63
6	26,257	24,560	16,000	35
7	35,506	33,654	21,210	37
8	40,537	35,667	29,912	16
9	33,573	28,459	13,500	57
13	59,184	38,523	20,047	48
Total inner city	194,811	178,607	107,325	40
Total Budapest	809,735	414,536	215,094	48

Source: Data from Budapest Municipal Housing Department.

The picture of different levels of residential privatization changed dramatically at the beginning of 1994, when the new Rental Housing Act gave the tenants the right to buy. As a consequence, indirect methods of protecting the public rental stock became illegal. A threshold no longer exists, so that if just one out of fifty tenants in a building wants to buy, the local authority has to turn the whole block into a condominium. Also, the role of prohibition lists will be insignificant as the legislation permits only a very limited number of situations where a house might be listed.

Many local government officials think that these new regulations damage the right of local authorities to dispose of their own property and transfer the real decision-making power to the tenants. This reduction of municipal power was the political goal of the ruling political parties when they replaced the limited right to buy, where local government had a decisive role, with the more open version, where tenants have the decisive role. The new regulation will obviously lead to a reduction in the public rental sector of housing—this share will be below 20 percent in Budapest and below 10 percent nationwide. Taking into account the fact that the private rental sector is still insignificant, these figures represent one of the lowest shares of rental housing in the whole of Europe.

The Privatization of Management

The central state subsidy for the maintenance of the public rental stock was completely eliminated in 1990. The new source of revenue from the privatization of rented dwellings has been considerably less than the former central subsidy because of the huge discounts on sales prices and the option to pay by installment.

The growing financial problems encouraged many of the state-owned management companies, the IKVs, to initiate internal reforms in the late 1980s. After the elections in 1990, the new local politicians made considerable efforts to reorganize these companies. A survey of 10 IKVs in Budapest in the summer of 1991 (Sullivan, 1991) reported the replacement of senior IKV managers in some districts, substantial cuts in administrative staff in others, and, in a few cases, the transformation of IKVs into joint companies owned by the district authority.

One district authority broke up its IKV into several joint stock companies, each responsible for a different aspect of management—for example, rent collection or major repairs. The objective of these reforms was to create separate limited companies that could work independently. The bulk of the shares is held by the IKV parent company, but typically the local management and employees also have some shares. The new companies work mainly for the IKV, but they also have the right to seek contracts on the market. The IKVs have gradually decentralized their technical departments and the satellite offices have increased their independence.

An alternative model for reforming the management of municipal stock is to transfer the role of landlord to the city administration—specifically, to its housing department, which would take on responsibility for the district's housing policy and planning strategy as well as management of stock. It would collect information on the rental stock and set up and operate a new management system. It would contract independent managing companies for other services, and it would delegate the task of allocation, maintenance, rent collection, and communication with tenants to IKVs or to other property management firms. Such a model has been implemented, with substantial USAID technical help, in the city of Szolnok (Baar and Mark, 1993).

In Budapest, some district governments tend to delay the reform of the IKV and have taken only small steps toward change. In most of the districts, the number of tenements and therefore the amount of the work available for the IKVs has been rapidly decreasing, owing to sales. As a result, most of the IKVs have been transformed into local government enterprises (limited liability companies with only one owner—the local authority).

Apart from the transformation of IKVs, the other main question regarding housing management is the efficiency of condominium management. There are three main forms of management in the owner-occupied condominium sector: (1) management organized by the apartment owners themselves through their elected representatives; (2) management by a private management enterprise—in many of the newly privatized condominiums, the local IKV initially kept its role until private ownership exceeded 50 percent; (3) the use of housing maintenance cooperatives.

In Budapest, there were in 1992 about 16 private companies providing management services for condominiums. Most of these were established by former employees of the IKVs. These private management companies are in most cases more efficient than the IKVs. Their services, however, are still relatively expensive, especially if compared to the costs of management organized by the owners themselves. In this case, management costs can be kept down through postponing necessary work and/or hiring cheap labor on the black economy.

The most important problem confronting the new condominium owners in Budapest is the poor condition of the housing stock, which is the result of the decades of neglect under public ownership. In this situation, there are three prerequisites for the successful maintenance of condominiums (Rabenhorst, 1992).

1. Owners must develop a sense of commitment to the improvement of their housing and a willingness to make monetary sacrifices to bring this about. The belief that it is worth while to invest in one's own housing is more and more general; however, only a fraction of the new owners are in a position to do so.
2. Skilled property management and construction contractors must be available and responsive to the needs of owners.
3. The condominium association must function in such a way as to foster feelings of confidence and stability among the members.

These three conditions, and especially the first, are fulfilled only in the case of buildings in "better neighborhoods." As a consequence, there is a substantial polarization to be expected among privatized houses: some will be brought up to a good physical standard, but in the case of the vast majority deterioration will continue or even speed up.

Decentralization of New Construction

Hungarian housing construction consisted of two forms of organization until 1993: large housing construction companies based on the production of prefabricated sections, and small individual builders. Under this system, project development was in the hands of the big companies who worked with local councils and the National Savings Bank. There were only limited possibilities for private developers, who were usually lawyers or building cooperative managers, to step into the market. Their main role was to organize the "building of communities," mainly in the suburban areas or in-fill development in the inner city, where large companies did not have an interest.

After the 1983 Housing Reform, and especially after the Small Enterprises Act and the Bidding for Public Construction Work Act, the construction companies themselves gained permission to develop residential projects, and the local council started to play an active role in the process by developing and selling serviced land to entrepreneurs. However, the process was very slow, partly because it did not have strong political support.

The demand for the products of the industrialized sector of the construction industry diminished as a consequence of extending subsidies such as the social policy (child) allowance to the self-help housing sector. Demand for prefabricated housing diminished even further after 1989, when the housing finance system was changed dramatically, eliminating the low interest rate on long-term loans. Consequently, the majority of all housing investment (around 80 to 90 percent) has been made by individuals since 1990.

The sharp drop in state investment has led to a market loss for the big producers of residential and communal buildings. In addition to the strict monetary policy that reduced subsidies, high taxes and a lack of long-term planning have produced negative effects on the construction industry. The overall consequence has been a sharp decline in output. Changes in housing policy brought substantial changes in the organization of the construction industry from 1985 onwards. Unused capacity was converted, and huge factories were sold off. The number of small companies increased from 74 in 1985 to 4,575 in 1992 as a result of the Act of Economic Enterprises. Yet employment in the construction industry declined by 33 percent between 1985 and 1992. By the end of 1991, organizations with fewer than 50 people made up 80 percent of the building industry, and their share of production made up 20 percent of construction industry output (Tables 4.4 and 4.5).

The transformation of the huge companies and their privatization took two forms: spontaneous privatization, in which the company was transformed by its staff and they became the new management, and state privatization, in which

Table 4.4. The Number of Firms in Construction Industry (by number of employees)

	>20	20–50	50–300	>300	Total	State Owned	No. of Employees
1985	74	98	257	164	593	189	275,136
1988	293	413	459	139	1,304	196	259,195
1990	1,541	847	638	143	3,169	0	227,000
1992	4,575	1,449	788	113	6,925	0	182,073

Source: Housing Statistics Yearbook, 1985–1992.

privatization plans were drawn up by independent consulting firms chosen by the State Property Agency and implemented.

A swift process of reform began in the middle of the 1980s. Those branches of the state companies that could function on their own were turned into independent companies by 1989. Although the new units are theoretically independent, the original state company remains the dominant shareholder, while the remaining shareholders are external parties, who are in regular business contact with the branch. Banks appear as external shareholders who assume the debt of the company for a share in the property. This system enables companies to reduce losses temporarily and avoid bankruptcy. The process of decline may have been slower than expected because companies sold their assets in order to compensate for operating losses (Table 4.6).

The new government made its privatization policy public in 1990. The state promoted a centrally supervised version of privatization by forming the State Property Agency (AVÜ), to prevent spontaneous privatization and to slow down

Table 4.5. Housing Construction in 1981, 1989–92

	No. of Units	Average Floor Space (m²)	Total Floor Space (1,000 m²)	No. of Second Homes
1981	76,975	70	5,388	4,675
1989	51,487	88	4,531	2,308
1990	43,771	90	3,939	2,285
1991	33,764	90	2,985	1,753
1992	25,807	93	2,400	2,081
1993	21,500	-	-	-

Source: Housing Statistics Yearbook, 1981–1993.

Table 4.6. Number of Construction Companies by Type of Organization, 1989–92

	1989	1990	1991	1992
Companies and co-operatives	167	151	146	131
Partnerships	552	1,930	3,930	5,582
Limited companies	500	1,871	3,845	5,479
Stock companies	6	26	57	103
Associations and other enterprises	1,187	1,181	1,149	1,236
Total	1,906	3,262	5,225	7,046

Source: Housing Statistics Yearbook, 1989–1992.

the process. The AVÜ is a centralized body with the necessary legislative authorization and staff to supervise all phases of privatization. However, the agency proved unable to conduct and manage the transformation of all the companies, so external consulting firms were invited to tender for work. These consulting firms—mostly foreign banks and well-known Western consulting firms—undertook the job of privatization on the basis of commission to be paid in the next phase, and their fee was determined as a certain percentage of future sales.

There is a fierce battle between the companies that have already been transformed and those that are currently being privatized. But for bigger developments the AVÜ demands that the construction company deposit funds, calculated as a certain percentage of the costs, as insurance. This cannot be afforded by the companies that do not have a sound financial basis. Small new enterprises, which lack finance, guarantees, and references, generally subcontract work from the bigger companies.

The number of small private construction companies has increased. In 1991, approximately 100 companies were in operation in the construction industry. By 1992, 61 construction companies were transformed, forming 800 new companies, many of them limited-liability companies. Foreign companies showed little interest in buying construction companies, but a number of smaller monopolies have come into being in the construction materials industry. This has had a serious impact on the price of the materials available.

THE IMPACT OF PRIVATIZATION MEASURES

In January 1992, the Metropolitan Research Institute and the Urban Institute carried out an extensive empirical research program to explore the plans and future expectations of tenants concerning the possibility of purchasing their dwellings (BRPS, 1992). The sample of addresses was selected from the January 1990 stock of public rental housing in Budapest. The timing of the survey coincided with the beginning of a rapid increase in the pace of privatization. The survey findings show that 20 percent of dwellings had been privatized. Another 20 percent of tenants were ready to buy immediately, 30 percent were considering it, and less than 30 percent of public tenants rejected the idea of buying.

In our evaluation of the survey results, we examined the motivation of tenant households (Hegedüs, Mark, Struyk, and Tosics, 1992). The decision of the household to buy or not to buy was a rational choice that was based in part on the uncertainty about the future regulation of the right-to-buy policy and future regulations on rent levels, allowances, and property rights in the rental sector. Households reported two strong motives for buying: to acquire the value of the property—that is, the difference between the value of the apartment as owner-occupied and its value under the state rental system; and to obtain a secure position against changes in rental policy. The control over maintenance was, according to the empirical results, a much less important motive for tenants. Those households who reported that they would not buy their dwelling were also motivated by two groups of factors: the lack of financial means and the rundown physical condition of the house—in other words, its low value as an investment.

The factors that determined which dwellings were sold and who bought them can be seen in Figures 4.1, 4.2, and 4.3. The trend is clear: the better housing units were bought and the buyers, and those who intended to buy, had a higher education level and a higher income.

The conclusion of the analysis was that the investment value and rent expectations were the most important determinants of the purchase, while the location of the unit could add a further incentive to buy. The social aspects of the process were less crucial, although there was a positive correlation between social status and the value. The other finding of the analysis was that a negative attitude toward privatization was less likely to be influenced by investment value, and more by social position and the poor quality of the rented dwelling.

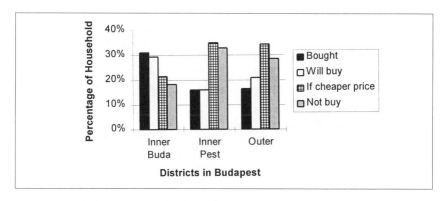

Figure 4.1. Privatization of Budapest public rental stock. (*Source: BRPS,* 1992.)

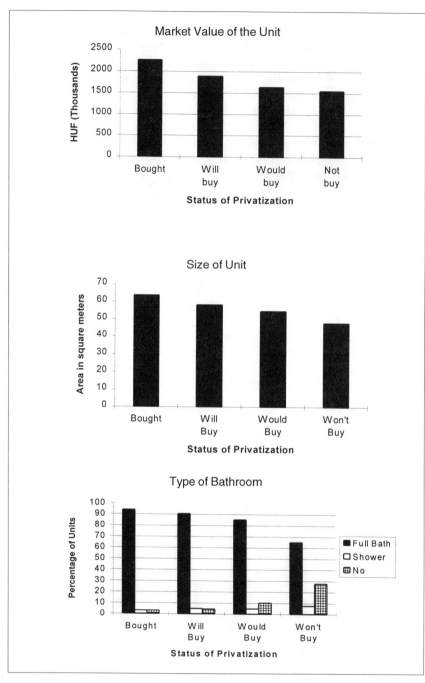

Figure 4.2. Characteristics of the public rental stock in Budapest by privatization status. (*Source: BRPS,* 1992.)

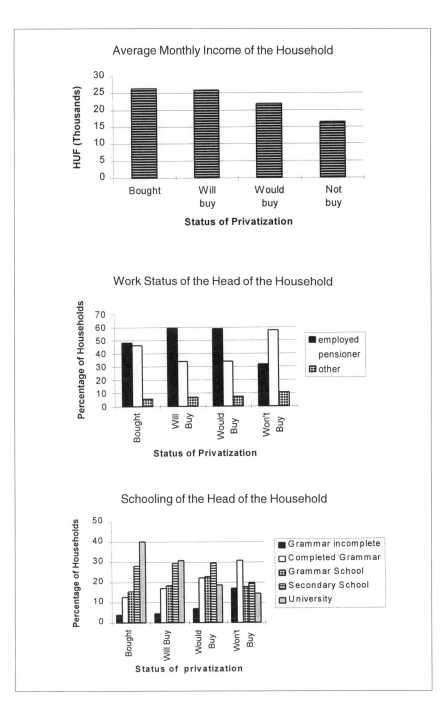

Figure 4.3. Characteristics of occupants of the public rental stock in Budapest by privatization status. (*Source: Budapest Rental Panel Survey,* 1992.)

Table 4.7. Privatization Process and the Equity Issue in the Budapest Public Rental Sector

	Scenario A: 1 January 1990	Scenario B: 1 January 1992		Scenario C: Everyone Buys Who Wants under Given Terms		Scenario D: Everyone Who Would Like to Buy under More Favorable Terms		Scenario E: Everyone Buys
	Rent Subsidy	Rent Subsidy	Value Gap	Rent Subsidy	Value Gap	Rent Subsidy	Value Gap	Value Gap
Low Income (below 25%)								
Per unit (HUF)	46,200	44,244	483,955	41,868	454,988	37,572	304,785	283,637
Sum (b.HUF)	4.6	3.7	7.3	2.9	13.2	1.5	21.5	28.2
% of Total	21.6	22.7	16.5	25.3	15.6	31.3	15.6	16.7
No. of Units	99,432	84,449	14,983	70,375	29,058	40,409	59,024	99,432
No. in Sample	219	186	33	155	64	89	130	219
High Income (above 75%)								
Per unit (HUF)	66,048	63,312	707,509	61,956	642,079	63,672	600,472	587,753
Sum (b.HUF)	6.7	4.9	17.7	3.0	34.4	0.8	53.7	60.0
% of Total	31.7	29.6	40.3	25.8	40.5	16.7	38.9	35.8
No. of Units	102,157	77,185	24,972	48,581	53,575	12,713	89,444	102,157
No. in Sample	225	170	55	107	118	28	197	225

Total Sector

Per unit (HUF)	53,208	50,496	596,138	47,904	542,250	43,728	477,073	421,980
Sum (b.HUF)	21.3	16.5	43.8	11.7	84.9	4.8	138.0	168.8
% of Total	100	100	100	100	100	100	100	100
No. of Units	400,000	356,447	73,553	243,360	156,640	110,783	289,217	400,000
No. in Sample	881	719	162	536	345	244	637	881
% of rental/ owner occup.	100	81.6	18.4	60.8	39.2	27.7	72.3	100

HUF: Hungarian forints.
Note: Condition: no change in present sale terms and rent subsidy.
Source: BRPS (1992).

75

We evaluated the equity consequences of "give-away" privatization. The privatization decision reflected decisions about two different types of housing subsidies—the rental subsidy and the investment value. We investigated how large the subsidy was, and who benefited by it. Regarding the rent subsidy, we based our estimate on the "fair rent" concept rather than on what the equilibrium rent would be if there were not a large shortage in the market. We supposed that fair rents would be determined on the basis of demand, which is limited by household income. A household cannot afford to pay more than 20 to 25 percent of its income on rent. In our estimate, we took 25 percent of household income as a fair market rent, using the upper limit because of the problem of income underreporting. The distribution of this subsidy is considered to be regressive— that is, the higher-income groups enjoy the larger part of the subsidy.

Table 4.7 presents the main results. According to our survey data, those in the top quarter of the income distribution receive 32 percent of the rent subsidy, while those in the lowest quarter of the income range receive 22 percent of the rent subsidy—less than their proportional distribution in the population. The question is how privatization modifies this regressive distribution of the subsidies within a diminishing rental sector and by the distribution of investment value subsidy to the buyers. "Give-away" privatization generates a huge equity problem arising from the difference between the market value and the discounted selling price. This can be conceived as a capitalization of inequality.

According to our findings, the investment value was distributed even more unevenly than the rent subsidy, which follows from the fact that the dwellings in the best condition were bought first. Of the total investment value, 40 percent went to the top income group, whereas the lowest-income group obtained 17 percent. The first two years of privatization thus continued the distribution pattern of the rent subsidy and transferred the unequal situation in the rental stock into the private sector. As the privatization process goes on, within the remaining rental sector the gap between the low- and upper-income tenant is decreasing. The reason for this is that upper-income tenants mainly leave the rental sector and consequently enjoy a smaller share of the rent subsidy. The price of achieving this lower level of inequality within the remaining rental sector is the huge amount of subsidy given to the tenants who buy, which is distributed in a regressive way.

To sum up: "give-away" privatization is a large gift to sitting tenants. The annual rent subsidy of 21 billion forints will be replaced by a once-and-for-all subsidy of 138 billion forints when the privatized share of the rental stock reaches its most likely peak of around 70 percent. Privatization increases inequalities favoring the higher-income groups of tenants. This, of course, gives political strength to the local officials and representatives. Moreover, privatization at a highly discounted price works against future housing policy. In addition to the emerging social problems and the decrease of vacant apartments available for social allocation, deferred maintenance is likely to remain a problem in privatized dwellings, as only a few of the new owners will be able to shoulder maintenance costs and meet the heavy financial burdens of renovation.

CONCLUSION: THE CHANGING ROLE
OF PRIVATIZATION IN HUNGARY

The give-away type of privatization of state rental housing was introduced in Hungary around the middle of the 1980s. The change in the political system brought in new regulations for the privatization of housing management and the construction industry, and with the transfer of rental housing to local governments the formation of housing privatization policy became increasingly a local task. As a consequence, substantial differentiation developed between local authorities in the speed and price aspects of privatization. By the time local authorities were in a position to establish their local housing policy (around 1993), central regulation of housing policy again became stronger. The new central regulations removed the decision-making rights of local authorities regarding privatization, which is one of the most important elements of their local housing strategy. The consequences of this recentralization of policy formation, particularly the introduction of the compulsory right to buy scheme, are dramatic. Certain strata of society have been favored, and it will be difficult for local governments to establish a healthy, self-sustaining local public rental housing stock. Without such a sector, the task of local governments to set up effective local housing policy will be very difficult to achieve.

ACKNOWLEDGMENT

The authors wish to thank USAID, which funded most of the work underpinning the findings of this chapter.

REFERENCES

Annual Handbook of Capital Government. 1992. Budapest.

Baar, T., and Mark, K. 1993. *Szolnok Pilot Asset and Property Management Program.* Washington, DC: The Urban Institute.

Budapest Rental Panel Survey. 1992. *Budapest Rental Panel Survey (Budapesti bérlakás vizsgálat) Preliminary Summary.* Budapest: Metropolitan Research Institute.

Buckley, R., Hendershot, P., and Villani, K. 1992. Rapid housing privatization: Pay the special dividend and get on with it. Paper presented to the AREUEA International Conference, Los Angeles 22–24 October.

Hegedüs, J., Mark, K., Struyk, R., and Tosics, I. 1992. *Transforming the Housing Management and Tenant Satisfaction in Budapest.* Mimeo.

Hegedüs, J., Mark, K., Struyk, R., and Tosics, I. 1993. Local options for the transformation of the public rental sector: Empirical results from two cities in Hungary. *Cities* 10 (3), 257–271.

Housing Statistics Yearbook [Lakásstatisztikai Évkönyv], 1980–1992. Budapest.

Rabenhorst, C. S. 1992. *Condominium Operation and Management in Budapest: Status and Implication for the Future of the Privatized Housing Market.* Washington, DC: The Urban Institute.

Sullivan, D. 1991. *A Brief Survey of 10 Budapest IKVs—July 1991.* Mimeo.

5

The Russian Federation

Mikhail Berezin, Olga Kaganova,
Nodezdha Kosareva, Andrey Pritkov,
and Raymond Struyk

This chapter examines the experience of housing privatization in Russia. The context is sketched in the first section, which covers the major political events and economic conditions in the break-up of the Soviet Union. This is followed by a review of the key housing policy changes from 1985 to the major political reforms in 1990, ending with a brief description of the characteristics of the Russian housing system at the end of that period. The rest of the chapter discusses the experience of privatization in housing from 1990 onwards, focusing, in particular, on the problems that have arisen. In conclusion, some thoughts are offered on the likely impact of these changes.

POLITICAL AND ECONOMIC BACKDROP

The final disintegration of the Soviet Union was marked by the following major events:

1. The free election of Soviet People's Deputies and live broadcasts of legislative debates. The first session of the Soviet People's Deputies Parliament already revealed a major political confrontation between proponents of a Western-style market economy and democracy, including A. Sakharov, Y. Afanasiev, G. Starovoitova, Y. Boldyrev, and later B. Yeltsin, and those wishing to "create order" by relying on already existing institutions in the Soviet Union. Those in the latter camp included Party leaders, representatives of military circles, and the KGB. Higher members of this latter group turned out to be implicated in the failed coup d'état of August 1991.

2. The December 1990 abolition of Article 6 of the U.S.S.R. Constitution, which stipulated the leadership role of the Communist Party in the political life of the nation, thus legally depriving the Party of its political monopoly.

3. The March 1990 free election of local bodies of power, making such powers dependent on voters' confidence. This gave rise to the political struggle between representative bodies and executive structures. St. Petersburg provided the best example of such a confrontation.

4. The declaration by the U.S.S.R. republics of their sovereignty, which led to the disintegration of the Union and to the divergence of political and economic viewpoints.

During this time, housing reform was shaped by four main economic issues:

1. There was increasing commercialization of economic entities due to the disintegration of administratively established economic relationships and to the implementation of new laws of the Soviet Union and the RSFSR (the former name of the Russian Federation), resulting in the removal of limitations on earnings, the creation of private contracts, and the extended rights of enterprises and managers to decide how to use former state property.

2. An expansionary monetary situation arose because of government attempts, despite income growth, to retain budget allocations for most enterprises and social programs, resulting in inflation that reached 240 to 500 percent in 1991, a shortage of goods, and an expansion of barter and black-market trading.

3. A recession occurred due to a number of factors, including the government administrative crisis and inflation.

4. The external debt grew, primarily due to reductions in exports. This resulted in stronger dependence on existing and potential creditors.

One phenomenon that cannot be attributed to politics or economics was the active commercialization of management structures. However, this commercialization primarily took the form of *nomenclatura* privatization in the sense that groups of still influential managerial and political leaders (known in Russia as the *nomenclatura*), together with new businessmen, appropriated pieces of state property. The state administration has been involved in commercialization by directly participating in *nomenclatura* privatization. It also established commercial ties between the public and various bodies of power. No statistics are available on the extent of *nomenclatura* privatization. However, it is believed to be widespread and the participants, on the whole, seem to have adhered to the prevailing laws. One example of such *nomenclatura* commercialization is a large construction and trade company set up by the Moscow City Council. In this case, complications arose over the question, "who runs the city—the city council or the construction and trade company?" This question arose because some of the individuals on the city council were also running the construction and trade company.

From early December 1991 on, the Yeltsin–Gaidar government in Russia attempted to balance the budget. This caused further confrontation between the government and sectors of the population oriented toward market reform, and between the government and those who wished to maintain certain basic social guarantees. As a result, most producers and local authorities encountered pressing financial problems.

Economic problems have been reflected in household incomes. However, despite the fact that average per capita income in Russia in 1992 was very low (about 1,175 rubles per month), and official estimates of a monthly subsistence pension of 612 rubles (*Trud*, 1992), 68 percent of St. Petersburg residents still supported the trend toward a market economy, while only 19 percent expressed a cautious or negative attitude toward this trend (*Smena*, 1992).

HOUSING POLICY FROM 1985 TO 1990

The first steps toward reforming the whole system of economic and social relations in the former Soviet Union were taken in 1985. The initial period of *perestroika* was mainly based on old standard administrative approaches to solving economic problems. One of the main social and economic undertakings was the Housing 2000 program, which was based on the plan formulated by the 1986 Congress of the Communist Party. Its goal was to provide every family with a self-contained housing unit by the year 2000.

In fact, attempts at practical solutions to the housing problem followed the old formal pattern. The state bodies in charge of housing policy believed that the housing problem would be solved if they could build apartments for every family and distribute them "fairly." Hence, a target was set of 2 billion square meters, or 40 million apartments, to be constructed in the Soviet Union between 1986 and 2000, based on 19 square meters of total space per person. However, there is evidence that the target should have been set much higher, at 2.6 billion square meters, given the needs of the population.

The calculations were far from accurate for two reasons. (1) They were based on a rigorous matching of type of housing supplied to each family based on need. Millions of extended families of two and even three generations living together in a single apartment were not provided for in this plan. The more accurate number of those who did not have a separate apartment was 35 percent of all households nationally and no less than 45 percent in the cities—much higher than the official 15 percent figure of the U.S.S.R. State Committee on Statistics. (2) These calculations made no provision for improving the housing conditions of families who already occupied a separate apartment, with kitchen and bathroom services for their exclusive use, but whose apartment was too small for the family. About 40 percent of all families fell into this category. The target also ignored any differentiation in the size and quality of the units that may be desired by the population.

The demand for apartments should be calculated on a more accurate basis for families and single persons. Survey evidence suggests that half of all unmarried family members who have come of age want to live separately. Given this assumption, the number of households in the Soviet Union wanting apartments will reach 111 million by the year 2000, rather than the 97 million calculated by the U.S.S.R. State Planning Committee. To meet this demand, it would be necessary to build at least 37 million dwelling units (or 43 million units if an allowance is made for reserves) over the 1990–2000 period. In 1990, the construction of only 30 million units was planned for this period.

During the first two years of the Housing 2000 program, the rate of housing construction in Russia increased somewhat. But after a peak of 20.1 million square meters of newly built floor space in 1987, construction began to slow down. By 1989, housing construction had fallen to 72.8 million square meters. Against the background of a general economic recession in 1990, housing construction only reached 89 percent of its 1989 level (Financy i Statistika, 1991). In 1991, housing construction volume decreased by another 22 percent (RSFSR State Committee on Statistics, 1992a).

The country was facing a deadlock: The "official" approaches had so far resulted in endless lines of families waiting for the distribution of state housing units. The then-existing system of distribution and rents stimulated excess demand for units and space and simultaneously produced low-quality housing because of the lack of incentives and funds for good construction and maintenance. Thus, the result of all of these initiatives was to make it even clearer that the housing situation would not materially change without fundamental reform in the sector.

In the next period of economic reconstruction (1988–90), the housing sphere gained political prominence, driven not only by the necessity of addressing pressing social issues, but also by the need for macroeconomic stabilization. Housing in Russia is a constant source of budgetary conflict because of its ever-growing requirements for both capital and revenue financing. From 1976 to 1990, 82 percent of housing was constructed through state investment and was allocated to the population free of charge. Housing expenditure accounted for more than 14 percent of total state capital spending. Another part of state expenditures went for housing maintenance.

In 1990, the president of the Soviet Union, Mikhail Gorbachev, issued the first formal proclamation on the necessity to shift to a market-based housing system. Based on this decree the U.S.S.R. government formed a housing policy for the period between 1990 and the year 2000. The main idea was to preserve the goal of providing every family with a separate apartment by the target year, but the responsibility for reaching this goal was to be shifted to the level of the republic. The policy called for privatization of the state and public housing stock by disposing of houses to their occupiers and the transfer of housing maintenance onto a self-financing basis. Help was to be provided to those undertaking individual and cooperative construction. Despite these declarations, the state approach to housing policy continued to be paternalistic; in fact no real changes took place.

In the fall of 1990, the Shatalin–Yavlinski "transition to the market" program, the so-called 500-day plan, was presented and debated, but not adopted. This program proposed selling the state housing stock to residents practically free of charge, but only over a one-year period, after which sales would be at market price. The plan was to change the system of providing households with free housing from the state so that, in the future, units would be targeted to lower-income families and unit size norms would be strictly enforced: the plan assumed increasing rent levels to cover operating costs and the demonopolization and privatization of housing construction.

Analysts have suggested that in a comprehensive program of transition to a housing market it is essential to include at least the following elements:

- clear establishment of the conditions under which state-owned and municipal houses may be privatized;
- a system of prices for housing;
- terms of leasing state-owned and municipal houses;
- a mechanism of financing housing and promoting housing credit;
- principles of socially guaranteed housing conditions for those in the low-income brackets and those on the waiting list for state-owned housing;
- altering the economic mechanism in housing construction;
- clarification of property rights for land and real estate.

Comparing Russia's current housing policy with the guidelines above, one could conclude that the only success so far has been in privatizing the housing stock and changing property rights. Despite economic reforms begun in January 1992, including price liberalization, true housing reform has not yet taken place. No one in Russia supports policies that would increase rents, change the subsidy system for housing maintenance, or reduce the rights of tenants to indefinite occupancy terms. The housing finance system remains undeveloped. The principles for allocating free state and municipal housing remain unchanged. Widespread privatization of the housing construction industry has been delayed until the second half of 1992.

Legislation has not resolved the problems of land rights or the right to buy and sell land, which are treated separately under the law. In particular, legislation dealing with urban land is undeveloped. This is why there is not yet any legal definition of "real estate."

HOUSING PROPERTY STRUCTURE

The present housing crisis has resulted from the housing policy conducted in the Soviet Union since 1917. It is characterized by the socialization of every aspect of the housing sphere, from monopolized state housing planning and construction to highly centralized housing provision and distribution.

Table 5.1. Ownership of Housing in the Russian Federation, by Size of Total Floor Area, 1990

	Urban	Rural	All
State housing	44	35	42
Departmental municipalities (local soviets)	35	2	25
All state housing	79	37	67
Public housing (trade unions and collective forms)	1	9	3
Construction cooperatives	5	0	4
Personal property	15	54	26
	100%	100%	100%

Source: Financy i Statistika (1990).

The housing ownership structure was created according to this policy (Table 5.1). State-owned property is not homogeneous. According to housing legislation, "state-owned housing stock was under the jurisdiction of State Committees, Ministries and Departments (including enterprises)" (RSFSR, 1986). Local soviets owned 25 percent of state-owned housing stock, while departments owned 42 percent.

The main feature of the departmental housing stock was that its construction was financed not only with funds from state departments, but also with central government money. In practice, departments tended to keep control of all property rights in housing placed at their disposal.

For example, when the process of housing privatization, including the sale of departmental housing, began, agencies, departments, and enterprises obstructed the process to the maximum degree possible. They have been most effective in delaying privatization of units of average quality, in order to retain a housing stock with which to attract workers. The best units are occupied by enterprise and government managers, and for them privatization is profitable. The owners of the worst units are happy to sell them, if they can find buyers.

Since the creation of the Law of Local Self-management in 1990, the Law on Property in the RSFSR in 1991, and the Russian Federation Supreme Soviet's Decree on Subdivision of State Property in the Russian Federation into Federal Property, State Property of Republics within the Russian Federation, Territories, Regions, Autonomous Districts, Cities of Moscow and St. Petersburg and Municipal Property in 1991, state residential stock under the jurisdiction of local soviets has been transmitted to municipalities. Housing construction and maintenance enterprises were also transferred. However, the residential stock of enterprises and organizations has remained state property. This stock will eventually be transferred to the state property of republics within the Russian Federation, territories, regions, autonomous districts, and the cities of Moscow and St. Petersburg. However, until the appropriate owner is identified, the stock remains federal property.

Public housing—that is, collective farms and trade union housing—comprises a relatively small share (3%) of the housing stock. In the countryside, such housing is the responsibility of collective farms [*kolkhozes*] or other cooperative organizations. In cities, it is under the jurisdiction of trade unions or other public and cooperative organizations.

We can get a clearer picture of the centralization of housing by examining the structure of housing construction in terms of ownership (Table 5.2). State construction accounts for 78 percent of total housing construction.

Living space in state-owned and public buildings is rented to citizens for permanent residence. The monthly rent was fixed as far back as 1928 at the rate of 13.2 kopeks per square meter and has never been changed. In higher-standard housing (with elevators and refuse chutes), it is 16.5 kopeks. The rent is approximately 1 percent of the average per capita income for factory and office workers' families. Over and above rent, families pay fees for municipal services, which, together with rent, make up 2.5 percent of family income. The rest of the cost of housing and municipal services is state-financed. At the same time, a family's spending on upkeep is not confined to rent and fees for municipal services. Renters have to pay for electricity, telephone, current repairs, and so forth. The total upkeep for, say, a two-room apartment costs an average family about 4.5 percent of their income in 1991.

Despite price reforms, rent levels have remained unchanged, and no part of the government has taken the initiative to change this situation. But since 1 January 1992 fees for communal utilities have increased three- to fivefold. Local budgets

Table 5.2. Housing Construction in the Russian Federation by Types of Property, 1990

State housing (departmental and municipal)	78%
Public housing	8%
Construction cooperatives	5%
Personal property	9%
	100%

Source: Financy i Statistika (1990).

have been used to make up for shortfalls in federal government subsidies to housing maintenance organizations. But these local budget subsidies now provide only one-third or less of the estimated subsidies needed, and even the estimates of needed subsidies have been insufficient for proper maintenance.

Under current economic conditions, preserving the existing system of subsidies for housing maintenance will only aggravate the inequality of various groups with respect to so-called "free housing." Under the current system, state subsidies for housing are distributed in favor of wealthier families (with respect to both housing and income), as rent collected is based on size of living area. Contrary to logic, the way the system now works, the larger the total floor space of an apartment and the higher its quality, the greater the state subsidy.

So-called "free" state-owned apartments are available to those whose living area is below the established level of 5–7 square meters of living space per person. This constitutes a large number of people, and the waiting list for improved housing conditions keeps growing. In 1986, 8 million households (23 percent of Russia's urban households) were waiting for improved housing. By the end of 1990, this number hit the 9.5 million mark (26 percent of urban households). The average time spent on the waiting list was seven to eight years.

The amount of living space now being allocated is strictly limited to 9–12 square meters of living space per person, which means that a family may count on obtaining a new apartment with fewer rooms than there are family members. At the same time, the higher the social status of a person, the greater the probability of obtaining a state-owned apartment of a larger size and higher quality in a prestigious residential area, without having to wait. In addition, the administrative distribution system is corrupt. "Free" apartments can be purchased despite the seemingly rigid public supervision of their distribution.

Studies indicate that occupants of state-owned units are not from the lowest income brackets of the population, but those who by virtue of their social position have access to them. Moreover, renters of state-owned housing treat it as their own property and often sublet it at market prices.

Apart from official opportunities to improve their housing conditions, families can exchange their apartments by paying cash to the seller based on the black-market price of a square meter of living space. The rules of exchange, however, are very rigid, and such exchanges only take place in the larger cities. Subletting is also possible at black-market prices.

Almost 26 percent of housing is owned by individual citizens (in cities the figure is 15 percent). In cities, long-standing bans on individual construction, difficulties with land allotment and with acquisition of construction materials and credits, and rural–urban migration have led to a situation where self-financed housing construction by individuals barely exceeds 10 percent. This housing is not of such high quality as the single-family detached homes known in the West.

The purchase or construction of an individual house has been very restricted. Land could not be bought or sold. Plots were allotted by local soviets to individual house builders based on strictly fixed quotas and waiting-list procedures.

It is only in recent years that restrictions on individual housing construction in large and medium-sized cities have been lifted.

The early 1960s witnessed the beginning of a housing construction cooperative movement whose share in the housing market is now approximately 6 percent. Only those whose living area does not exceed the fixed level (8–9 square meters per person) could become members of these cooperatives. In 1990, cooperatives built 50,000 apartments (5 percent of the total number of units built). Most individuals who wished to buy cooperative apartments were not from high-income sectors of the population. Rather, they came from families on average income levels.

Families in cooperative apartments and privately owned houses ended up paying all capital and maintenance costs, which, according to our estimates, amounted to seven or eight times the expenditure of residents in state-owned houses. In the past, however, these families did enjoy favorable interest rates.

Until very recently, the state granted personal credit to purchase a cooperative apartment at 70 to 80 percent of its cost at an annual interest rate of 0.5 percent over 25 years. However, interest rates have now risen; as of early 1992, the RSFSR Savings Bank was offering credit for 20 to 25 years at a 20 percent interest rate. Loans for individual housing construction were being offered on the same terms.

THE PROBLEMS OF TRANSITION
TO A HOUSING MARKET

Existing mechanisms of distribution and corresponding relationships of ownership only exacerbate the housing problem. People in acute need of better housing have practically no chance of improving their situation. Those who have less than 5–7 square meters of living space may have a chance of something better, but only after many years of waiting. The vast majority of the population has no real prospect of improvement. Today, 26 percent of urban families are on official waiting lists for housing, while according to our estimates no less than 60 to 65 percent of all urban families needing better housing stand no chance of improvement under the existing distribution system.

Within the population, 58 percent believe the existing housing distribution system is unjust, and only 27 percent consider it basically or completely fair (*Voprosy Ekonomiki*, 1990). Respondents associate housing privileges with groups employed in the Party and Soviet administration, leaders and directors, and the highly paid.

The previous housing system completely ignored the huge volume of potential effective housing demand. Based on our most conservative estimates for the former Soviet Union, unsatisfied effective demand comprised 70–100 billion rubles at the end of 1991; 9–11 billion rubles are accounted for by those in the waiting line to purchase a cooperative apartment, and 18–22 billion rubles were ready to be paid by those who wished to join this line. Potential allocations for individual construction now exceed 27 million rubles. As our survey data show, residents of state-owned buildings are prepared to pay from 17 to 43 billion rubles to improve their housing standards.

Thus, the creation of a housing market could attract at least 54–60 billion rubles. Privatization of existing state-owned housing, depending on its terms, could draw in 17–43 billion more rubles from the resources generated by effective demand.

PRIVATIZATION

As of spring 1992, lawmakers and economists have only been paying attention to policies concerning privatized housing, which is only one aspect of housing reform. The major drawback of all housing programs has been the lack of a *comprehensive* approach to housing reform.

The first steps toward privatizing housing were made in late 1988. Ownership of apartments in housing and housing construction cooperatives that had been fully paid for was turned over to residents. An attempt was made also by a further resolution in 1988 to let people buy the apartments they occupied in state-owned and public buildings, as well as vacant apartments in buildings subject to reconstruction or major renovation. When selling apartments into private hands, the original principle was retained: one family could have only one apartment or individual house.

In the Russian Federation, the selling price of an apartment was based on its depreciated cost in current prices, taking into account major renovations required. The present owners of buildings—the executive committees of local soviets, government departments, and enterprises—could establish the selling price of an apartment taking into account its quality and location. In practice, however, the lack of effective valuation mechanisms sometimes produced unrealistic prices.

The initial conditions for privatization were developed with a single aim: namely, to eliminate from state responsibility the oldest housing, which was also the cheapest in terms of price but at the same time the most expensive to maintain. As a result, the process failed to gain widespread acceptance. In 1989, only 10,500 apartments in state-owned and public buildings were sold to citizens in Russia (RSFSR State Committee on Statistics); in 1990, the figure was 43,000 (Table 5.3). By 1991, sales were increasing. From January to October 1991, some 81,000 apartments were privatized (Table 5.4). By the end of November 1991, that figure increased to 90,000 apartments, with an assessed value of 505 million rubles. Thus, by the beginning of December 1991, 0.04 percent of all state and public units had been privatized—a small beginning.

From the beginning of 1992 onward, the housing privatization process has been organized through the new rules adopted in the Law on Privatized Housing in the RSFSR of July 1991. But up to now we do not know of any city in Russia

Table 5.3. Sales of Apartments to Individuals in the Russian Federation, 1990

Vendor	No. of Flats	Total Space (m²)	Assessed Value (mil. rubles)	Revenue From Sales (mil. rubles)
Local soviets	24,500	1,055,000	112	86
Ministries and agencies	18,500	,937,000	94	46
Total	43,000	1,992,000	206	132

Source: Financy i Statistika (1990).

where privatization has become a widespread phenomenon. Moscow is probably most active in this respect. Moscow authorities decided to give the apartments to their occupants free of charge. By the end of February 1992, more than 35,000 apartments had been privatized. By early May, 100,000 units in total (about 45 percent of the municipal stock) had been transferred to their occupants. The general delay in moving ahead with privatization seems to be mainly due to problems in determining the exact procedures. For instance, one city has been unable to decide on what year to base the price of apartments; another has not yet decided whether to charge buyers the cost of documentation, and so on.

In St. Petersburg, approximately 75,000 applications to privatize apartments had been submitted by the end of February 1992. By the middle of 1992, not all district offices had started handling documents. Despite the fact that the Law on Privatization of Housing Stock required district offices to prepare transfer documents within two months from when they receive applications, office clerks estimated it would take them almost a year to handle all the applications received by the middle of 1992.

Table 5.4. Sales of Apartments to Individuals in the Russian Federation, January–October, 1991

	No. of Flats	Total Floor Space (m²)	Average Assessed Value (rubles)
St. Petersburg	41	54	5,202
Moscow	945	60	9,327
Russian Federation	80,910	48	5,593

Source: RSFSR State Committee on Statistics (1992b), pp. 9–14.

Below are examples of how much apartments are selling for according to the evaluation procedure adopted in St. Petersburg:

- for a household of two, an apartment built in the 1940s or 1950s (during the Stalin era), with 103 square meters of floor space, costs 34,000 rubles;

- for a household of four, an apartment built in the 1960s (during the Khrushchev era), with 53 square meters of floor space, costs nothing, although it is valued at about 12,300 rubles;

- for a household of one, a recently built unit with 81 square meters of floor space costs 21,000 rubles.

The reasons for these prices are attributable to a combination of central legislation and local authority practice.

OPTIONS FOR HOUSING PRIVATIZATION

Under the Law on Privatized Housing in the RSFSR, every citizen of the Russian Federation has the right to buy the apartment he or she occupies, on the following terms: each person in a household is given, free of charge, at least 18 square meters of total space. Each family then receives 9 square meters on top of that. The price of each square meter given free of charge is based on the price of average-quality housing in the city. There are limits on what the household gets for free. The family must pay for the portion of the assessed value of the unit that exceeds the voucher given them free of charge. The Councils of Ministers of the RSFSR determine the rules for assessing the costs of privatized housing.

It is expected that during the transitional period the terms and procedures for providing housing to families needing it will remain in force. At a later stage, state-owned and municipal apartments will be granted only to low-income families (whose income does not exceed certain minimums), invalids, and veterans of the Second World War.

Under the privatization law, most cities (for example, St. Petersburg, Novosibirsk, Ekaterinburg, and Omsk) have developed their own models of privatization, which they began to implement in early 1992. But even implementation of these programs has not quietened debate about housing privatization. In Moscow, housing privatization has been a source of sharp conflict between the city administration and the city soviet.

The common element in all privatization proposals was that the tenant has the right to purchase his or her apartment. Proposals for the sale of whole buildings or purchase of units by outsiders have not been put forward, and the possibility of returning nationalized units to their former owners has never been discussed in Russia. All housing privatization proposals are based on the principle that privatization will be voluntary. The aim is to extend the sphere of market relations and help increase investment in housing construction.

The privatization programs, of which we are aware, can be grouped into four options, all based on the basic principle of a tenant's right to purchase his or her housing unit.

- *Option 1: Free transfer.*   All housing shall be privatized to the full extent possible through free transfer to residents; only floor space in excess of fixed quotas will be sold at depreciated (or otherwise low) cost.
- *Option 2: Buying out.*   The estimated cost of all apartments will be paid with only minimum discounts; in other words, residents will purchase from the state the right to own their apartments.
- *Option 3: Being socially just.*   A fixed amount of living area will be freely transferred to residents; "prohibitive" prices will be charged for extras beyond that fixed amount of space.
- *Option 4: Being conservative.*   The housing market will be developed primarily through new housing construction.

It is argued by its proponents that Option 1 (privatization "at any price") is a *sine qua non* for a large, quickly growing market. This is the only mechanism that would trigger a boom in housing construction. In practice, it suggests a free transfer of housing within certain fixed amounts of living space (associated with average city-wide costs per square meter). It also suggests a buy-out of extra living space at depreciated or slightly higher cost. Close to this variation are the privatization schemes being worked out under Russian Federation housing privatization law.

The concept of privatizing state-owned and municipal housing in Moscow as originally proposed by the city government was fully consistent with the principles of this option. The average cost of one square meter of total space was set at 203.5 rubles. For every family residing in Moscow the first family member was to be granted a portion of the apartment approximating 6,105 rubles. Each additional family member was to receive 3,366 rubles. This corresponded to 18 square meters of total usable space per person and an extra 12 square meters per family at the price of 203.5 rubles per square meter. The estimated cost of the entire apartment was based on its depreciated value with regard to required renovation, layout, amenities, and public utilities, and its location within one of the three large town planning zones (the center, the middle, and the periphery). All in all, 12 indicators of housing quality were taken into account.

The most extreme form of this option is the free-of-charge model proposed by G. Popov, the mayor of Moscow. This housing privatization proposal has now been implemented in Moscow. The main arguments for free privatization are: the difficulty in effectively using the proceeds from privatization sales under inflationary conditions; the danger of leaving the population without any savings in an inflation environment; and the impossibility of avoiding corruption in the valuation of apartments (Popov argues that Moscow can achieve social justice in the future through the imposition of a property tax).

Option 2 assumes a replenishment of the budget from privatization. It calls for tenants to make full payment for ownership of their units. For example, the first proposal for privatized housing in St. Petersburg would have used the present technique of estimating prices based on housing quality. A city resident would have been entitled to free floor space worth only 1,000 rubles—that is, 3–10 square meters of total floor space. In practice, this proposal amounted to full payment for privatization.

Option 3 is based on strict observance of principles of social justice, which could lead both to economically inefficient results (as prohibitive prices will simply stop the process of privatization) and to negative effects with regard to forming a new social structure. For example, originally the Moscow Soviet calculated freely transferred floor space in a similar way to the plan envisaged in the RSFSR Law. However, buying out extra or excess space or higher-quality housing calls for payments progressively increasing with the amount of space above the norm, which reduces privatization to the purchase of extra housing at market or even higher prices—out of reach for most of the population.

There are several serious problems with Option 4. (1) It is difficult to run an apartment building in which apartments belong to several different owners—the state, the municipality, and private residents. Under such conditions, the various owners become coproprietors of the building's engineering equipment and common rooms. (2) Departments that have jurisdiction over the best state-owned houses can be expected to resist privatization. (3) Some fear that privatization might reduce the volume of cheap municipal housing needed for the poor, thus requiring new construction.

EFFORTS TO ORGANIZE A HOUSING MARKET: THE CASE OF MOSCOW

Despite antagonism and disputes between local legislative and executive authorities, a housing market has begun to emerge in Moscow. It is very small in scope and operates almost exclusively through US dollar transactions. For instance, according to available data from late 1990, the basic price per square meter of living area averaged roughly US$192. This extremely narrow market created prices that are absolutely out of reach for most city residents.

According to data from February 1992, prices per square meter of usable floor space have risen to the US$300–600 range. It has become more popular to lease apartments than to sell them. In 1992, the annual rent per square meter averaged US$150 and higher.

Auctions for apartments have constituted another step toward a housing market. Such auctions began in Moscow in April 1991, when the executive committee of the Moscow City Soviet sold at auction the leasing rights to 10 apartments to Moscow-based enterprises and organizations. Only enterprises with registered lists of employees waiting for improved housing were permitted to bid.

The leasing price per square meter of usable space averaged roughly 5,000 rubles, a 10- to 15-fold increase over the original price, equivalent to the mean estimated cost of housing construction in Moscow. The auction prices coincided with the market housing prices in Moscow in terms of hard currency prices converted to rubles.

By the second auction in June 1991, prices had jumped by 300–400 percent. In October 1991, the average price of leasing rights for a square meter of usable floor space in Moscow municipal apartments rose to 17,900 rubles.

Somewhat later, auctions were also organized for private apartments and houses. Citizens with residential registration in Moscow were permitted to take part in the sales. In September 1991, the maximum price of space per square meter hit the 51,000 ruble mark. In January 1992, the price per square meter of usable space reached as high as 150,000 to 200,000 rubles. In late February, one could observe some price decrease (presumably as a result of the fall in the dollar exchange rate). Prices of low-comfort apartments on the outskirts of the city were 1.2–2.2 million rubles. However, comfortable apartments in good locations cost 8–10 million rubles (100,000–150,000 rubles per square meter).

THE OUTLOOK FOR FUTURE PRIVATIZATION EFFORTS

We predict the following course for housing privatization over the next two to three years. Privatization of state- and municipal-owned housing stock will continue because state and municipal entities do not have the resources for maintenance and repair. In cities such as Moscow and St. Petersburg, a quarter of this housing stock may be privatized. This portion may be higher if city authorities encourage the process.

Private companies, individuals, and joint stock companies will own a certain percentage of this housing stock and will do a good job of maintaining it. This could stimulate more interest in buying larger portions of buildings, or entire buildings. In St. Petersburg, for instance, there are now plans to sell at auction portions of buildings under repair and buildings that have been recently built. This move was motivated by dramatic city deficits and the desire to facilitate joint ownership of buildings.

Conflicts between building owners and tenants will create the need for groups to protect both landlords' and tenants' rights. Such conflicts will also create competition between maintenance service firms. Conflicts will also arise over semilegal and illegal house sales. This will require setting up a centralized registration office to record legal real estate transactions.

Prestigious residential areas will emerge in the suburbs, although due to housing construction costs and general inflation, these areas will be limited in number. Some residential areas will turn into slums. This is likely to happen to areas with housing built during the Khrushchev era, and in St. Petersburg and other large industrial cities, and to areas bordering industrial zones with pre-1917 housing.

Most contractors specializing in prefabricated construction will soon be out of work. Some construction firms will be privatized and will produce needed items, whereas others will lose their current contracts. Competition in the industry will facilitate the emergence of small construction companies oriented toward cheap building technologies and materials. There will be a drastic drop in investment in new construction. The state and municipalities will, instead, focus on developing engineering infrastructure.

Population growth in large cities will slow, and the populations of cities such as Moscow, St. Petersburg, and Ekaterinburg will drop. However, the population on the outskirts of these cities will continue to grow, as will the density of development on already developed land.

To facilitate Russia's attempts to move from a central to a market economy in the housing sphere, several priorities should take precedence. First, there is no alternative to increasing rents and house prices to market levels over the next three to five years. Much educational work, best channeled through the media, will be needed to win people over to this idea. Both those who have great hopes for the positive changes that a market economy can bring and those who continue to rely on the now disappearing state need to be convinced of the necessity of this course. Families unable to afford an apartment providing them with some fixed number of square meters of space per person should receive subsidies from the government or municipality. The Hungarian experience should be useful to us in this respect (Struyk and Telgarsky, 1991).

The second priority is to offer incentives for government authorities to be more interested in providing better-quality management. Bureaucratic battles, low salaries, and contradictory regulations have contributed to low morale and a lack of devotion to work among local officials. One improvement would be to decrease the number of deputies in local soviets, a step already taken in St. Petersburg. Doing so increases the responsibility given to smaller groups of decision makers, which in turn heightens interest in their work. Another improvement would be to clarify the relationship between state and commercial activity—currently a sticky area for local officials. Other issues that must be addressed include land management and housing finance.

Despite history, sociological surveys indicate that Russians still have faith and hope that their life will improve (Matchevitch, 1992). But they need reassurance that policies aimed at market reform will benefit them. The Russian people still harbor much anger over their misfortunes and are used to blaming others for their fate. Housing privatization policies must, therefore, take into account both the emotional and the economic obstacles to housing reform.

REFERENCES

Financy i Statistika. 1990. *Narodnoe Khozyaistvo RSFSR v. 1990 g., Statisticheskil Sbornik* [The national economy of the RSFSR in 1990, a statistical handbook]. Moscow: Financy i Statistika.

Financy i Statistika. 1991. *A Brief Statistical Handbook*. Moscow: Financy i Statistika.

Matchevitch, M. 1992. Nadezhdi malenky orkestric. *Smena* 34 (6 March).

Pravda. 1990. O novykh podkhodakh k resheniya zhilishchnoi problemy v strane i merakh po ikh praktitcheskoi realizatsii [On new approaches to solving the housing problem and measures to implement them] (20 May).

RSFSR. 1986. *Housing Code of the RSFSR*. Moscow: Juridichsekaya Literatura.

RSFSR State Committee on Statistics. 1989. The housing conditions of the USSR population. *Statistical Yearbook 1989*.

RSFSR State Committee on Statistics. 1992a. The social and economy situation of the Russian Federation in 1991. *Ekonomika i Zhiza* 4.

RSFSR State Committee on Statistics. 1992b. *Statischeskiy Press Bulletin* 1.

Smena. 1992. Politichesky Barometr (28 February).

Struyk, R., and Telgarsky, J. 1991. *The Puzzle of Housing Privatization in Eastern Europe*. Washington, DC: The Urban Institute.

Trud. 1992. Zhit chtobi vizhit, ili chtobi zhit [Living to survive or surviving to live] (17 March).

Voprosy Economiki. 1990. Raspredelemie zhilya i socialnaya spravedlivost: tochka zreniya naseleniya [Distribution of housing and social justice: The public's point of view].

6

Bulgaria

*Sasha Tsenkova, George Georgiev,
Stoicho Motev, and Dimitar Dimitrov*

INTRODUCTION

Recent housing reform in Bulgaria introduced a number of privatization measures aimed at the establishment of a market-oriented housing sector. This chapter will examine the steps and policies of privatization that attempted to change the form and extent of state control and regulation over the housing market. It will analyze systematically the privatization of the production, finance, management, and consumption of housing.

To enable a better understanding of privatization processes, the impact of economic restructuring and political change in the wider context is considered first. Second, the major characteristics of housing provision under the socialist system are presented, with particular emphasis on housing production, allocation, costs, and tenure patterns. Furthermore, the politics and economic rationale of privatization alternatives are briefly discussed. Third, the analysis focuses on the particular aspects of privatization with specific importance for the Bulgarian housing sector. Emphasis is placed on a whole set of interrelated issues, which include the restructuring and privatization of production, the deregulation of prices and elimination of subsidies, the operation of the housing market, the restitution of property, and the sale of public housing. Finally, the impact of privatization measures on housing supply and demand is evaluated, and attention is drawn to the major problems and policy failures in the process of privatization.

POLITICAL AND MACROECONOMIC REFORM

Bulgaria is in the process of transition from a centrally planned to a market economy. In the last three years, major political and economic reforms have taken place. Reform initiatives were launched in November 1989 by the Communist Party, which on reelection in June 1990 emphasized a commitment to free markets, competition, decentralization, and financial reform. As a result, various policies were discussed and some were implemented. These included the liberalization of prices in February 1991 and legislation on the privatization of state firms in May 1991. However, radical changes were avoided.

In the election of October 1991, the first nonsocialist government since 1944 was elected. This was the Union of Democratic Forces, which was a coalition of former opposition parties that indicated a preference to move toward a more dynamic and radical change. Tight fiscal and monetary policies were introduced, together with further deregulation of prices and interest rates. Small-scale privatization in the service sector was initiated. A package of restitution laws was passed through Parliament regarding the restoration of property rights over expropriated agricultural and urban land and commercial, industrial, and residential property. Private sector activity was encouraged, and state enterprises were restructured on market principles.

It should be noted that Bulgaria's market reforms were implemented under extremely unfavorable external conditions and considerable dislocation in the domestic economy. The poor economic performance of state enterprises, a substantial budget deficit, and accumulated foreign debt were, and still remain, the overriding economic problems. The contraction of all economic sectors resulted in a 12 percent drop in output levels in 1990, followed by another 23 percent drop in 1991 (Word Bank, 1992). A main macroeconomic concern was the inflation rate—471 percent in 1991, 79.5 percent in 1992. Unemployment reached 14.8 percent in 1992. An income policy to regulate increases in wage levels in the public sector was adopted. The living standard of the population changed dramatically. It is estimated that over 90 percent have incomes on or below the minimum level.

The transition to a market economy has proved to be particularly difficult, and the social costs of the market reform in Bulgaria have been extremely high. Problems are further aggravated by political instability and the lack of continuity in managing the reform processes. The first democratic government faced a political crisis at the end of 1992 and was forced to resign. It was succeeded by a new government of experts, which announced the revision of previous policies and legislation. Politically it was a step back to a more conservative approach in the transition to a market economy. The political priorities of the government are now the restructuring of the economy, privatization, the facilitation of economic growth in the private sector, liberalization of foreign trade, and investment.

The transition to a market-oriented housing sector was associated with wider processes of radical economic restructuring, deregulation, and the elimination of subsidies. Policy reform emphasized the importance of housing markets, private sector resources, and initiatives in the provision of housing. The chronic housing shortages made housing a politically sensitive issue in the reform process. Policymakers reacted under constant pressure from various well-organized social groups with different and often conflicting interests, which explains the controversial character of the housing policy reforms. It is against this background of radical economic and social restructuring with the attempt to eliminate the long-standing imbalances and distortions in the economy and its immense financial problems that the reform of the Bulgarian housing sector should be understood.

HOUSING BEFORE THE CHANGES IN THE POLITICAL CONTEXT

The Housing Problem

An overview of the housing situation in Bulgaria requires some reference to the qualitative and quantitative characteristics of the existing housing stock. This certainly says very little about the real housing problem, but it is a good starting point from which to orient succeeding discussion.

Investment in housing was smaller than in other East European countries, but more or less stable in the 1980s, at 12.8 percent on average of the total investment outlays (Renaud, 1991). According to the preliminary data from the 1992 Census of Population and Housing, the housing stock amounted to 3,061,000 dwellings, which was 6.1 percent more than in 1985; 55 percent of the housing stock was built after 1960. The average dwelling space per person increased from 11.1 square meters in 1965 to 18.9 square meters in 1985, while the average number of inhabitants per dwelling in the urban areas changed from 4.2 in 1965 to 3.26 in 1985 and 2.8 in 1992 (Central Statistical Office, 1965, 1985, 1992). This major improvement was mainly the result of increased state involvement in housing and the commitment of resources for new housing construction. The overall housing shortage in Bulgaria was approximately 320,000 units. If structural and qualitative characteristics of the stock are taken into account, the housing deficit could be 600,000 dwellings (Konaktchiev, 1990).

In terms of technical equipment and infrastructure, 35.4 percent of the dwellings lacked sewerage system, 33 percent had no water supply, and 1.9 percent were without electricity (Central Statistical Office, 1985). Furthermore, due to deferred maintenance and the poor initial quality of the existing stock, the 1985 assessment indicated that 25.5 percent needed urgent improvements and major repairs, and 4.3 percent were identified for slum clearance. Examining the structure of the housing stock, it should be noted that although 56.8 percent of the dwellings had 30–90 square meters of residential space, the proportion of small dwellings under 29 square meters was substantial—30.8 percent in 1985 and 23.3 percent in 1992 (Central Statistical Office, 1993).

Major Characteristics of the Housing System

Until 1989, Bulgaria was similar to other countries with a centrally planned economy in terms of the structure and the performance of the housing sector. The state had a strategic responsibility for the whole housing system.

State institutions and enterprises had a key role in planning and carrying out the actual production of housing. Economic management of the housing system was accomplished through central planning and implemented at the local level through five-year housing programs, which set the planned targets for the state construction and building materials industry. The plans were based on demographic forecasts for population structure, data on housing needs taken from the waiting lists of the municipal authorities, and the technical capacity of the industry. There was plenty of evidence for the apparent failure to meet unrealistic and often politically set targets in the five-year programs.

The balance between central control and local initiative on the part of housing authorities and individuals varied over the years, but one common feature was the central determination of investment decisions and the explicit control over the allocation of resources for housing production and housing finance. Macroeconomic regulation was achieved through planning targets for the output of the construction and building material industry, and control over the prices of basic inputs of land, materials, labor, and the completed dwelling.

In the actual operation of the system, market allocation of housing had been replaced by a socialist administrative method of distribution according to need. Apart from the power to control exclusively the supply side, housing demand was also controlled through wage policies, which kept wages low and more or less equal in all economic sectors (Tsenkova, 1991b).

The consumption of housing was restricted in accordance with national housing standards, which set maximum living space per person and household, taking into account household structure and age and number of children. Housing was a constitutional right, but households could own only one dwelling, and could exchange it only with the approval of local housing authorities. There was a three-year period to arrange for the disposal of a second residential property acquired through inheritance or marriage. In addition, households could own a summer house or "villa."

Housing Provision

Apart from the general characteristics of a housing system in a centrally planned economy, Bulgarian housing provision had certain specific features. Housing production was concentrated in 88 large construction enterprises, employing 6.5 percent of the national workforce, which produced prefabricated panels for housing. Highly centralized and industrialized housing production replaced traditional Bulgarian house building of low-rise, single-family houses. It was suitable for large-scale public development schemes on the urban fringe to house the rapidly increasing urban population. Due to migration to the industrial urban centers, in 1990 urban population reached 70 percent, compared to 24 percent in 1946 (Central Statistical Office, 1993).

Output levels realized a peak in the 1970s but have gradually declined since then. Annual housing production in the different forms of provision for the 1965–88 period is presented in Figure 6.1. State producers dominated the supply of new housing, but the share of cooperative and individual housing production was substantial before the introduction of market reforms. However, even with the massive investment in new housing provision, the growing needs could not be met. The usual criticisms were aimed at an insufficient budget allocation, a chronic shortage of building materials and labor, a mismatch between suppliers of materials and construction enterprises, low quality, and inefficient management.

On the whole, the socialist planned economy was an "economy of restricted supply." In an attempt to solve the problem, the Bulgarian government took a more pragmatic view, deliberately expanding private sector housing provision (Carter, 1990). Whilst retaining crucial control over the system, it allowed housing cooperatives and individuals to finance and promote housing for their own consumption, provided that they were registered with the local housing authorities as being in housing need. Enterprises were also encouraged to provide housing for their employees. The opportunity for enterprises to channel profits into enterprise funds for social development and housing was different according to the status of the enterprise and its sector. This allowed control to be extended over workers' behavior through lower wages and the restriction on labor mobility. It also created an additional stimulus for career advancement, in that enterprises provided mostly housing for sale.

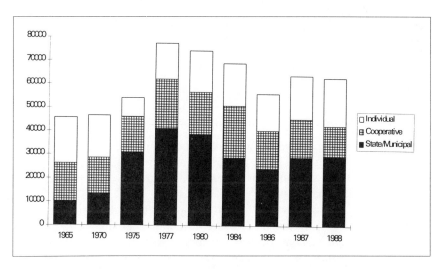

Figure 6.1. Output of new housing in Bulgaria, 1965–88. (*Source:* Central Statistical Office, 1989.)

Housing policy focused exclusively on new-house–building programs, in which the provision of housing for sale was the dominant form. Private ownership of housing was encouraged, resulting in 86 percent private ownership by 1988. Thus housing costs, maintenance, and management responsibilities were shifted to the individual households (Tsenkova, 1991b).

Public sector housing provision was predominantly for sale. The developers were local housing authorities, state enterprises, and public institutions. Construction was financed through short-term loans at an interest rate of 4 percent from the State Savings Bank and carried out by state construction enterprises. Land was either publicly owned or compulsorily purchased by local authorities. Since 1975, the state had invested in the construction of 511,196 new dwellings, of which 485,450 were sold to households on local authority waiting lists. Investment patterns were different in rural and urban areas. Public development was dominant in the larger towns.

Despite the fact that most of the new housing development was initiated by the public sector, a significant proportion was financed and carried out by cooperatives and individuals. The main difference between public and private (or market) forms of provision was in the level of involvement and direct contribution to the promotion and construction of housing. Future homeowners were often involved in labor-intensive finishing work. Self-build was a major form of private housing provision, with a strong tradition in rural areas and small towns. It was largely facilitated through the mobilization of resources by the extended family. Most young households would have relatives to help them with money and/or the construction. Local authorities facilitated the process through the provision of land often free of charge or at symbolic prices.

However, housing cooperatives and individuals received lower priority in access to land or long-term construction loans; they were less likely to obtain contracts with state construction companies; they also faced major difficulties in obtaining building materials, often on the black market, and meeting transport and labor costs. The importance of the second economy for this form of provision was great.

Tenure Structure and Property Rights

One of the distinguishing characteristics of Bulgarian tenure structure is the continuing high degree of home-ownership and the polarization of tenures— public renting vis-à-vis home ownership. Private renting has been marginal. The evolution of tenure patterns is shown in Figure 6.2.

The growth of home ownership has taken place under different conditions, largely determined by the decisions of state institutions and supply-side agencies. Under state socialism, home ownership was seen as socially and economically beneficial. It provided security and comfort but was also an economically feasible alternative, since access to public renting was strictly limited and private renting was practically nonexistent. Home ownership could validly be regarded

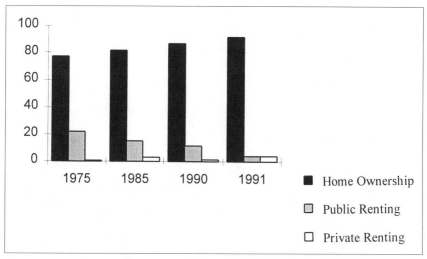

Figure 6.2. Housing tenure in Bulgaria, 1975–91. (*Source*: United Nations, 1985; Hoffman et al., 1992.)

as a logical preference, given the circumstances and a strategy of wealth accumulation under state socialism.

It should be noted that there was a major contradiction in the allocation policy. If a household was successful in the queueing process, it could then consume practically an unlimited amount of housing and pass it on through inheritance. Control was exercised exclusively on access to housing, but not on its subsequent consumption. This resulted in distributional inefficiencies in both the owner-occupied and the rented sectors. There was plenty of evidence of households that were overhoused, especially elderly people.

Home owners in housing cooperatives had individual ownership over the units and a share of the common space, roof, lifts, stairs, and land. They could transfer or sell their property without the approval of the cooperative. In the new housing estates, where state-built apartments were sold to households or public sector tenants, home owners had the same property rights as cooperative members, without exclusive ownership over the land. Public sector tenants had unlimited rights, basically the same as home owners. Once public housing was acquired, it could be transferred to family members, provided that they were in housing need. It could be exchanged with the approval of the local housing authority.

Housing Costs and Subsidies

As a result of central regulation, housing for rent and for sale was affordable, and housing costs were 4–5 percent of the average annual household income. The rent in public sector housing for an average household with two wage earners, in an apartment of 58 square meters, was 4 percent of the net income, whereas the average amount spent on all housing costs—that is, the rent and utilities—was 11 percent (Grigorov et al., 1987). State housing was so cheap that it did not require financial accumulation. The same household, if successful in the queue for public housing for sale, would spend 5 percent of annual income on mortgage payments (Tsenkova, 1991b).

Low housing costs were a major achievement of the socialist housing policy. Housing was sold and/or rented at prices set by the central planning system, with little variation according to size, quality, or location. Household income differences were not taken into account. State-produced housing was sold at a price from 136 to 170 leva per square meter. Rents were fixed in 1967 at 2.0 leva per square meter in the private sector and at 0.19 leva in the public sector. Due to the extreme housing shortages in larger towns, unofficial private sector rents were much higher.

Costs of basic inputs were regulated. Building materials and fuel costs were subsidized, but land had practically no value and presented an insignificant proportion of the development costs. The amount of subsidy directed to housing between 1985 and 1989 was relatively constant between 0.52 and 0.6 percent of the state budget. It was used to cover the growing difference between the construction costs and the sale price. Thus the subsidy per square meter in 1985 was 33.12 leva, while in 1989 it was 85.73 leva (Hoffman, Koleva, Ravicz, and Mikelsons, 1992). As Renaud (1991) argued, production subsidies allocated to the building material and construction industry were not used in a cost-efficient way, and a significant proportion financed production inefficiencies.

Home owners also benefited from a traditional source of consumer subsidy—25-year mortgages up to 18,000 leva at 2 percent interest rate. Housing cooperatives and individuals received long-term construction loans under the same conditions to finance private housing provision. However, as a result of the systematic bias against the private sector, private housing provision was 2.7 times more expensive, as a result of differences in the price of building materials, transport costs, and labor (Word Bank, 1990). A substantial amount of personal savings was required to balance the gap between the loan and the actual construction costs of the development. The advantages of private housing provision were better quality and a higher standard of housing, as well as a shorter waiting period.

Apart from general consumer subsidies, individual grants were made to young families with two or three children and to households in economically assisted regions, with waivers for mortgage down-payment requirements on part of the loan. Special grants from a compensation fund were available to owners to balance the difference between the price of new housing and the value of their property where it had been compulsorily purchased by local authorities for public development.

Housing Management and Maintenance

The management of privately owned stock was the responsibility of individual home owners or voluntary associations in the case of multifamily buildings. Everyday maintenance and minor repairs were often carried out on a private or self-help basis by members of the association. Major repairs and improvements were contracted to municipal maintenance firms but carried out after substantial delay. The State Savings Bank issued five-year loans up to 3,000 leva for the renewal and improvement of housing. Since the government was obsessed with setting up politically attractive targets for new construction, very little was done to provide any subsequent financial, technical, or organizational support for the maintenance and management of private housing. There was a constant shortage of materials, equipment, and labor for maintenance work. The lack of an adequate legal framework to define the responsibilities of home owners in terms of management and maintenance also presented a serious barrier for its efficient organization, especially for housing in multiple ownership (Tsenkova, 1991a).

The public rented sector was managed by municipal maintenance and management companies. The maintenance of housing was an insignificant part of their activity, which was focused almost exclusively on the servicing of the technical infrastructure of the municipal area. As a result, the maintenance of the housing stock was given a low priority and was almost "privatized." Urgent repairs for the maintenance of the dwellings and their common areas had become the tenants' responsibility over time by default. However, major structural repairs were financed from local authority budgets and carried out by the municipal maintenance companies in accordance with their five-year plans. Rents were insufficient to cover these costs (Tsenkova, 1991a).

Housing Allocation and Exchange

Political changes after 1944 gradually led to the complete destruction of the preexisting housing market. Free-market property transactions were not allowed. The legal framework referring to individual or property rights gradually established local housing authorities as key agents in the access and transfer of housing. A household could own one dwelling and one summer house. New housing for rent or sale could be acquired in accordance with the waiting lists, in which households were grouped into a number of "privileged" and "unprivileged" categories. Existing housing, if vacant, could be transferred also with the assistance of local housing authorities. Since the prices were fixed by state tariff, there was very little incentive for home owners to sell a second dwelling, however acquired, or to move to a smaller one. Property tax or maintenance and utility costs were not a financial burden either. In rural areas with no housing shortage, "free" transactions of vacant properties and serviced land could be made, provided that buyers were eligible according to official requirements for housing need.

WHY WAS PRIVATIZATION NEEDED?

In Bulgaria, the privatization of the housing sector involves general policies that aim to reassert market forces and reduce state intervention. The policy promotes deregulation in the provision of housing, an increase in the role of private sector institutions, and a reduction in public expenditure. It can be argued that the process of state withdrawal from direct housing provision and the shifting of the responsibility to the private sector was initiated in the 1980s as an attempt to improve the socialist housing system. The Bulgarian government deliberately expanded the private sector in place of its public counterpart. It also encouraged home ownership as a strategy designed to avoid a long-term financial commitment to management and maintenance.

In terms of ownership, privatization implies the transfer of public assets such as public rented stock and state enterprises into private ownership. The practical implementation of the privatization policy should be discussed together with new directions in housing policy, the process of economic restructuring, and the wider context of social and political change.

Privatization was motivated by the pressure to reduce the budget deficit and to move away from central regulation and a directly subsidized housing supply to a market-oriented system. In the context of fiscal constraint, privatization was seen as economically attractive and a feasible alternative. The aim of privatization was to improve the economic and social diversity of the housing system and to abolish long-standing imbalances and distortions. Privatization strategies and measures in the housing sector stemmed, to a large extent, from broader economic and political changes in society. The restructuring of the housing sector in accordance with market principles was necessary for its integration into the economy as a whole. The main objectives were to keep the sector vital, to maintain the value of existing assets, and to benefit from investments already made.

Since housing is a very sensitive political issue, it attracts considerable attention. However, the platforms of the major political partners, the Union of Democratic Forces and the Bulgarian Socialist Party, had lacked a clear philosophy on future housing policy and privatization and are extremely vague in terms of programs and details. After the political changes in 1989, successive governments undertook various reform initiatives aimed at transforming the housing sector along market principles. Among the most significant reform measures were the liberalization of house prices and private sector rents, the revival of the housing market and the privatization of public housing. These issues are analyzed in greater detail in the following section.

The unstable political context in Bulgaria influenced the scope and the pace of privatization. Political uncertainty made it easier for particularly well organized interest groups to exercise pressure over the decision-making process, thus leading to various conflicting policies and ad hoc solutions.

PRIVATIZATION MEASURES AND THEIR IMPLEMENTATION

In a narrow sense, privatization in Bulgaria was the transfer of public assets into private ownership through the sale and/or the restitution of property. In the wider sense, it implied the deregulation and the privatization of production and the exchange and consumption of housing. At the risk of oversimplifying complicated issues, this analysis focuses on the policies that give a specific dimension to the privatization process in Bulgaria—that is, the market adjustment of housing production, subsidies and housing finance, the operation of the housing market, and the sale of public housing.

Restructuring of State Enterprises

The construction and building-material industry has been publicly owned. Privatization, through the sale of shares and the establishment of joint ventures, is expected to be implemented under the supervision of the National Agency of Privatization. The political context and the availability of domestic capital will determine the extent and form of their privatization.

Meanwhile, monopolistic enterprises have been broken down into smaller autonomous units operating on market principles. The production of building materials in 1990 was concentrated in 6 firms, but in 1991 their number had increased to 36, with the expectation that 40 more would be formed (Hoffman et al., 1992). The decentralization of housing production, as an initial step in privatization, resulted in the subdivision of construction enterprises into 350 economically autonomous units. It is proposed that 125 will remain under state control and the rest will be transferred to local authorities for subsequent management and/or privatization (Krastev, 1992). A major strategy for their economic survival and adjustment to market provision is the restructuring and flexible use of their technological capacity. Most of the enterprises are large, with over 1,000 employees, equipped to produce up to 2,000 prefabricated units per year. Their monopolistic position in the supply of housing contributes to the distortion of prices due to production delays and inefficiencies, overrunning costs, and bad management.

Reviving the Private Sector

The private building industry consists of small, badly equipped firms, all operating on a small scale. It is estimated that they currently hold 2 percent of the total construction industry assets (Hoffman et al., 1992). Most of the firms channel their activity into renovation, repairs, and finishing work. Private firms, involved in new house building, often act as developers in small housing schemes, where the risk is manageable and the profits secure. They also fill the gap in the provision of maintenance and repair services for home owners and act as subcontractors for municipal maintenance companies. Restrictions on the private sector have been abolished and discrimination in access to materials, credit, and equipment eliminated.

Price Reform

Macroeconomic regulation in housing was removed, at the same time as the liberalization of prices was introduced. Freeing the prices in February 1991 resulted in an initial 10- to 15-fold jump in the price levels of building materials, equipment, and labor. A further increase in prices followed a rise in fuel costs and continued to keep pace with high inflation. However, the positive effect of the change was the elimination of long-standing shortages of basic inputs for housing on the market. Regulations stating the fixed prices for housing and land were abolished. House and land prices were determined by market forces. Rents in the private sector were deregulated. In the public sector, even though tenants faced an 800 percent increase, rents are still 15–20 times lower than the market rent.

Subsidies and Housing Finance

In the struggle to reduce subsidies and the budget deficit, production subsidies in housing were eliminated. Households had to face the true cost of their housing. No subsidy is allocated for new provision of public rented housing or for maintenance and management of the existing public sector housing: it is expected to be self-financing. Direct budget allocation for consumer subsidies, in the form of tax allowances for home owners or shelter allowances for households in the rented sector, does not exist.

Since the beginning of 1991, when it was affected by the monetary reform, the mortgage interest rate has stood at 49 to 54 percent. However, outstanding mortgages issued prior to the reform had a fixed interest rate of 10 percent. The difference amounts to 123 million leva per month. It is financed through cross-subsidization by other borrowers and is not recorded as an on-budget subsidy (Ravicz, 1992). As of May 1993, old mortgages have a 25 percent interest rate. In expectation of further changes in housing finance, most borrowers repaid the old loan in advance of these unfavorable financial terms. It is estimated that almost 90 percent of home owners now own their property outright.

As far as new construction loans and mortgages are concerned, the high interest rate certainly discourages borrowing. What is more, the State Savings Bank (SSB) did not adjust its portfolio to market prices. Although all commercial banks can officially provide credit for construction, SSB still continues to be the major source of housing finance. It is currently offering loans of up to 100,000 leva, which is sufficient to buy 10–15 square meters of a dwelling at market prices. The introduction of indexed mortgages, which are more suitable to a high inflationary environment, is being considered by the SSB and the Postal Bank. Lack of credit supply is a major problem for new housing construction. It is estimated that currently there are 50,000 units that cannot be completed as a result of inadequate finance. Private developers operate with 50 percent of the market house price—that is, cash or personal savings, provided up front by the prospective owners (Tsenkova, 1991b).

Housing Markets

As a result of amendments in the Property Law in April 1990, local housing authorities have lost their strategic power to control access to housing. Individuals have been allowed to exchange and possess an unlimited number of properties. Since the share of new housing is insignificant, housing market activity focuses on the existing stock. There is little reliable information on actual prices of urban land and housing, due to the lack of information and monitoring systems. Infrastructure to facilitate housing market transactions is emerging. Real estate agents and appraisers are gradually developing local and regional networks and a database to facilitate the sale and/or exchange of housing. Previous uniformity in prices has changed into a diversified system that reflects the location, amenities, quality, and accessibility of the area. Over time, various housing submarkets have been formed, with substantial differentiation in prices. Information on house and land prices is given in Table 6.1.

Characteristic geographic patterns have been established, determined by the rapidly increasing prices in larger towns, especially in Sofia, and the more stable house prices in rural areas and small towns. Moreover, apartments in high-rise buildings on the urban fringe sell at prices two or three times cheaper than apartments in the central areas or the single-family houses in attractive urban locations. Newly built dwellings are 30 percent more expensive than existing ones. In general, prices in 1991 rose well above the rate of inflation and continue to escalate. Thus an apartment of 60 square meters on a housing estate in Sofia might have sold for 90,000 leva in March 1991, whereas in the first quarter of 1993 the price was likely to be 380,000–400,000 leva. Possible explanations of this phenomenon are the chronic shortages of housing, the lack of other investment opportunities in the economy, and the possible opportunity to convert housing into office space, which is in high demand at the moment.

Since the Bulgarian housing market is targeted exclusively toward home owners, its efficient operation is badly hindered by the lack of mortgages to finance housing purchase. A sales tax of 9 percent and an estate agent's fee of 1.5 percent also present a financial problem. But the core of the crisis lies in the extremely low effective demand. Currently the ratio of annual income to house price is 1:14 to 1:20.

The variation in private sector rents is also significant, suggesting the formation of submarkets in rented property. Rent levels have increased 15- to 20-fold compared to 1989 "black-market" rents. Currently in Sofia and other regional

Table 6.1. Market Prices for Housing and Urban Land, in Bulgaria (Bulgarian Leva)

Settlement	Year	Apartments	Houses	Urban Land
Sofia				
Centre	1992	6,000–1,600	4,000–1,000	550–1,000
	1993	13,000–20,000		1,000–1,300
Housing estates	1992	2,800–6,200	3,800–6,200	200–800
	1993	7,500–9,500	4,000–7,800	300–1,000
Suburban	1992	1,800–4,000	2,300–5,200	50–800
	1993	3,500–5,000	4,000	–
Villa zones	1992	3,500–6,000	5,500–8,600	300–500
	1993	14,000–21,000	12,000–20,000	500–700
Elsewhere				
Regional towns	1992	1,800–5,000	1,500–5,000	200–400
	1993	8,000–10,000	8,000–10,000	–
Other towns	1992	1,200–3,000	1,200–5,000	120–250
	1993	4,500–7,300	4,000–7,500	–
Villages	1992	–	1,000–4,500	20–350
	1993	–	2,500–5,000	–
Resorts	1992	–	1,800–5,300	80–500
	1993	–	–	–
Villa zones	1992	–	1,500–3,200	50–350
	1993	–	2,600–3,600	–

Note: In 1993 there were 38 leva to 1 U.S. dollar.
Source: Architecture and Art Exchange (1992); Dimitrov (1993).

towns, average rents vary between 35 to 60 leva per square meter; an average household with two wage earners would have to spend 50 percent of its income on rent.

Privatization of Public Housing

The policy was initiated for political purposes at the end of 1989 by the last socialist government and energetically implemented by the local bureaucracy. The political elite frenetically took advantage of the right to buy at below-market prices, thus transferring political into economic power. The transfer of housing into private ownership was seen as the most obvious and simplest way of removing financial burdens and responsibilities from the state. Public sector tenants could buy their dwelling at 1977 prices, provided that they had applied to exercise the Right to Buy before March 1991. The gap in privatization and market prices was enormous, as illustrated in Figure 6.3. Despite the increase in the basic price per square meter in August 1992 from 131 to 1,120 leva, it still remains six to ten times lower than the market price. There were no restrictions on selling the dwelling on the open market and thus realizing substantial capital gains.

The results of the privatization of public housing in terms of the costs and off-budget subsidy were summarized by Hoffman et al. (1992). In 1989, the subsidy per unit as a percentage of unit costs was 33 to 131 percent, depending on location, size, and quality. With the sale of 21,000 units for the year, the subsidy was estimated at 240 million leva, which amounts to 0.6 percent of the GDP. In 1990, the gap in prices increased dramatically; at the same time, the volume of units sold increased to 90,000. Thus the subsidy peaked at 11.6 percent of the 1990 GDP. In the first half of 1991, the price gap was over 1,300 percent. The state sold 20,000 units, resulting in a huge off-budget subsidy which was approximately 6 percent of the GDP (Hoffman et al., 1992, p. 30).

The sale of public housing raises a number of issues about fairness, equity, and the long-term consequences of the policy. Obviously it failed to provide revenue

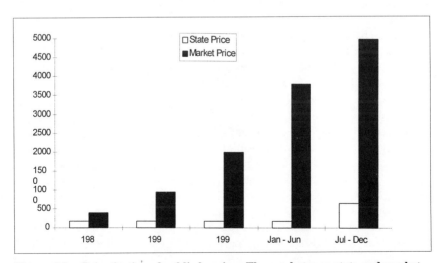

Figure 6.3.   Privatization of public housing: The gap between state and market price, in Bulgarian Leva per square meter. (*Source:* Hoffman et al.,1992; Dimitrov, 1992, 1993.)

and reasonable financial return on past investments. In social and economic terms, there were gainers and losers in this process of redistribution of public wealth. In a way, the sale of public housing perpetuates past housing inequalities as high social status families with higher income have been able to obtain better-quality housing at symbolic prices. The extent, form, and costs of the privatization of public housing are totally inconsistent with the generally stated principles of the market reform.

Restitution of Housing

This is another form of privatization of publicly owned housing. It was not expected to have such a dramatic impact over tenure patterns, since it included only some 10,000 dwellings (Dimitrov, 1993). In December 1991 and February 1992, a package of Restitution Acts, which directly affected the housing sector, was passed through parliament. Property title to buildings and urban land that had been subject to compulsory purchase for public development was to be restituted, provided that development had not been initiated. In effect, expropriated property could also be returned to former owners if it was in public ownership. In the case of properties occupied by public sector tenants, a three-year period has been allowed before property can be repossessed: in the meantime rent is paid to the original owners or their heirs. Local authorities are encouraged to provide alternative accommodation for low-income tenants. Most of these residential properties are in the central areas and consist of one or several units, which will probably end up as commercial space or mixed-use development. It is unlikely that the restitution process will lead to a substantial increase in private rental housing.

It should be noted that the actual implementation of these Acts is a complicated and extremely bureaucratic process of clarifying property rights, endless legal procedures, and arguments with local planning authorities and other public bodies whose interests are affected. In the implementation process, the struggle over property and urban land, in particular, is a whole saga of overcoming bureaucracy.

This form of privatization demands further intervention in order to achieve a more equitable and socially fair solution. It raises a number of questions. Whose interests are served? Certainly in most towns the old commercial centers have changed ownership patterns dramatically. After the restitution the "new owners" receive substantial revenue from the hundreds of small businesses established in their shops and offices. However, the majority of owners whose property was expropriated or compulsorily purchased do not qualify under these laws. In the course of 45 years, expropriated properties were sold on to other private owners or rebuilt as a result of urban renewal or urban land redevelopment. How and when are these people going to be compensated?

ASSESSMENT OF PRIVATIZATION MEASURES

Impact on Housing Supply

Housing supply was favorably affected by the privatization processes. New actors and structures emerged, and existing institutions with long-term interests in housing acquired new roles and responsibilities in the process of adjustment to a market environment. The changes facilitated a more diversified structure in housing production. Figure 6.4 illustrates major trends in the provision of new housing.

Public construction enterprises still have a monopolistic position in the supply of housing with a substantial share of housing output. However, the private sector has reasserted itself, and its importance is growing. Private speculative house building has emerged. Both private and public developers face increasing financial difficulties, high inflation, and a lack of an adequate credit supply. The liberalization of prices was a significant step toward the establishment of a market-oriented housing sector, but the price of building materials and dwellings has escalated far beyond their real value. Further increases were brought about by cuts in the production subsidy, high fuel costs, and high interest rates. Land supply became a major problem for private development as land costs, on average, account for 50 percent of the final costs. The number of housing starts fell dramatically, reaching its lowest level in the last 50 years.

As far as the existing stock is concerned, the emerging housing market was expected to stimulate a more efficient use of housing and eliminate distributional inefficiencies in the previous administrative system of housing allocation. Certainly vacant units, especially in areas with housing shortages, were traded up.

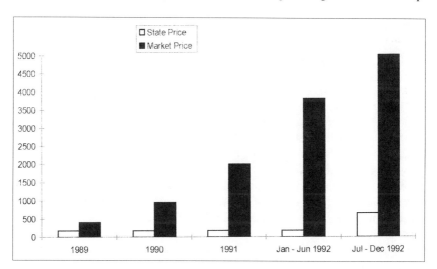

Figure 6.4. The output of new housing in Bulgaria, 1988–92. (*Source:* Dimitrov, 1992, 1993.)

Since the supply is limited and the housing deficit has persisted for a very long time, free-market prices have reached unprecedented levels. This further escalation of house prices, coupled with the lack of mortgage finance, blocked the efficient operation of the market.

The public rented sector contracted as a result of the privatization measures. Local authorities are left with the worst parts of the stock, which is in substantial need of repair and improvement. Privatization also changed the social profile of the tenants. Only tenants on very low income did not take advantage of the right to buy. Although rents are substantially below market rents, municipal management companies report 20 percent rent arrears. Meanwhile, private renting has expanded to 2 percent of the stock due to the deregulation of rents. With the general squeeze on wages and rising utility costs, many home owners on fixed low incomes are letting part of their dwelling as a strategy for economic survival.

Housing Demand

A market-oriented housing sector depends on the role of the individual household and its ability to exercise housing demand through its purchasing power. Individual choices and preferences feed back into the system through these price signals, to which the suppliers of housing respond. The process of economic restructuring and control over the increase in public sector wages imposes a limitation on the aggregate housing demand. Rising unemployment also reduces income levels and creates economic uncertainty.

Even though households were prepared to pay higher costs for their housing, they found themselves squeezed out of the market, with very little chance to improve their housing situation. The gap between income and entry costs has increased dramatically, suggesting a future deepening of the housing crisis. A study exploring the range of affordable housing for families in five income quintiles presents a good snapshot of the affordability gap at the moment (Ravicz, 1992). It concludes that the current mortgage arrangements, income levels, and house prices make housing unaffordable to practically all households.

The income data refer to the income of a family with two wage earners and two children. House price data refer to house price variations within the range from 4,200 to 12,000 leva per square meter for new units and from 2,500 to 10,000 leva for existing dwellings. In the smaller cities, the price range is reported to be between 1,500 and 5,000 leva. Even at the lowest possible prices only households in the highest income quintile can afford to buy 54 square meters. For the first time, the Bulgarian dream of becoming a home owner is questioned by large sections of society as the previous housing shortage has been replaced by a shortage of affordable housing. Under such circumstances, social pressures to compensate various groups still in line for housing under the old system are understandable.

Typical housing prospects for the enormous number of homeless households would be either to share housing with parents or in-laws—the so-called "hidden homelessness"—or to rent privately, spending a huge proportion of income on housing costs and utilities. Obviously housing conditions will worsen in qualitative and quantitative terms. The increasing costs of deferred maintenance and repair of the existing stock, especially in multifamily housing, will present a major problem. Housing output is most likely to continue to decline, due to the lack of effective demand. Escalating prices and declining incomes will increase the social pressure on local authorities who retain the statutory responsibility to house people on a low income and those who are socially disadvantaged.

CONCLUSION

The political instability and the magnitude of the economic problems have pushed housing aside from the top of the political agenda. Privatization was not carried out as a comprehensive reform, but as a sequence of various measures and policies, leading to *ad hoc* and often conflicting solutions.

It has been argued here that, due to economic difficulties and fiscal constraints, state financial commitment and involvement in housing provision had decreased before the political changes in 1989. The socialist state still retained control over crucial aspects of housing provision, such as the distribution of housing, housing production, and finance. At the same time, it had deliberately expanded private sector activity in the provision of new housing by cooperatives and individuals and in the maintenance and management of housing. It had also encouraged home ownership within the context of public ownership of production and the central regulation of prices.

Privatization measures in housing responded to macroeconomic changes in society. They favorably affected the structures and forms of housing provision, leading to more diversity and consumer choice. The emergence of a housing market was a major factor in the process of adjustment by housing suppliers and consumers. The move to a market-oriented system presented new problems and challenges (Hegedüs and Tosics, 1992). The drastic elimination of production and consumption subsidies, the deregulation of prices, and the high levels of inflation led to the escalation of house prices.

Although the systematic bias against the private sector was abolished, there was very little competition on the supply side. Public enterprises and institutions held a monopolistic position in housing production and finance. This contributed to further price distortions. Despite several adjustments, the privatization of the state construction industry still did not gain momentum. Housing output decreased dramatically.

While the socialist system was associated with images of housing shortages, long waiting lists, price rigidities, bureaucracy, and planning, the new notions of decentralization, of individual freedom in the decision-making process, of democracy and competition, raised great expectations among consumers. In the free market, however, these rights are associated with the ability to pay for housing services. The scale of the present affordability problem has led to questions about the social efficiency of the privatization measures. The apparent failure of the privatization policy to address the whole complexity of interrelated problems has been demonstrated clearly by the evidence on decreasing output and the growing affordability gap, homelessness, deprivation, and deterioration of the owner-occupied stock.

Privatization in the housing sector included the massive sale of public rented housing to sitting tenants at prices below market value. Apart from being a political issue, this privatization measure had both an economic and a social dimension. In economic terms, the form and cost of privatization as measured in terms of an off-budget subsidy were shown to be inconsistent with broader reform objectives. It was argued that, in social terms, it has deepened social inequalities. On the whole privatization has favored the "haves" and deprived the "have-nots." The "haves" benefited from the increasingly socialized housing costs under the previous system, and later increased their profits in a market-oriented sector. The operation of the market legalized and deepened housing inequalities. It turned home owners into mini-property speculators desperately trying to determine the value of their assets and realize their capital gains. At the same time, the homeless have no prospects for alternative provision of shelter in the existing totally unsubsidized and unregulated housing market.

REFERENCES

Architecture and Art Exchange. 1992. Information on "free-market" land and house prices (21 April).

Carter, F. 1990. Housing policy in Bulgaria. In J. Sillince (ed.), *Housing Policies in Eastern Europe and the Soviet Union.* London: Routledge.

Central Statistical Office. 1965. *Census of Population and Housing.* Sofia: Central Statistical Office.

Central Statistical Office. 1975. *Census of Population and Housing.* Sofia: Central Statistical Office.

Central Statistical Office. 1985. *Census of Population and Housing.* Sofia: Central Statistical Office.

Central Statistical Office. 1989. *Statistical Yearbook.* Sofia: Central Statistical Office.

Central Statistical Office. 1992. *Census of Population and Housing.* Sofia: Central Statistical Office.

Central Statistical Office. 1993. *Census of Population and Housing.* Sofia: Central Statistical Office.

Dimitrov, D. 1992. *Monitoring of the Housing Sector: Current Data on Housing.* Sofia: National Center of Urban and Regional Development.

Dimitrov, D. 1993. *Monitoring of the Housing Sector: Current Data on Housing.* Sofia: National Center of Urban and Regional Development.

Grigorov, G., et al. 1987. *Human Settlement Situation: Trends and Policies in Bulgaria.* Sofia: National Monograph, Committee for Regional and Urban Planning, Council of Ministers.

Hegedüs, J., and Tosics, I. 1992. Conclusion: Past tendencies and recent problems of the East European housing model. In B. Turner, J. Hegedüs, and I. Tosics (eds.), *The Reform of Housing in Eastern Europe and the Soviet Union*. London: Routledge.

Hoffman, M., Koleva, M., Ravicz, M., and Mikelsons, M. 1992. The Bulgarian housing sector. An assessment. *Bulgaria Paper No. 1C*. Washington, DC: The Urban Institute.

Konaktchiev, D. 1990. The housing problem in the transitional period. *Architectura* 5–6, 25–26.

Krastev, L. 1992. Present constraints from past policies. *Architecture and Art Exchange* (6 June).

Ravicz, M. 1992. *Alternative Mortgage Instruments for Bulgaria. A Compilation of Eight Studies*. Washington, DC: The Urban Institute.

Renaud, B. 1991. *Housing Reform in Socialist Economies*. Discussion Paper 125. Washington, DC: The World Bank.

Tsenkova, S. 1991a. Maintenance policy in a context of socio-economic transition. Paper presented at the International Workshop on Building Maintenance Strategies, HABITAT, May 1991, St Kirki, Bulgaria.

Tsenkova, S. 1991b. *Bulgarian Housing Policy Reform*. MA Dissertation, University of Sussex.

United Nations. 1985. *Compendium of Human Settlements Statistics*. Geneva: United Nations.

World Bank. 1990. *Bulgaria Housing Memoir, World Bank Environment and Infrastructure Mission, 25 June–6 July*. Mimeo.

World Bank/CECSE. 1992. Bulgarian market reform: Beating the odds. *Transition* 6, 5–6.

7

Poland

Edward Kozlowski

INTRODUCTION

When postcommunist countries started the transformation process of their political, economic, and social systems from the centralized toward the market-oriented formation, it seemed to be possible to formulate a basic, general model, which held for all these countries. Later, the transition process took a different form as each country has taken its own direction. As the years passed, it has been recognized that the transformation not only differs from country to country, but also depends on the political forces and groups that hold power. This process can be very well observed in Poland, and housing is one of the best examples.

The transformation of the housing sector can be described in terms of its constituent parts—that is, the finance system, the savings system, the taxation system, rent policy, the privatization principles, and the social aid and allowance system.

In the transition process, it is necessary to define the strategic points and steps, the main goals and the rules for each of these parts. The next step is to change the legislation and then to establish or transform the new institutions. But, first of all, housing policy assumptions should be related to financial possibilities. Even the best and most complex program for the housing sector is worth nothing if no simulations of its financial consequences are made.

This chapter describes the housing situation at the end of the 1980s, the government housing programs, and the dilemmas of housing privatization in the early 1990s, and it provides some conclusions.

HOUSING BEFORE AND AFTER THE CHANGES
IN THE POLITICAL SYSTEM

The situation in the housing sector is very complex. The model of housing policy in Poland, as in other postcommunist countries, was the result of the whole socioeconomic system with its strong social pressures and biases. It resulted from several basic decisions taken after 1945: (1) housing policy was subordinated to general economic policy and very strongly to employment policy. Housing decisions were taken by the centralized administrative authority. (2) Under the policy of satisfying housing needs, market principles were almost totally eliminated. Housing was considered to be a social right, and houses were part of public property. Outlays for housing construction were planned and decided centrally and did not depend on demand. Rents were also centrally fixed at a very low level. (3) Private ownership of multifamily residential buildings and private construction of dwellings for rent were treated as inappropriate within the system. State authorities had the right to allocate private apartments. Private construction companies were replaced by very large state-owned construction *kombinats* and design offices. (4) A central cooperative investment organization was established.

During the entire postwar period, a steady improvement in housing standards took place, although at different rates across Poland. Table 7.1 provides some details on the overall standard of housing in Poland in 1988.

At the end of the 1980s, the tenure structure of the housing stock was diverse in Poland. Table 7.2 shows that more than a quarter of urban housing was owned and managed by the municipal authorities; about half of these units were built before 1945, another 39 percent between 1945 and 1970, and only 11 percent during the past two decades. It means that this stock was in very poor physical condition, with many deteriorating buildings. The amortization of the stock was estimated at 80 percent. Of existing stock, 12 percent was built and administered by state enterprises. This large group owns and rents out about 700,000 tenements in towns and about 500,000 dwellings in rural areas. About 43 percent of these units were built during the past 20 years, and all this stock was modernized more frequently than was communal housing. As a result, these units are gener-

Table 7.1. Selected Indicators of the Housing Situation in Poland, 1988

	Urban	*Rural*	*Total*
Number of persons per room	0.96	1.10	1.01
Usable area per person	16.8	17.6	17.1
Number of households per dwelling	1.14	1.20	1.16
Dwelling equipped with bathroom (%)	78.9	43.0	68.9

Source: Data from 1988 National Population Census.

Table 7.2. Occupied Dwellings by Sector, Poland, 1988

	Urban	Rural	Total
Private	23.7%	81.8%	41.7%
Cooperative	36.7%	0.5%	24.3%
State/municipal	27.8%	3.4%	19.3%
Enterprise	11.8%	14.3%	12.1%
Total no. (thousand units)	7,039.8	3,676.9	10,716.8
	(100%)	(100%)	(100%)

Source: Data from 1988 National Population Census.

ally of better quality. Cooperative stock is the newest form of housing and accounted for about one-quarter of all stock in 1988. It is well equipped, and generally built in multistory apartment blocks.

At the end of 1992, the housing stock in Poland consisted of about 11.3 million dwellings, which included 7.5 million in towns and 3.8 million in rural areas. In towns, the significant majority of the housing stock—more than 80 percent of dwellings—was in apartment buildings. In rural areas, on the other hand, most dwellings—that is, about 90 percent—were single-family houses.

By the end of 1992, out of a total number of 11.3 million dwellings, about 4.9 million were private single-family dwellings, 2.9 million belonged to housing cooperatives, and 3.4 million were apartments in rented housing. The largest stock of rented apartments was in buildings owned by municipal authorities. In these buildings, there were about 1.8 million rental units and about 200,000 units bought by the municipal tenants. Private individuals owned about 300,000 of the dwellings available for rent; however, they did not have the right to dispose freely of these properties.

The most important feature of Polish housing is the shortage of dwellings, which has remained high for many years. According to the data from the 1988 National Census, the number of households and inhabited apartments showed a statistical deficit in the number of available dwellings (Table 7.3), equal to the deficit of 20 years earlier. On the basis of demographic projection, it is estimated that by 2020 the population increase and the housing shortage will lead to a deficit of between 4.3 and 4.9 million units, of which about 80 to 85 percent will be in the cities. Most of the projected housing needs will occur in urban areas, where they will be most difficult to satisfy, since the concentration of these needs will vary geographically: 9 of the 49 administration areas with the biggest urban complexes comprise 53 percent of the urban housing need.

As well as the housing needs arising from the demographic changes, there will be needs arising from the conditions and amenities of the housing stock. As a result of inadequate renovation and modernization, and the lack of appropriate

Table 7.3. Number of Households and Number of Available Dwellings, 1988 (thousands)

	Total	Urban	Rural
Households	11,970	7,864	4,106
Inhabited dwellings	10,717	70,404	3,677
"Statistical deficit of dwellings"	1,253	824	429

Source: Data from 1988 National Population Census.

maintenance for many years because of insufficient resources, the estimated requirement for stock renewal is much higher than the actual deficit in the housing stock. This means that much obsolete housing remains in use. However, the extent of the problem will vary in intensity in different areas of Poland.

Of course, in the period up to 2020, major changes are likely to occur in the relationship between housing needs and quality standards. This means that there will be different expectations in respect of the size of dwellings and the use of space as well as in the provision of utilities, installations, furniture, and other household equipment.

The shortfall in housing is related directly to the capabilities of the housing construction industry, and in particular to the rise in the expected standard of housing. There has been a huge breakdown in the organization of the construction industry since the 1970s. The number of building enterprises fell from 1,652 in 1985 to 1,145 in 1991, while the average number of employees in each company fell from 5,602 in 1978 to only 176 in 1991. The output fell from the level of about 280,000 dwellings in the peak year of 1978, down to 88,000 in 1993. In the 1970s, average annual completion rates of new housing amounted to 6.2 dwellings per 1,000 population. By the 1980s, this had fallen to 5.0 per 1,000, and by 1993 to fewer than 2.3 per 1,000. Tables 7.4, 7.5, and 7.6 show a very

Table 7.4. Number of New Dwellings Completed in 1992 and 1993, by Type of Investor (thousands)

Type of Investor	1992	1993	1993 as a % of 1992
Communal/enterprises	11.8	8.3	70.7
Housing cooperatives	84.3	45.8	54.3
Private	36.9	33.9	92.0
Total	133.0	88.0	66.2

Source: CSO (1994).

Table 7.5.   Total Usable Floor Area of New Dwellings Completed in 1992 and 1993 by Type of Investor (in thousands of square meters)

Type of Investor	1992	1993	1993 as a % of 1992
Communal/enterprises	700	480	68.6
Housing cooperatives	5,137	2,782	54.2
Private	4,130	3,983	96.4
Total	9,967	7,245	72.7

Source: CSO (1994).

rapid decline in recent output and the virtual withdrawal of the state authorities from house building. The crisis in housing construction is very deep.

The general economic breakdown during the 1980s multiplied difficulties in the system required to satisfy housing need. Low standards and high depreciation characterized particularly those buildings constructed in the interwar period, and especially those in the private rented sector.

Since 1990, the transformation of Polish housing into a market system has been regarded as a necessary component for the market reform of the whole Polish economy, and it has also been used as an instrument for the rationalization of the housing sector. A number of actions were taken to shape a new system capable of meeting housing needs. The dominant characteristic of the transformation was the change in the role of money from a passive to an active element; this brings into focus the housing finance system, including the credit system.

Previously the housing finance system had a passive role. Planning was limited to considerations of the physical stock. The financial system was characterized by high direct subsidies, indirect subsidies through low prices, and the transfer of income through the credit system by means of negative rent interest on savings for housing credits.

As a consequence, the financial burden on those households that did obtain housing was low; rent levels accounted for between 1.5 to 2.5 percent of house-

Table 7.6.   Changes in the Profile of Investors in Housing Construction by Sector in 1952, 1978, and 1993

Sector of Investment	1952	1978	1993
State/communal/enterprises	70.6%	18.4%	9.4%
Cooperative	—	55.4%	52.1%
Individual	29.4%	26.2%	38.5%

Source: CSO (1954, 1979, 1994).

hold expenditure in 1978, compared to 4 percent in 1993. This system generated inflation and shortages, which led to a long waiting list for housing. The reform of the credit system, which started with the introduction of the Law on Regulation of Credit Relationships in December 1989, introduced positive interest on deposits. This was an indispensable condition for encouraging savings, but for those who made savings, their ability to pay more for housing was reduced.

Another problem arose from the high nominal interest on loans, which drastically reduced the term of repayment. As a consequence, the burden on household budgets grew significantly. The proposed system of capitalization and annulment of most of the interest (60 percent capitalization, 32 percent subsidized, 8 percent actually paid by the borrower), while not guaranteeing stabilization of this burden under high inflation conditions, caused serious problems for the banks' liquidity, and the burden on the state budget grew arithmetically as new generations of credits were created (Table 7.7).

Table 7.7.   Changes in Terms of Construction Credits in Poland, 1983–90

Terms of Credit	1983–87	1988	1989	1990
Prepayment (% of construction costs)				
tenancy type	10	10	10 ⎫	
ownership type	20	20	20 ⎭	30
Construction Credit (% of construction costs)				
tenancy type	90	50	60 ⎫	
ownership type	80	80	80 ⎭	70
Subsidy (% of credit)				
tenancy type	50	40	30 ⎫	
ownership type[b]	20	30	30 ⎭	(a)
Period of Repayment				
tenancy type	60 ⎫	40	up to 40	up to 40
ownership type	50 ⎭			
Interest Rate (%)				
tenancy type	1	1	3 ⎫	
ownership type	1	1	6 ⎭	115

[a] 60 per cent: capitalized, to be repaid by the borrower later, even if the central budget will buy this capitalized part of interest rate from the bank; 32 per cent: subsidy paid from the central budget; 8 per cent: to be paid by the borrower currently.

[b] Only if the construction credit was repaid by the owner, before the dwelling was inhabited.

The solution for this problem was a system based on capitalization of the nominal interest, with liquidity support from the budget (interim purchase of interest). This system linked loan repayments to the average salary, guaranteeing greater stability for the household budgets. However, since the loans were contracted by cooperatives proportionally to the size of apartments, they usually had to be paid off in a lump sum. Under the then existing conditions (the relationship of dwelling cost to income, real interest rate, prospects for income changes), these credits would pay off if the average household designated 25 percent of its income for the loan repayment. This law was issued in spring 1991 and regulated the repayment of loans that had been converted into mortgages by the end of 1990.

The system requires liquidity support from the state budget in the first years of its implementation and provides guarantees for borrowers and banks in the event of rapid change of economic parameters, because the credit repayment is not related to changes in the capital market but to wage changes.

A consequence of raising the economic parameters to real levels in 1991 was a further growth of prices in residential construction and further increase in the real interest rate. This resulted in a fast-growing share of subsidies (loan annulment) for housing construction from the state budget.

A more serious problem was caused by the increasing number of defaulting loans that had been contracted according to social need, based on dwelling size and not on market criteria such as household income and repayment capability. This was a major threat, both for the people's savings and the state budget. If the old credit terms and contracts were continued, people would lose 70 percent of their savings, or the state budget deficit would grow by another 15 percent, causing hyperinflation. Under these circumstances, the only solution was to convert old loan contracts into mortgage loans under the law of January 1992, which amended the Budget Act and other laws. At the same time, a new system of housing loans, based on a dual index mortgage, was prepared. This system allowed for the protection of deposits by adopting a positive interest rate, and also the protection of the borrower, since the rate of repayment is set at 25 percent of the borrower's income and is indexed periodically, based on the average wage index, thus separating it from the fluctuating inflation rate.

The creation of an overall, market-oriented system of finance for house construction requires a number of further actions to reform both the credit system and the overall financial system. Work toward the solution of the remaining problems is still in progress.

The association of household income with the cost of housing is inappropriate and is the cause of the greatest problem. Since possibilities for subsidy are limited, the solution lies in the development of more efficient construction technologies and more rational designs and construction processes. On the one hand, the potential of the construction industry is very great, since the production base consists of *kombinats* producing concrete panels, although this type of construction is about 30 to 40 percent more expensive than alternative technologies. On the other hand, the discontinuation of indirect subsidies to the price of construction materials has brought about an increase in construction costs.

Additional costs have arisen because of the rise in the price of land, which had previously been transferred for a symbolic payment, and the rise in infrastructure costs, which under the old system had been financed from the state budget. These factors, together with the rise in real interest rates, have compounded the problems.

HOUSING PRIVATIZATION PROGRAMS

There are over 150 registered political parties in Poland. Those currently active can be divided into three groups, based on their standpoint on housing issues: the first group supports the need for state intervention in the housing sector; the second group opposes state intervention; the third group has no views on this matter.

A majority of the political groups see the need for state intervention to solve the housing problems. The Democratic Union stresses this the most. It foresees the possibility of a breakthrough within three years, if their policy is adopted. It advocates securing land available for construction, supporting for communal social and rental construction, low interest rates on housing loans, and the annulment of housing debts. It also proposes priorities to be given to housing production, the partial valorization of old housing savings, and a development of a system of rent subsidies and tenant protection. Similar proposals have been put forward in the programs of the Citizens' Association Centrum, the Alliance for the Democratic Left, the Homeless Association, Trade Unions for the Protection of Society, the Christian–National Union, and the Christian Democracy and Labor Solidarity Party.

On the other hand, the Union of Real Policy is against any government intervention in housing policy; it supports privatization and stresses the freedom of owners of private residential buildings and the development of individual housing construction. The Conservative–Liberal Party has a similar policy: "Everybody has the apartment that he or she deserves" is a common slogan.

Groups such as the Liberal–Democratic Congress ("a poor society cannot afford construction") and the Confederacy of Sovereign Poland ("any working person should have such income that would allow him/her to buy an apartment on the market") do not have a detailed view on these matters (Jarzabek, 1991).

Decisions on the transformation of parts of the housing sector are made after much resistance and lengthy discussions. These discussions have focused on a number of issues, such as finance and the credit system; a whole set of issues regarding the availability of land for residential construction; the development of rental systems for communal and company housing stock; a system of payments for community services; and all the issues relating to changes of ownership.

The government and parliament, as well as individual owners and users of housing stock at the local level, have tried to move ahead of existing legal regulations and change the status quo. These attempts do not tackle all the problems; however, some tenants have purchased their apartments, as Table 7.8 shows.

An example of indecisiveness at the parliamentary level is the discussion of new versions of the housing law, which has dragged on for years. In 1993, the government published *Basic Principles in Housing Policy*, also known as the New Housing Program, on the directions and strategies for the solution of these housing issues. Part of this program addresses the problems of restoring order to the confused ownership rights and obligations.

It is a legacy of the past to treat the ownership of housing as a means of satisfying solely the needs of the owner and his or her relatives. The introduction of market economy principles into housing requires change. The ownership of housing is an obligation, and therefore it is permanently and inseparably tied to the obligation of management and maintenance of the property, either directly or through participation in joint ownership of the whole property.

The program for restoring order in ownership relations in housing aims to establish an owner for each separate apartment or housing unit, and to define

Table 7.8. Proportion of Housing Stock by Sector, Showing Proportion Purchased by Tenants

	1988 (%)			1993 (%)		
Sector	Rented	Owned	Total	Rented	Owned	Total
Central government (before 1990)	34.5	0	34.5	0	0	0
Municipal authority (after 1990)	0	0	0	15.0	1.8	16.8
Enterprise	6.6	0	6.6	11.5	0	11.5
Cooperative	26.4	0	26.4	13.3	11.5	24.8
Total proportion in public sector			67.6			53.1
Single-family dwelling	0	26.4	26.4	0	43.4	43.4
Rental apartment	6.0	0	6.0	2.6	0	2.6
Total proportion in public sector			32.4			46.0

Note: A Law of March 1990 transferred the ownership of state housing to local authorities.
Source: Data from 1988 National Population Census; CSO (1994).

precisely the rights and obligations of each owner. It is most important that the ownership of housing is inseparably tied to the duty of managing and maintaining the property.

The current laws are not sufficient for the regulation of rights and duties of owners. A new act on home ownership will fully restore rules for the individual ownership of apartments and also provide for joint ownership of real estate, including common parts of buildings and common land. This law will correct more recent solutions, which gave the joint owners the right to perpetual usufruct, but only of the land on which the building stood. This led to conflicts as to how to separate the communal land—for example, the sidewalks and streets—from the land necessary for access to the whole building.

Under the proposed legislation on housing ownership, owners of separate housing units would constitute a housing community, sometimes within a condominium, that would be responsible for the management and maintenance of the whole property. It has not been decided whether the management will be undertaken by individuals on behalf of the community, or whether the coowners will delegate this responsibility to a legal entity such as a housing cooperative or specialized company. The owner of a housing unit need not be the user of the unit but must participate in the management and in the full cost of maintenance of the property. The coverage of full maintenance cost of the property will be the responsibility of the owners and will thus be separated from the rent, which is paid by the tenant to the owner.

The establishment of the act on housing ownership will allow for choice in the transformation of the current cooperative sector. By law, the present ownership right to a cooperative unit will be transformed into this new form of housing ownership, based on general ownership rules. Owners of housing units within housing cooperatives will be able to participate in the management and maintenance of their condominium.

Social and economic conditions have led to legislation allowing the legal separation of the enterprise-owned housing stock from state-owned enterprises. An act has been proposed to permit local authorities to take over the ownership of enterprise-owned housing.

It is necessary to add that there is a lack of financial needs and consequences in the New Housing Program. Even the chapter, "Reforms of the System of Housing Finance," which describes ideas and proposals, omits any calculations of its effects on central, local, or household budgets.

The program was accepted by the government, but most of the parties whose representatives are in the parliament have not accepted it. Only the Democratic Union has offered the program full support. ⁄

PRIVATIZATION MODELS: THE DILEMMA

The concept of development in the centrally planned socialist economy was based on the domination of the state and on quasi-state ownership, and this led to the central allocation of housing. This was coupled with a centralized system of management based on the so-called socialized ownership, which in reality was state ownership, and the takeover of most private property. This enabled housing policy to be used as the strongest tool in employment policy and facilitated the implementation of social policy.

The current policy of transformation in East European countries, which was brought about by the failure of the planned economy, also forced the transformation of the housing sector. This has caused a number of problems, of both an economic and a social nature, because the socialist economy was constructed as the opposite of market-based system. Some of these problems relate to the issue of privatization.

Privatization is understood as the sale or takeover of public property into private ownership, usually in exchange for payment or certain services. Privatization is a necessary precondition for the introduction of an effective market system in housing. The reform of the system should meet several objectives. (1) It should limit the scope of subsidies to housing, at the same time increasing investment and the effectiveness of the maintenance of existing stock. (2) It should provide the opportunity for greater spatial and vertical mobility in society through the establishment of a housing market, which, in turn, will improve the effectiveness of the use of existing stock. (3) These reforms should guarantee a better allocation of capital for housing, which would support regional development. (4) Privatization should motivate employees to aim toward a model of housing consumption; this would support economic development and lead to the easing of social tensions.

Privatization may relate to real estate or the rights and laws pertaining to property. Privatization processes relating to real estate may include the sale of individual housing units, the sale of individual commercial units such as shops or offices, the sale of whole buildings, or the sale of land together with residential buildings. The privatization of rights pertaining to real estate is limited to the conveyance of the rights of ownership to private property which was previously nationalized by the public housing economy, and to the management of housing units and housing complexes. The privatization processes in real estate relate almost exclusively to the urbanized regions of Poland.

So far in the transitional economy, the model of limited privatization was used only to favor persons with connections, by selling nationalized housing units at a fraction of their market price. The current proposals of privatization, despite the widespread market rhetoric, have a clear political purpose. The main objective is to "buy" social calm through the donation of state housing units to their tenants. At the same time, the need for a rationalization of rental policy and the regulation of the legal status of occupants, especially in apartment buildings, has been overlooked.

The proposals prepared by the Ministry of Construction contained some new, positive elements. The draft law "On Regulation of Some of the Ownership Relations in the Housing Economy" focused on two groups of issues, as outlined earlier. These related to the transformation of the cooperative form of ownership as limited property rights into private ownership and those relating to the privatization of apartments in company-owned buildings. The direction of those reforms—that is, the privatization of part of the housing stock and the discontinuation of socialist cooperative property—raised no doubts about the move toward the creation of a market economy. However, certain detailed comments could be raised about the proposed solutions.

The government was right to oppose the solidification of the cooperative ownership system through the concept of the right of lien and limited property rights, proposing, instead, full private ownership and, consequently, the right to mortgage the property. However, the proposed law made no provision for any organization of homeowners, which would be capable of creating a system for the management of common areas. The draft legislation proposed that home owners would have to decide the form of management within six months from the sale of the last apartment. The experiences of market-economy countries show that large residential buildings are prone to deterioration if the owners avoid payment of the growing costs of maintenance of common areas—for example, the external fabric, stairwells, corridors, sanitation and utilities, and surroundings. This occurs in spite of a precise legal framework for common maintenance. The lack of such a legal framework in Poland would mean that the process of deterioration would be much faster. In the course of parliamentary discussions, it was stressed that the right solution would be the creation of an Association of Homeowners as a legal body, which would choose its own management and supervisory board for the condominium. This form of management should be introduced by the existing owner, whether it is a cooperative or an enterprise, in such a manner that power in the association is gradually transferred from the current owner to the homebuyers, as they purchase their apartments. Only when the last unit is sold may the new owners decide to introduce a different form of management to make the management structure effective and well-grounded.

Certain other reservations arose concerning the privatization of the housing stock. The most important was the definition of the price at which the apartments, cooperative or company-owned, were to be sold to their tenants. One proposal was that the price of cooperative apartments would be equal to the nominal rather than the real value of annulled credits. As a consequence, payments would be a fraction of the real value.

Under this proposal, the nominal value of cooperative apartments to be sold to cooperative members depends on the terms of credit that were given for the construction of this stock, especially the proportion of government subsidy and the interest rates used in different years. It also depends on whether the apartments were built for rent or ownership.

Privatization of the state-owned housing stock by selling to tenants has been possible for over 20 years. Now, every municipal authority has the right to establish the price of the apartments, and the prices vary widely between districts in the same municipality. Some prices are very low; for example, in some municipalities there are proposals to set the price for a whole apartment below the market price of one square meter of the apartment. However, the value of the "gift" will vary considerably from place to place, according to the market value of the property.

Very low selling prices would lead to the privatization of rented housing to low-income households, who would not be able to afford the maintenance, and, due to the high standard of these apartments, they would not be eligible for social assistance. This could well speed up the process of deterioration in the housing stock and also put much pressure on state and local budgets. Moreover the gift of this property to particular persons would vary considerably in value, due to the operation of the housing market.

Similar comments could be made about the concept of privatization of company-owned housing. This stock is relatively new and in quite good physical condition, as there has been sizeable investment in maintenance during the last 10 years. As research has shown, the tenant structure is bimodal (Kozlowski, 1990; Kozinska et al., 1992). On the one hand, some tenants are upper-level managers, whose allocation of housing has been based on their occupation and their usefulness to the company. On the other hand, some tenants are in a very difficult financial situation, as they have been allocated the housing on the basis of their social need. For the group, privatization will transfer ownership to those who will not be able to afford maintenance of their housing, nor will it assist the state budget, either in the short or in the long run.

It seems that the main rule of privatization of housing stock should be to adhere strictly to market prices. Where it is difficult to define the prices and to limit abuse, upper and lower limits could be set, based on the costs of "replacement"—that is, the cost of constructing a new building of the same type. This price could be the starting point for discounts, inversely proportional to the value of the apartment, and based on their size and standard. The ultimate goal should be the privatization of whole buildings, not single units, together with proper protection of the mutual rights and duties of their owners. Discussions indicated that the real value of an apartment should constitute the basis for reconciliation with the state budget in the case of credit annulment for state buildings. The only point for negotiation concerns the preferences and manner of repayment. To protect the household budgets and the interests of the state budget, the repayment could be calculated either according to a dual-index system, with repayments linked to the price inflation rate and the index of minimum wage or retirement pension for retired families, or according to an income index alone, which would be a better solution for the homebuyers, given the high rate of price inflation.

It was suggested that in the case of company apartments, due to the rather uniform legal status of their tenants, it would be wiser to transfer them to local authorities. In future, they would be subdivided into two categories, of low and high value. The first type of apartment could be used for social renting purposes, with the costs of maintenance being generated from income from the high-value apartments. The argument about high subsidies for company stock would then lose part of its validity. The need to set rents based on real costs was suggested, together with targeted social assistance. As discussed above, these apartments are generally in good physical condition, so there is no fear that high subsidies will be required to meet the costs of major renovations for low-standard apartments, as has happened in state and private rental stock.

In general, differences of opinion on the housing situation are likely to lead to an individual approach to particular cases by the local authorities. Thus, the law should sketch a framework in the form of legal and economic limits and design a certain direction for these processes, without going into details, in order to permit local discretion.

The proposals, as well as the experience gained from other countries, raise some general questions about the widespread and accelerated privatization of existing stock. Simple answers to these seem hardly possible. Will such a broadly understood privatization really create a housing market, or will it stabilize the existing structures, increasing the political pressure for larger subsidies, when poor people become owners? For apartments located in multifamily buildings, will it not mean a slow depreciation of the stock as it deteriorates, leading to a crisis in the market price? What will be the consequences for the financial and banking systems and for the state budget? How will it influence housing construction, general consumption, and demand? How will these consequences spread out in time? What will be the spatial and social benefits as a result of privatization?

So far no estimates of the scope and consequences of the proposed changes have been attempted. Only preliminary research of potential beneficiaries has been conducted (Zaleska, 1992). The results confirm that older people and those in lower-income groups fear these changes.

CONCLUSION

Basic economic change was introduced in Poland in 1989. The central planning system is now being replaced by a market economy with self-regulating mechanisms. Profit and efficiency have replaced the former means of evaluating organizational effectiveness, which was the planning target. Ownership transformations have commenced at the local level, when the ownership of state property was transferred to local authorities.

The banking system has improved considerably since 1989. Almost 100 private banks have been opened, although the public PKO (Common Savings Bank) still controls about 90 percent of the mortgage loan market.

A crucial factor in the transformation process is the creation of an effective capital market—first of all a primary market but also a secondary one. Warsaw Stock Exchange has been opened, and now it has the largest turnover of all the postcommunist countries.

At the same time, substantial changes have taken place in the administration and power structures. A president's office was instituted. A parliament with two houses was established. Central administration is being reorganized. A motion was submitted for the reinstatement of 294 *poviats*—the former administrative authorities, the middle administration level between a *gmina* and a *voivodship*.

Major changes have been implemented in the housing finance system. In November 1990, the Polish Council of Ministries created the Government of Poland and the World Bank Housing Finance project, which has been preparing the credit system based on the World Bank Loan and using the instrument of a dual index mortgage. The system of payments and rents is being reformed. Property tax has been established, and the personal tax system has been reformed by the introduction of a general, progressive income tax. At the same time, tax allowances were introduced for those who invest in housing.

In the rented sector, the level of rents is centrally set up for municipal and enterprise apartments. These rents cover about 30 percent of the maintenance costs. However, every housing cooperative has the right to set its own rents, and these rents should cover the full cost of maintenance. In 1993, the Ministry of Spatial Economy and Construction prepared proposals for decentralizing the rent system, which would give local authorities the right to set the rent level.

The existing land registry is facing two problems: (1) there are cases where the legal status of ownership is not clearly defined, and (2) the registers contain only 15 percent of immovable property and are therefore incomplete. All these changes are accompanied by transformations of legal regulations from the Constitution of Condominium Law.

A characteristic of the present political situation is the profusion of different parties, groups, orientations, and coalitions. Trade unions have been fully democratized. All this change is accompanied by constant shifts in government administration.

In May 1993, the Polish president announced the dissolution of the parliament. Four months later, there was a new election, and a new government was chosen, based on a coalition of former socialist parties (the Alliance for the Democratic Left and Peasant Party). This meant the termination of that round of transformations, and the start of a new cycle.

The transformation of Poland is an ongoing process; however, in the housing sector some considerable progress has been made, and privatization is in progress, despite many legal, administrative, and political obstacles. Already, the proportion of private dwellings is 57 percent—close to the situation in some West European countries.

REFERENCES

Basic Principles in Housing Policy: Government Proposal for the Parliament of the Republic of Poland (The New Housing Program). Warsaw, 1993.

CSO. 1954. *Statistical Yearbook.* Warsaw: CSO.

CSO. 1979. *Statistical Yearbook.* Warsaw: CSO.

CSO. 1994. *Statistical Bulletin V. XXXVIII.* Warsaw: CSO,

Jarzabek, Z. 1991. *Program Mieszkaniowy w Programach Partii i Stronnictw Politycznych Uczestniczacych w Wyborach Parlamentarnych* [Housing policies in the programs of political parties and associations]. Warsaw: IGM.

Kornilowicz, J. 1993. "The housing rental policy in Poland." Workshop on Management and Effective Use of Existing Housing Stock. Warsaw: HIR.

Kozinska, D., Kowlowski, E., and Kulesza, H. 1992. *Gospodarstwa Domowe i Rodziny Wedlug Tytulu Zajmowania Mieszkania* [Households and families by title of occupancy]. Warsaw: IGM.

Kozlowski, E. 1990. *Zroznicowania Spoleczne Sytuacji Mieszkaniowej w Polsce* [Social differences in the housing situation in Poland]. Warsaw: IBPiK.

Local Self-Government Act. 1990. *Journal of Laws* No. 21, pos. 123 (with later changes).

Zaleska, E. 1992. *Preferencje Spoleczne w Zakresie Przeksztalcen Wlasnosci i Zarzadu Czynszowych Zasobow Mieszkaniowych* [Social preferences in ownership transformation of rental housing stock]. Warsaw: IGM.

8

Czechoslovakia

Peter Michalovic

INTRODUCTION

Toward the end of 1989, Czechoslovakia, like many other countries of the former "Eastern Bloc," set a course for political and economic reforms. The basic goals of the reforms were to introduce democracy and to provide a means to return to political pluralism and a market economy. A return to a well-proven model of an effective administration was seen as the way out of a deformed and disturbing reality.

This is an appropriate time to review and evaluate the first results of these changes, as it is almost three years since they were implemented. Moreover, completely new elements of social development are appearing now. The separation of Czechoslovakia into two republics and the search for new forms of cohabitation within one economic space will certainly influence social policy, including housing policy, in the future. Further developments will follow from the many positive phenomena that have emerged in the recent past. However, the act of separation into the two states will bring heavy financial burdens, with consequences for both sides.

The changes in the political structure and the national economy have prepared the way for the introduction of market relations and regulation. During the first stage, the preexisting production sector was profoundly restructured. In Slovakia, for example, the number of state-owned companies in the construction industry skyrocketed in a relatively short time from less than 50 to more than 400. Moreover, hundreds of small private construction firms emerged, many of which have grown successfully.

Another way of adjusting the economy to regulation by market forces is through privatization, which, in the Czechoslovak Federal Republic (CSFR), has taken three forms—the restitution of property, small-scale privatization, and large-scale privatization.

The process of restitution is regulated by two laws. First, the Law on Certain Property Injustice Mitigation was passed and remained in force for six months from November 1990 until the end of April 1991. It had particular relevance for housing, as it remedied some of the problems arising from the nationalization decrees that had been introduced after February 1948, which had led to the removal of ownership rights over movable and immovable assets.

Second, the Law on the Modification of Land and Other Agricultural Property Ownership Relations, which was passed in 1991, related to agricultural land, farms, and dwellings on their original site. Claims could be made under this legislation until the end of 1992. Restitution is made by returning the asset to the original legal owner, by making a financial reimbursement, by returning the selling price of the property, or by making a payment to cover the difference between a financial reimbursement and the selling price.

The small- and large-scale privatization schemes relate to property in state ownership. They differ in form and character, depending on their scale. The small-scale privatization that was implemented from the beginning of 1991 until June 1992 was achieved through the sale or lease of property, directly or by auction.

Large-scale privatization was achieved mainly by the so-called "coupon technique." This coupon privatization, which was offered in two waves, enabled citizens to obtain free shares in companies of their choice. This offer was open to all citizens who were over 18 years of age, permanently domiciled in CSFR territory, and legally entitled to take up the offer.

The positive developments achieved so far include a rapidly expanding private sector, a quite favorable balance of trade, and, most importantly, the development of financial systems. Despite pessimistic forecasts, which were based on developments in Hungary and Poland, the rate of inflation has been kept low. Although inflation rose steeply to 30 percent following price liberalization in November 1991, the situation stabilized, settling at an annual rate of less than 10 percent; indeed, the monthly inflation rate was down to less than 1 percent in the latter half of 1992.

On the other hand, the developments of the past three years have also resulted in a great many problems and negative effects. The new situation has placed an emphasis on individual responsibility and on the need to change conventional patterns of behavior. It requires people to reorientate themselves and adjust to the new conditions. New social phenomena have emerged—unemployment, the rise in the crime rate, the development of social differentiation, which conflicts with ideas about social equity and growing manifestations of anomie. Other problems arising from the cohabitation of several nationalities within one state have been neglected.

Naturally, this chapter is not intended to evaluate the overall development of Czechoslovak society; rather, it intends only to point to the interrelationships between the political and economic changes on the one hand and those in the housing sector on the other. Housing obviously could not remain untouched by the on-going reforms: in future, housing will be regulated by market principles.

The principles of housing policy reform were laid out in government decrees in June 1991. This legislation defined the main goals of the reform and set out the first steps toward its implementation. The individual issues connected with these reforms are discussed in the second section of this chapter.

It is interesting to note how the elements of housing policy have changed in importance over time. Housing issues were disregarded in the run-up to the first free elections to the federal and national Czech and Slovak parliaments in June 1990. The election programs focused mainly on guarantees of political freedom and individual rights, as well as measures for the establishment of a market mechanism within the economy. Later, in the 1992 election campaign, housing issues had a more important place, as was evidenced by the activities of the government, parliament, and the political parties.

Of course, the opinions and ideas on individual issues were very much differentiated according to the orientation of each political body. Sometimes the opinions occupied clearly opposing views. For example, there were two contrary opinions on the issue of whether local community dwellings should be sold to their users. One proposal was to sell apartments to the maximum number of interested occupants, even at a minimal price. A proposal from the federal government in 1993 spoke of a contractual price that should not be higher than three times the annual rent in 1990, which would be generally about one-fifteenth of the market price, or one-twentieth in metropolitan areas. At the opposite extreme there was a proposal not to sell the dwellings at all (*Narodna Obroda*, 1992).

It is important to have a discussion of these housing issues because it influences the position given to housing on the agenda for government programs. All efforts have to be concentrated on finding solutions to the accumulated problems. They must be resolved at a new level of quality, preferably by a systematic approach that takes into consideration the interrelationships between housing and planning, housing administration and maintenance, social affairs, and ecology.

HOUSING BEFORE THE CHANGE
IN THE POLITICAL SYSTEM

The development of housing in Czechoslovakia has passed through several stages since 1945 (Michalovic, 1989). Most of Czechoslovakian housing stock in the cities was nationalized after 1948, when it came under the administration of the municipal councils, which allocated housing in the public sector. A right of ownership was changed to the right to personal use. This affected mainly the one-family houses in country areas, but also city dwellings to some extent. The form of ownership for the total housing stock was narrowed to two sectors: state-owned apartments and one-family houses for personal use.

Until the late 1950s, new construction continued in both sectors at an average annual completion rate of 55,000 dwellings. About two-thirds of the new buildings were state-owned dwellings, built according to plan by state-owned, nationalized construction companies. The other third was built individually, for personal occupation, almost exclusively in country areas.

As a result of the easing in the political climate in the late 1950s, the structure of the housing sector changed, and two new types of housing tenure emerged: a cooperative sector and a sector of dwellings owned by state-owned enterprises. Both of these types of housing had traditions rooted in the period before 1948.

The cooperative housing movement, which was renewed in 1959, developed fast. Initially, people with a common interest and a self-help orientation established small associations within different state institutions and enterprises. In 1965, cooperative dwellings accounted for the highest proportion (49%) of all newly built dwellings. This expansion was the result of favorable finance arrangements. About one-third of the costs were covered by the state as a non-returnable contribution, about one-fifth was paid by members as a membership fee, and the remainder was paid by the member in the form of an annuity. In the initial period, cooperative housing brought a higher quality of housing and a higher standard of living for occupants. Only in the 1970s, as the result of the political frost, did the movement have to comply with general bureaucratic regulations from the planning authorities and begin to be dependent on the mass production of the state construction industry. Some small cooperative housing associations continued to build dwellings to a high standard, providing, for example, detached one-family dwellings.

The development of housing by state enterprises continued up to the end of the 1980s. In essence, these dwellings were rented units, built by an enterprise for its own employees. If they were intended for the members of the "specialistic" oligarchy of the organization, the quality standard of the units was high. The fact that such dwellings were not personally owned was not a handicap. On the contrary, the user received an apartment without any down payment, at a low rent, and with strong tenant protection.

It is important to remember that a perception of "ownership" hardly existed. As an illustration, the same unofficial compensation money—that is, "key money"—was given for an apartment regardless of tenure, whether it was state-owned, enterprise-owned, or belonging to a cooperative unit. Not even a user of a cooperative apartment could sell the unit. It could only be transferred to another family member or an inheritor. In the case of a member who moved away, the apartment was returned to the cooperative association, and the membership fee was returned to the member. Of course, this solution did not provide any profit or gain to the user. For that reason, most of those who moved offered their apartment to a waiting applicant in return for some financial reward. This transfer had to be officially authorized by the cooperative board, but in practice this happened automatically. Another strategy was to keep the apartment and rent it out until the children grew up, even though people were not legally allowed to have more than one dwelling.

The development of the two sectors—the cooperative and the enterprise-owned—led to an expansion of building activities. The construction process was accelerated by the industrialization of the building industry, which began in the late 1950s and resulted in an annual increase in the proportion of new building produced by panel technology. Building activity reached a peak in 1975, when 144,678 dwelling units were produced in total. During the early 1980s, the yearly average building output fell to 91,000 dwelling units. The proportion of newly built dwellings produced by panel technology reached 90 percent of all the dwellings supplied by state-owned building companies, at a time when it had already been abandoned in other advanced countries. Hand in hand with this development, the construction companies grew in size to become huge, monopolistic, inflexible organizations.

These developments were the same in both parts of Czechoslovakia. The structure of housing tenure, however, shows some specific differences. In Slovakia, the proportion of dwellings in personal ownership—that is, one-family homes—is larger, due to the higher proportion of rural settlements there. In the Czech lands, there is a higher proportion of state-owned apartments as a result of the stronger urbanization and high-rise construction that has taken place mainly since 1948. The structure of CSFR housing tenure, showing each type of housing in the two republics immediately after the November revolution at the end of 1989, is given in Table 8.1.

The administration of this housing stock has developed in a similar way as the sectors themselves. Initially, "housing administration units" were established at the level of the local municipal authority to administer and maintain state-owned apartments. They gradually grew into independent state-owned "housing enterprises," whose location corresponded with the preexisting structures of the state administration—that is, each district operated one housing enterprise. However,

Table 8.1. Housing Stock in Czechoslovakia, 1989

Housing Sector	Czech Lands	Slovakia	Total
State-owned	27.4%	17.4%	24.1%
Cooperative	17.5%	20.1%	18.3%
Enterprise-owned	9.7%	6.8%	8.9%
User-owned	45.8%	55.7%	48.7%
Total no. of units	4,082,357	1,777,929	5,860,286

Source: FSU (1990).

their monopolistic position and heavy state subsidies contributed to overstaffing and to a low level of efficiency in these organizations.

Housing enterprises did not function as investors in their stock. The construction of housing stock was planned by the Central Planning Commission and financed from the state budget by the Ministry of Construction. The buildings were finally handed over for administration to the local housing enterprises.

Housing cooperatives performed their own administration and the maintenance of stock. The original character of the cooperatives, with their clear specifications on costs of individual buildings and their careful accounting, contributed to a greater efficiency in their administration and to higher standards for tenants in the cooperative sector. Nevertheless, in 1982 all cooperatives in each administrative area, except for those providing self-help buildings, were merged into one huge cooperative association. This concentration had a negative impact on the quality of administration, and the advantages of cooperatives in comparison with housing enterprises decreased.

The enterprises created their own housing administration units to administer enterprise-owned apartments. If the dwellings in one residential area or building complex were owned by different enterprises, usually the company owning the highest proportion established the administration unit, which secured services for the other companies on a contractual basis.

The generally low efficiency of the administration and maintenance, especially of state-owned housing stock, was directly encouraged by the economic regulations, distorted prices, and the system of state subsidies. The low rents, which had not been increased between 1964 and 1991, were not able to cover the costs of providing services such as heating and warm water supply. The state compensated for the incurred losses in order to achieve the promised level of social security. At the same time, the state created social inequity by providing privileges to households who obtained state-owned dwellings regardless of their higher income and by creating differences in the level of service provided in the state, cooperative, or private sector.

An unclear ownership framework led to limited housing mobility. The negative factors for long-term development were related to problems in the sale of apartments at market prices, the small differences in rent between units of different size, the strong motivation to keep an apartment for offspring, and the restricted opportunity to develop a housing career due to the uniformity of housing built using mass production.

The results of an interview survey conducted with 2,000 people in a representative sample of dwelling units in Slovakia in 1991 showed that only 32 percent of households were living in adequate accommodation, 26 percent were living in underoccupied apartments, and the remaining 42 percent of households contained more members than the total number of habitable rooms in the dwelling (Michalovic, Papanek, Simunek, and Handiakova, 1991). These data confirm that much of the existing housing stock was overcrowded.

The restricted opportunity for housing mobility also affected the local real estate market. There were in reality no real estate institutions, except for the efforts made by some communal institutions to organize the exchange of apartments for a fee. In Bratislava, the capital of Slovakia, in the second half of the 1980s, 275 to 841 apartments were purchased annually for personal occupation or to be registered as family houses. This accounted for between 0.2 and 0.5 percent of the total stock of 160,000 permanently occupied apartments in Bratislava. It is estimated that additional apartments were sold for "key money," but the relevant data are not available.

THE PRESENT SITUATION: REFORMS IN HOUSING AND PRIVATIZATION

In June 1991, the governments of both republics adopted the Principles of Housing Policy Reform, which outlined the main objectives of the reform. A new mechanism using market relationships was to replace the existing administrative and distributional system of construction and the allocation of dwellings. Also, the role of the citizen, the community, and the state in the provision of housing was to change. The citizen would take on the responsibility of securing accommodation, whereas the state, the republic, and the community would develop the conditions necessary for the creation of a housing market. With these reforms, housing would become accessible to all social groups in the population.

In addition, the housing market would be influenced by state policy on income, prices, finance, and social affairs. The social policy would guarantee that the cost of adequate housing for each citizen would not lead to a living standard below the socially accepted minimum. The role of the municipal authorities and communities was to implement this housing policy as an organic part of their comprehensive responsibility for general development in their area (Uznesenie Vlady SR, 1991).

This document also defined the first steps necessary in specific policy areas, in legislation, in the economy, and in social policy, if the objectives were to be achieved. Some of the steps that were implemented brought a substantial change to the housing situation. We examine the impacts of these changes on specific housing sectors, on housing management, and on the real estate market in the next section.

Changes in the Housing Sector

The first changes occurred in the state sector. Some of the state-owned apartments were given back to their original owners, under the Mitigation Law of 1990. This kind of restitution applied only to urban housing stock built before 1948. Most of the state-owned housing stock was transferred in May 1991 to local authorities. From this time on, the state sector ceased to exist. Some of its property was transferred to the private sector but most of it went to the local authorities.

The changes also affected the enterprise-owned apartments. With the privatization of the state enterprises, this sector will disappear. Some properties are likely to be privatized or sold to sitting tenants, whereas others will be transferred into a public rented sector administered by the municipal authorities.

An amendment to the Civic Code came into effect at the beginning of 1992, affecting the third sector of dwellings for personal use. The previous right to personal use of property was modified to become an ownership right. These ownership rights apply to all dwellings, buildings, and their respective plots, which were previously in personal use.

The newly created housing structure in CSFR consists of four main sectors: (1) communal apartments, which were formerly the state-owned apartments administered by the local authorities or housing enterprises; (2) apartments owned by state organizations, which were administered by state enterprises up to the time of their privatization; (3) cooperative apartments owned by building and self-help housing cooperatives; (4) private apartments, which were previously for personal use but are now in private ownership. It is difficult to put forward reliable figures for housing with the exception of the cooperative sector, because of the changes that took place in the three years up to 1992. However, Table 8.2 provides a comparison of the proportions of housing in each sector in 1980 and 1992.

Between 1987 and 1992, the proportion of new building funded by public investors fell from 69 to 65 percent. The total overall output of new building also fell, from 79,625 in 1987 (5.2 dwellings per 1,000 population) to 62,535 in 1991 (4.0 per 1,000). Although nearly two-thirds of the investment in new dwellings between 1987 and 1991 was in the public sector, the overall proportion of housing in the public sector did not change substantially due to the balancing process of privatization.

A census was conducted in 1991 for the whole of CSFR (FSU, 1991), but it failed to map all the described changes. However, the results are interesting from another point of view. The urbanization process has resulted in the depopulation

Table 8.2. Proportion of Housing in Each Sector in Czechoslovakia in 1980 and 1992 (in percent)

Housing Sector	1980	1992
Public rental: local authority	23	21
Enterprise-owned	10	9
Cooperative	16	18
Private rental	0	3
Owner-occupied	51	49

Table 8.3. Housing Stock in Czechoslovak Federal Republic, 1970–91

Date of Census	% of Occupied Dwellings	% of Unoccupied Dwellings	Total Dwellings
1.12.70	96	4	4,406,415
1.11.80	93	7	5,277,783
3.3.91	91	9	5,845,415

Source: FSU (1991).

of the rural areas. The number of unoccupied dwellings had grown during the past 20 years from 176,000 to 525,000, most of them located in rural settlements (Table 8.3). The data show that the percentage of permanently occupied dwellings continued to decrease, despite the intensive construction of one-family homes, which accounted for more than one-third of new building in housing. In the past, most of the empty homes were located in country settlements and served as second homes for recreational purposes. In 1991, just over half the uninhabited houses were used for recreational purposes. It is an open question whether this growing trend will continue when there are better opportunities for investment in a first home.

Changes in Housing Management

With the changes in the structure of the housing sectors, especially for the local authority housing stock, the problems in their administration needed to be resolved. Housing management enterprises had previously carried out the administration and maintenance of state-owned housing stock, now known as communal property. They had been responsible for the repair and maintenance of the stock and of the heating equipment, and for the provision of services such as heating and the supply of warm water. They had also been responsible for these services in 90 percent of the cooperative sector.

Housing management companies were, without exception, owned by the state up to the end of 1991, and the state subsidy system led to their low economic efficiency. The privatization process also influenced these enterprises. Unlike the situation in the past, when they took on the administration of newly built apartments from the state, in future these organizations will have to assume the role of the investor in the construction of rented accommodation.

After the abolition of state administration at district level, housing management companies were restructured and transformed. For example, at the beginning of 1992 there were 95 companies in Slovakia, employing some 18,000 people who managed 300,000 apartments in communal ownership, whereas during the previous year, 1991, there had been 38 enterprises with 27,000 employees. The number of employees has been permanently reduced, and repairs and maintenance activities have been privatized or contracted out. Most housing management enterprises came into municipal ownership, some of them being privatized in the first wave of privatization. Decisions about the form of administration needed for communal apartments is the responsibility of the local authorities. Housing services in the community can also be offered by the newly created private management firms. As competition emerges, the quality of services and the efficiency of the management will be positively affected.

Changes in the Real Estate Market

The restructuring of the housing sectors and the changes in the concepts of ownership have, of course, had an impact on the real estate market, as the experience of Slovakia shows. The prices of dwelling units, one-family houses, and building plots have increased, particularly in Bratislava, where average prices have increased threefold during the past three years. However, the demand for housing has not decreased as other factors have come into play, such as the growing differentiation in incomes, the increase in the number of people wanting to invest in real estate, and the return of some wealthy emigrés.

The institutions necessary to support these changes have started to develop. In Bratislava alone, 37 real estate firms were operating by the second half of 1992, not counting the number of lawyers who have taken on work in this area. There has also been a growth in property advertisements in papers and journals. In Slovakia, more than 20 advertisement journals are published, and many of these specialize in real estate. Business in real estate has become highly lucrative for those firms who have concentrated their attention increasingly on the purchase of plots of land suitable for large-scale construction.

Privatization and Sale of Apartments

The general process of privatization in the various sectors of Czechoslovakian housing was described in an earlier section. A particular process that has led to an increase in the proportion of apartments in private ownership has been the sale of apartments to sitting tenants. This sensitive issue has been the focus of much discussion. The transfer of cooperative apartments is already regulated by legislation, while the legislation dealing with the other two types of rented dwellings—community-owned and enterprise-owned—is at an advanced stage of development.

The sale or transfer of apartments in a cooperative property is regulated by the Law on Property Rights Modification and Arrangement of Property Titles in Cooperatives which came into effect in early 1992. Members of a cooperative who lived in their apartment were entitled to apply for a contract with the cooperative, under which transfers from the cooperative were free of cost to the individual, for six months from the date when the law was implemented. The contract had to include provision for the user's obligation to repay to the cooperative a proportion of the investment remaining unpaid. The contract now also includes provision for the users of a cooperative building to become joint owners of the common, nonhabitable space in proportion to the size of their respective apartments.

Some issues relating to sales in the communal sector have not yet been decided. The main problem is the regulation of the selling price of the dwellings, which is a matter to be decided by the federal government. In any case, a sale needs two actors—a buyer and a seller. It seems that there exists a great deal of interest on both sides. Many city mayors in Slovakia have declared that they expect up to half of the existing municipal housing stock to be sold. The municipal authorities are willing to sell because they need to acquire further financial resources, both for the maintenance and modernization of the remaining stock and for the construction of new social housing.

The interest of potential buyers can be assessed from survey findings, which indicated that only 22.1 percent of respondents were interested in purchasing their rented apartment. However, the average price these respondents were willing to pay for their apartment was almost 89,000 crowns—that is, seven times more than the regulated price proposed originally by the federal government (Michalovic et al., 1991). The rather low level of interest among tenants was probably due to the lack of information on the proposed conditions of sale. These findings also suggest that potential buyers were more likely than the government to be influenced by existing market prices.

The time schedule and the conditions for the sale of apartments owned by the state enterprises will depend on which wave of privatization these enterprises are included in and the administrative arrangements for the disposal of the property. In practice, there are likely to be only two alternative routes. In situations where the privatization project has the approval of the local authority, the enterprise-owned dwellings could be transferred free of charge into communal ownership. Alternatively, the dwelling could remain the property of the enterprise, which would retain responsibility for its management; in this situation, the dwelling could be sold at any time under existing legislation.

FUTURE DEVELOPMENTS IN THE HOUSING SECTOR

As a result of the changes described in the previous section, the total housing stock will comprise two basic forms: user-owned (owner-occupied) dwellings and rented dwellings. Suitable conditions are needed to encourage the gradual development of these two forms of housing. The transition to market regulation in housing has brought forward a need to develop and implement the new mechanisms for state involvement, especially to provide solutions to problems produced by the sharp rise in rents, to evolve a system to provide security for tenants, and to review the new situation of households with low incomes.

Table 8.4.   Dwellings Completed by the KBV System, 1987–91

	Dwellings Financed by the KBV System			Total Dwellings Completed		
Year	Czech Lands	Slovakia	CSFR	Czech Lands	Slovakia	CSFR
1987	15,688	9,118	24,806	49,000	30,625	79,625
1988	14,730	9,679	24,409	50,700	32,210	82,910
1989	16,838	10,539	26,777	55,073	33,437	88,510
1990	17,172	10,365	27,537	44,594	24,705	69,299
1991	15,044	6,177	21,221	41,719	20,815	62,535

Under the old system, known as the KBV System, or Complex Housing Construction System, state resources were allocated to finance house construction. Today state finance is available only for work to complete unfinished buildings. Other new construction, apart from dwellings for personal ownership and cooperative housing stock, has stopped. The new forms of state support for house construction and guidelines for implementation are still being discussed and developed. The cessation of construction of new housing for rent, apart from the completion of buildings in progress, has, of course, influenced the total yearly production figures for housing. The output in 1991 is only three-quarters of the average output in the 1980s (Table 8.4).

One of the first steps toward working out a new system of finance for house construction and for the modernization of dwellings and the related infrastructure was taken under the new legislation on house construction support, which came into effect in January 1993 under the provision of housing policy reform. This legislation incorporates several objectives of housing policy. It identifies support for housing construction as a crucial task for the national, regional, and community authorities. It requires that support for housing construction is focused on the need to create housing opportunities for households on a low income who could not otherwise secure adequate housing for themselves. It nevertheless aims to strengthen personal responsibility to resolve individual housing needs.

State support is to be provided by direct means such as returnable and nonreturnable grants, and by indirect means such as tax rebates and preferred loans. The implementation of these specific instruments will create the conditions necessary to encourage the construction of new dwellings, which will be available to let at a regulated but nevertheless economic rent. These conditions should also encourage the construction of dwellings for personal ownership by low-income households. Moreover, the legislation is intended to support the construction and modernization of the related infrastructure.

A specialized finance institute is to be established as a public–juridical institution to support the construction and modernization of housing in Slovakia. However, the development of this project has been curtailed and delayed for the present by the limitations of the state budget.

Another form of state support, which will facilitate long-term personal strategies for housing provision and for improvements in owner-occupied dwellings, is the establishment of a home savings scheme. The enabling legislation came into force in June 1992, and the first Slovak building savings bank opened on 1 November 1992. Saving conditions are set for individual accounts for specified time periods, and during that time not only does the state provide some contribution in the form of a benefit, but the savings bank also gives savers preferential treatment with regard to building loans.

Particular problems have been created by the transition to a system of economic rents. A stepwise rise in rents is intended to achieve a situation where the rent covers all investment, management, and maintenance costs of the landlord. A new decree from the federal and republic ministries of finance has amended a previous decree of 1964 regarding rent payment and related services. Four steps are advocated, but the decree specifies only the first two. As from January 1992, the "net" rent remained at its previous level, but the so-called "economization" of housing-related services was implemented. This led to an increase of 80 percent in overall rent payments. Six months later, the upper limit on net rents was increased by 100 percent, which led to a further rise. Overall, rents increased by 180 percent in 1992. The next steps, which took place in 1993, were less severe and took account of the prevailing economic conditions.

Although the average rent has historically been a small proportion of the average household income, the steep increases in rent have, of course, had serious social consequences for some groups, mainly those people whose income does not allow them to absorb such large price rises easily (Table 8.5). As price changes should not endanger the satisfaction of basic living needs, especially for those people who are not able to be economically active, there have been plans to develop a narrowly directed housing allowance system.

The present system of allowances is governed by the law on minimum income, which came into effect in December 1991. Under this law, a person or household in need with an income of less than 900–1,300 crowns per capita is eligible for an allowance for food and other basic needs from the state. This allowance may

Table 8.5. Average Rent for Public Sector Tenants as a Proportion of Household Income

	1987	1992
Average net rent	335 crowns	682 crowns
Average household income	5,500 crowns	7,088 crowns
Rent as % of household income	6.1	9.6

include a contribution for necessary household expenditures if the difference between per capita income and total household income is less than 500–900 crowns.

The implementation of economic mechanisms selected to support the development of the housing sector has to be undertaken with extraordinary sensitivity. It is, therefore, necessary to undertake a preliminary analysis of the existing structure and consider all the implications of the proposed changes, including an examination of the many alternative solutions.

CONCLUSION

This chapter has described the present stage in the privatization of the housing stock in Czechoslovakia. It shows one possible approach to the transformation of housing sectors in the transitional countries of Eastern Europe. The relations of ownership were settled rather quickly in the private and the cooperative housing sector. The private sector was reestablished with the reintroduction of the principles of ownership and by the restitution measures. The overwhelming proportion of the private sector is represented by owner-occupied dwellings; formerly rented apartments that have been bought by sitting tenants make up a very small proportion of this sector.

In the cooperative sector, the level of privatization has depended on the decision of the tenants. Their decision will have been influenced by the amount of outstanding debts in relation to the construction of their building. In the older housing stock, where the entire costs have been paid off, the transfer of ownership occurs free of charge.

The privatization of the other two sectors—communal and enterprise-owned—will depend on the introduction of new legislation on the ownership of dwellings. It is expected that the implementation of this new law will create the conditions necessary for the partial privatization of both communal housing stock and enterprise-owned housing stock.

The privatization of communal apartments is one of the most discussed questions. The officers of the municipal authorities maintain that the sale of communal apartments is motivated by the need to raise finance for the repair and maintenance of the communal housing stock, which has been neglected, and, to a lesser extent, to raise finance for the construction of new housing for rent.

Questions relating to the privatization of enterprise-owned dwellings are expected to be resolved in the future. In a situation where the rent, regulated by the state, does not fully cover the administration and maintenance costs, many enterprises see a way out by offering to transfer the dwellings into communal ownership. Other enterprises, mainly those that own housing in the larger towns, are waiting for the privatization of their business, after which they intend to sell the dwellings to tenants at a profit. Only a small proportion of enterprise-owned dwellings are expected to remain in enterprise ownership and available for rent.

This model depends to a large extent on the overall economic and social situation in the country, as well as on the political climate in which the principles and instruments of the housing policy are developed. It seems that the approval of basic goals by competent political subjects is a much simpler matter than their realization; this process is much more complicated and will require more time than originally thought.

REFERENCES

FSU. 1990. *Statisticka Rocenka CSFR 1989* [Statistical yearbook]. Prague: FSU, SU, SSU.

FSU. 1991. *Scitanie Ludu, Domov a Bytov: Predbezne Vysledky* [Census of people, houses and flats: Preliminary results]. Prague: FSU.

Michalovic, P. 1989. Housing dynamics in Czechoslovakia: What brings the mass housing construction. In Galland (ed.), *Housing Evaluation.* Lausanne: CIB.

Michalovic, P., Papanek, F., Simunek, I., and Handiakova, A. 1991. *Vysledky Empirickeho Vyskumu Subjektivneho Prezivania Meniacich sa Ekonomickych Podmienok Byvania* [Results of an empirical study of personal perception of changing economic conditions in housing]. Bratislava: UEOS.

Michalovic, P., Papanek, F., and Simunek, I. 1992. *Bytove Potreby a Potencial Trhoveho Spravania Uzivatelov Bytov* [Housing needs and market behaviour potential of flat users]. Bratislava: UEOS.

Mlada Fronta Dnes. 1992. *Ekonomicky pokles—stavi se mene* [A recession in the economy—there is less construction] (18 March).

Narodna Obroda. 1992. Obecne byty tvrdym orieskom [Communal flats as a hard nut] (27 March).

Uznesenie Vlady SR. 1991. *Zasady Reformy Bytovej Politiky v Slovenskej Republike* [Principles of housing policy reform in the Slovak Republic]. Bratislava.

9

Slovenia

Srna Mandič

This chapter describes how the policy of privatization was implemented in the housing sector in Slovenia by mid-1992. The self-management model of housing provision, which is the organizational legacy of former times, is being reshaped according to new schemes leading to the emancipation of the private sector in Slovenia.

The recent changes in housing were only part of the general transformation of Slovenian society, which is seeking a new social paradigm. The events described in the following paragraphs represent the milestones in the historical process. Slovenia entered the period as a unit of a federal state built on a philosophy of self-management under socialism, but ended the period as an independent state with a parliamentary democracy.

The Slovenian Parliament passed Amendments to the Constitution of the Republic of Slovenia in November 1989. This initiated two basic changes: (1) The previous one-party system was replaced by a multiparty system, enabling the newly formed political parties to enter the parliamentary elections. (2) The Amendments granted more autonomy to the Slovenian parliament, which provided the legal basis for the ensuing series of changes initiated independently of the federal legal and political context. From today's perspective, this appears to have been the opening act in a process that led to the gradual disintegration of the Yugoslav federation, a process in which the republics autonomously started to abandon socialism, each in its own way and at its own pace.

Many new pieces of legislation were brought forward, following the introduction of the amendments to the constitution. Self-management was substantially reduced in enterprise companies and abolished in the welfare services, which had been known as "self-managing interest communities." The administration and funding of the welfare services was centralized and transferred to the state.

When parliamentary elections were held in April 1990, the Communist Party lost its ruling position. A new ruling coalition of five parties from the center and the right of the political spectrum was formed. This coalition group, Demos, appointed the new government.

On 23 December 1990, a referendum on the sovereignty of the Republic of Slovenia was held. Slovenia then proposed that each republic should have autonomy in its own affairs. This autonomy could only be restricted by, or delegated to, the federal government by consensus. This proposal was not accepted by the other republics, who brought forward alternative proposals to extend centralization at the federal level.

The Republic of Slovenia made the decision to become independent. However, the proclamation of Independence in June 1991 was initially followed by a short period of military conflict, the so-called "weekend war." The changes introduced thereafter were intended to give Slovenia the necessary attributes of an independent state. A new national currency, the tolar, was introduced in October 1991. The following month the new Constitution was established, and in January 1992 Slovenia was recognized as an independent state by most countries in the international community.

The ruling coalition, Demos, started to disintegrate in the spring of 1992, and this lead to a serious government and parliamentary crisis. The government fell following a vote of no confidence in May 1992, and a new government was formed from the new ruling coalition of Social Democrats, Liberal Democrats, and Democratic Renewal Party, formerly the League of Communists. However, in the heavily polarized Parliament, each side could block the proposals of the other, and the pattern did not change much after the parties of the previous opposition and the ruling coalition changed places.

What were the major political and economic priorities throughout the transitional period? Once the possible threat of war was over and Slovenia gained international recognition as an independent state, public attention gradually turned toward domestic problems. The major issues during this period were the privatization of organizations and systems in the economy—that is, the transformation of industrial ownership and the restitution of assets to former individual owners. These issues continue to be fundamental to parliamentary argument.

The term "privatization" is generally used in Slovenia to denote the transformation of social ownership. This process has not made any systematic progress during the last two years, but it has become the source of permanent conflict between the political parties, and so far not one of the proposed models for the implementation of privatization has gained sufficient support in Parliament.

There are proposals for two different models put forward by opposing political parties. One model is supported by the "social democratic block," comprising the Liberal Democrats, the Socialists, the Social Democrats, and the Democratic Renewal Party. The other model is supported by the "conservative block," made up of the Slovenian National Party, the Slovenian Folk Party, the Liberal Party, and the Christian Democratic Party. The social democratic block promotes a model of privatization that is autonomous in a gradual process, with employees and managers becoming the most important shareholders. Managers who are already experienced in market-oriented entrepreneurship under self-management, it is argued, are an important resource that should not be ignored in the Slovenian process of privatization.

This model was criticized by the conservative block, which claimed that the existing "red" managers could not be trusted because of their previous loyalty to the socialist regime. They argued that the process of privatization should be carried out faster. It should rely on investors becoming the most important shareholders, with the state taking on the important role of providing capital and appointing directors.

The key difference between the two models is centered on the question of which group should gain the decisive role in the privatization process—the existing managers and employees in the first case, or the new elite of government administration in the second case. A new compromise model is being prepared, which would provide a wider range of inheritors to the social ownership of industry, including citizens, employees, investment funds, government development funds, pension funds, reimbursement funds, and private investors. In the meantime, the only model of privatization in operation is one established by the Markovic administration, and it is used infrequently because it relies on added capital alone. Some firms have experienced practical privatization because of their insolvency and subsequent sale.

The other major issue has been the restitution of assets to the original prewar owners of private property expropriated in the 1950s. The term "denationalization" is used to denote this process on Slovenia. Denationalization has been given priority over privatization. In other words, the transfer of ownership of assets that were previously nationalized is subject to a moratorium until the claims for restitution are settled.

The Act of Denationalization, which was passed in November 1991, did not attract very much attention at the time. It was discussed in terms of "injustices raised by the socialist regime." In contrast to some other ex-socialist countries, the notion has prevailed in Slovenia that these injustices have to be corrected and the property returned. Where it is not possible to return the property, compensation is to be provided. A two-year period has been set for the presentation of claims, and during that period all transactions relating to the property are under a moratorium, waiting for the "old" owners and their heirs to establish their claim.

Local government departments and courts have been increasingly burdened by claims for restitution, which have involved the development of procedures to examine complex evidence. The reimbursement scheme, which will impose a heavy financial burden on the state, has not been established, and, given the severe economic recession, it seems unlikely that it will be set up in the near future.

After the Act of Denationalization was passed, public opinion became increasingly critical, and efforts were made to change the legislation. Since the Slovenian National Party, which was the main promoter of the Act, has left the ruling coalition, the restitution process has lost some of its initial impetus.

The new Housing Act passed in October 1991 initiated some drastic changes. However, it did not become a focus for discussion, as public attention was focused elsewhere on the issues of national independence, the war, and industrial privatization. Housing debates were overwhelmingly concerned with details. They tended to focus on the particular terms of sale for the social rented stock and displayed a relatively weak concern for the more general issues relating to future housing policy. Generally, housing was treated as a major problem, unconnected to other economic and social issues. Only two housing issues—the strengthening of the private sector and the restitution of real estate property to its original owners—arose directly from the general debates on the economy and the suppression of the injustices of the socialist regime.

HOUSING BEFORE THE CHANGE

The State's direct involvement in housing provision in Slovenia, as in the rest of the former Yugoslavia, was not as significant as in other East European countries. This was due to a system of self-management, which created a complex network of institutions that took on many of the state's responsibilities, thus allowing decision making to be made at different levels. Individual enterprises were given an important role as the "grassroots" element of the whole system, known as the Basic Organization of Associated Labor.

This model led to organizational solutions in housing, which were specific to Slovenia and Yugoslavia. The most distinctive feature of the self-management model of housing was the devolution of responsibility for the provision and allocation of housing to the enterprise. In effect, decisions about the provision of housing for rent and the provision of home loans for employees were the employer's responsibility. These relatively autonomous decisions by enterprises on the use of housing funds made a substantial contribution to the growth of home ownership.

The social ownership of rented stock was another feature of the self-management system. "Social ownership" was a concept that defined "the working class as a whole" as the owner of the property, but the rights, powers, and obligations of ownership were attributed to a variety of institutions, which operated on the principle of self-management. Housing committees in individual enterprises, their delegates to municipal Self-managing Interest Communities for Housing, and Housing Councils made up of tenants all had a part to play.

The performance of the Slovenian housing system was in many respects similar to other national systems operating under state socialism, even though it was based on institutional arrangements specific to Slovenia, which, in principle, organized housing resources as an employment benefit (Szelényi, 1983). There was a permanent shortage of rented housing, rents were very low, but the property was poorly maintained—these issues were being raised constantly by the groups pressing for housing reform. Moreover, there was unequal access to the rented sector, and higher socioeconomic groups were overrepresented amongst tenants. Data from the 1984 Quality of Life Survey confirm this: 14 percent of adults with primary school education, 20 percent of adults with secondary education, and 31 percent of adults with university degrees had become tenants in social rented property. So, although adults with a university degree accounted for only one-third of tenants, they were proportionately overrepresented in this sector in comparison with less well educated adults (Mandić, 1991). More highly educated adults had a better chance of entering the rented sector, because housing opportunities were closely related to employment opportunities. This was seen as evidence that the system was unable to promote social equality, and, indeed, unequal access to social housing contributed significantly to the popular perception of the social injustice of the socialist system.

Housing Ownership and Tenure

Just before the housing legislation came into effect in 1991, the tenure structure was weighted toward owner-occupation, with two-thirds of housing stock in home ownership and the remaining third in the rented sector.

The social rented stock contained two segments. The largest segment, which represented 88 percent of social rented stock, was owned by enterprises for allocation to their employees. The remaining 12 percent was owned by different state agencies, including the municipal authorities, who were the successors to the previous Self-managing Interest Communities for Housing. Most of this stock was acquired under the Solidarity program and was allocated to "persons in need" who could not be housed by their employers. A very small section of the social rented stock was previously acquired by expropriation from private, pre-war owners. Under the new legislation this property, known as "general peoples' property," is subject to restitution to the previous owners.

The supply of social rented housing was permanently too scarce to satisfy the demand. It was therefore allocated via a system based on the principles of "need" and "merit." For each housing unit, points were given according to its facilities, the area of its floor space, its age, and its amenities. The value of the points was determined by the municipal authority. Rents were relatively low. Individual housing allowances in the form of rent subsidies were means-tested and available to a very small proportion of tenants. However, tenants were granted a tenancy right in perpetuity, which was transferable to other members of the household. Moreover, house exchange agreements were legal and disallowed only in a very limited number of circumstances.

The home ownership sector, in comparison, was much larger than the rented sector throughout the postwar period. Private ownership was restricted to two housing units, but not limited in any other way. The major method of entry to home ownership was by self-help construction. Home ownership was strongly encouraged by the provision of very cheap housing loans from employers and the enormous amount of help in kind and in labor provided by kinship networks.

It is worth noting that cooperative forms of tenure were not developed, and housing cooperatives operated only as temporary organizations to support the construction of housing units for private ownership.

Production

There were formerly two different forms of housing production—the social and the private. They differed not only in the type of producers and investors involved, but also in the type of housing unit produced. Private construction was almost exclusively limited to individual detached one-family houses. It was the individual potential homeowner who played the roles of the "developer" and "investor." Self-help practices were combined with work by small private contractors in house construction. Traditional construction techniques and materials were normally used. Such private construction was generally not discouraged by official procedures or shortages in materials, but in urban areas limitations on access to building land placed constraints on development. Finance was raised from a variety of sources such as personal savings, which could include substantial contributions from older generations and housing loans from employers and banks. Funding from all these sources was usually combined to finance the venture.

Social production, in contrast, was concentrated in urban areas, where the multifamily housing unit, usually in large housing estates, was the prevalent form of construction. The organization of this type of production was constantly under discussion (Mandić, 1992). Different models were used to combine the skills of a variety of social agents in the roles of developer and investor; building enterprises in social ownership, municipal departments dealing with land policy and housing policy, and the purchasers were all encouraged to play a part. However, even the final model, known as "socially directed housing construction," did not prove efficient, and the prices asked for by the building enterprises were seen to be unreasonably high (Kos, 1992). Some of these newly constructed housing units were sold to private persons and some to enterprises and municipal authorities. Purchasers under this system were usually preregistered and were required to pay part of the price in advance.

Finance raised from a variety of sources was combined to fund this type of construction: building enterprises' own capital, short-term loans from banks, funds from enterprises, and Self-managing Interest Communities for Housing, savings, and housing loans raised by individuals could all be used (Mandić and Rop, 1993).

This type of construction frequently used prefabricated sections. The types of apartments produced were highly standardized but of relatively low quality at a very high price. However, the system that provided access to building land favored social rather than private production of housing.

The social production of housing was most affected by the economic recession and the gradual social changes in the late 1980s. The output from this form of housing development rapidly decreased, with the number of units completed dropping from 7,000 in 1980 to 2,200 in 1990. Private production over the same 10-year period was significantly less affected, although its output dropped from 6,700 in 1980 to 5,500 in 1990.

Housing Management

Private owners were responsible for managing their own housing unit when, as in most cases, it was an individual dwelling. Management of collective types of housing required a more organized approach. All the stock—that is, both privately owned and socially rented units, contained in buildings under social ownership—was compulsorily managed by a municipal agency. The agency was responsible for repair and maintenance of the building and for the collection of rents and amortization payments from private owners. It was often criticized for its bureaucracy, high costs, and inefficiency in providing repairs. Only part of the rent collection from tenants living in a building was used for the repair and maintenance of that building, and in this the Housing Councils were given only a symbolic role in decision making. The larger proportion of the rent money was pooled at the municipal level to provide funds for major repairs, renewals, and improvements to the infrastructure of the area. This meant that some of the money collected in rent leaked out of the housing sphere and was used for other purposes. The priority given to the renovation of buildings in the municipality was often determined by "important persons" acting in the interests of a particular building or neighborhood in which they lived.

Real Estate Market

Two district real estate markets were in operation with their own logic, institutions, and price-setting mechanisms. First, there was the market for new housing units constructed by large enterprises in social ownership. The supply of these units was, until recent years, well below the level of demand. There were waiting lists of potential purchasers who usually had to preregister an interest and pay part of the purchase price in advance. There was a very complex methodology for price determination, operating with terms like expected price, net price, final price, and approved price. This system, which involved the registered purchasers and the municipal authorities, was supposed to control the process of construction and the price, but this never worked properly. Price-setting mechanisms remained blurred, and the high inflation rate made things worse. However, in the last few years the slowing down of the economy, together with the contraction in the number of sources for housing finance and the decrease in wage levels, all led to a decrease in the demand for house purchase and subsequently to a decrease in real estate prices.

The market in second-hand housing units for private ownership operated entirely differently. Prices were freely determined, and the most important source of information was newspaper advertisements, although many private real estate agents set up business in the last few years. After 1990, the sale of housing units in social ownership became legal within strict regulations. Under the Housing Act 1991, tenants gained the right to buy their social rented home.

WHY PRIVATIZATION?

Before discussing the question of privatization in housing, let us examine the preceding policy of socialization. The previous section has described how the Slovenian system of housing provision was crucially influenced by the social sector—that is, by enterprises in social ownership. They were the key actors in many sectors of housing policy and provision. In the construction sector, many building enterprises were in social ownership; in the area of housing management, many municipal management enterprises were in social ownership; and there were enterprises in social ownership involved in investment in rented housing and its subsequent allocation. Thus the social sector was a dominant influence in housing. "Socialization" was the official term used to describe the introduction and expansion of the social sector.

Were there any particular reasons for introducing the social sector and social ownership into housing? Looking back at the series of housing reforms, each of them initiating a particular form or extension of socialization, one can see how they corresponded to the broader political and economic changes taking place at that time. There were certainly many specific arguments in favor of these innovations in housing, yet the basic force of the movement was to encourage the spread of socialization. Housing reform followed on the same ideological and organizational pattern as was first adopted in the social reforms at the macro level.

The same pattern of change appears to have taken place in the process of privatization. Privatization, in the sense of a further emancipation of the private sector, is perceived as offering a general solution to the problem of lack of economic efficiency in enterprises under social ownership. It is argued that inefficiency will be discouraged by the introduction of private owners, who will be more strongly motivated to promote efficiency. After the concept of social ownership was rejected and general economic discussion focused on the positive benefits expected from the private sector, it was only a matter of time before techniques were developed to introduce the privatization process into housing (Kovac, 1991; Mencinger, 1991). The recent housing debates demonstrate that the issue is not why privatization should be pursued, but which particular form it should take in housing policy. Many specific debates centered on a discussion of the terms for sale for the transfer of ownership of social rented stock to tenants.

The Housing Act of 1991 did not need to promote the movement toward privatization. A general statement to the effect that it will "radically increase the social and economic efficiency of housing provision" was sufficient. The legislation corresponded to the general underlying expectation that private owners and private firms would take better care of housing maintenance and that private building firms would act more efficiently than enterprises in the social sector had in the past.

Political parties had somewhat different proposals on the terms of sale for the disposal of rented property and other proposed reforms, yet they did not disagree in their general expectations of housing privatization. They did not articulate any specific objectives of privatization or, indeed any objectives for housing policy in the future.

However, it was the reform of rented housing in Slovenia that "broke the ice" and the system of social ownership first started to be converted. The issues raised by the privatization of industrial enterprises have proved more contentious for political parties, and it has been harder and taken longer to reach agreement on those issues.

THE MOVES TOWARD PRIVATIZATION

The basic pattern of privatization in housing was outlined under the provisions of the Housing Act of October 1991. The section of the Act that relates to "privatization" deals only with the conversion of the social rented stock, but the Act generally makes provision for the enlargement of the private sector in housing.

Reallocation of Responsibilities and the New Institutions

Under the new legislation, neither the employer nor the enterprise takes on responsibility for the provision of rented housing. Moreover, the municipal authorities no longer have the role of housing providers; rather, they have the task of supporting several other agencies, who are prepared to make provision for rented housing. This reallocation of responsibilities is intended to encourage a pluralist structure in the provision of rented accommodation. A comparison of housing tenure over time is presented in Table 9.1.

The basic principles of tenure are legally defined as follows. Social housing is to be provided by the municipal authorities. It will be targeted on specific household groups on the principle of means-tested incomes and the size and structure of the household. This is very similar to the previous arrangement known as "solidarity housing." Social renting will become a marginal tenure, serving the housing needs of marginalized sectors of the population.

The most distinctive feature of the new policy is the introduction of three different types of private renting—commercial, nonprofit, and employer-owned property—in place of the one general category. Nonprofit renting is expected to be provided by nonprofit housing organizations, with the rents set at a nonprofit

Table 9.1. Percentage of Housing Stock in Different Tenures: Past, Present, and Future

	Before Privatization	After Privatization	Projection for the Year 2000
Owner-occupied	85	67	75
Social rented, owned by enterprises		29	1
Social rented, SICH or municipality	2	4	4
Private rented	0	0	5
Nonprofit rented	13	0	15
Totals	100	100	100

Source: Ministry of Environmental Protection and Regional Planning (1991).

level and a tenancy agreement that is permanent in principle. These same rights are legally guaranteed to all tenants who choose to remain tenants in the former social rented sector. However, tenants in property rented in the private sector or from employers have less security of tenure as their tenancy agreement may be terminated. Providers of this type of housing will be free to set rent levels, although the municipal authority will retain the power to intervene in extreme cases.

Municipal authorities will have the power to create their own housing funds, which will become a major source of investment finance for social housing, nonprofit housing programs, and home-ownership loans. The growth in these funds was fueled by the sale of the municipal housing to tenants.

The National Housing Fund is an important innovation. Its initial capital has been created by the sale of social rented property to the sitting tenants, the Fund receiving 20 percent of the selling price. The Fund is responsible for low-cost housing loans for homeowners and, more importantly, for funding for nonprofit housing organizations. This financial support will be supplementary to municipal housing funds and finance from private sources.

Removal of Legal Restrictions on the Private Sector

The Housing Act 1991 ceases to define housing management or housing development in such a way as to favor any one sector, as previous legislation did. There are requirements relating to standards of maintenance and the registration of firms who manage larger buildings, but otherwise private contractors may be freely chosen.

There are no restrictions placed on the number of housing units owned by a private individual. However, there are some limitations arising from tenants' rights, which are defined in the tenancy agreement.

Conversion of Social Rented Stock into Private Property

The Housing Act has provided two models of conversion of socially rented housing into private property. This first is to sell the property to the sitting tenants, based on their "right to buy" and popularly called "privatization." The second method is through the restitution of expropriated property to the original prewar private owners or their heirs, and this is called "denationalization." It has won priority over the right to buy in the sense that the social housing, which was obtained by expropriation of private owners, cannot be sold to the sitting tenants but has to be restituted to the original private owners upon their claims.

The terms of sale are laid out in detail by the Housing Act. Each tenant with a formally validated housing right was given the right to buy. The right, which is transferable to other members of the household, may be exercised for a two-year period.

The price of the unit is determined in the following way. First, a discount of 30 percent is granted on the original value of the unit—that is, the book value already used for rent calculations. Tenants are free to choose between an outright purchase and payment by installment over a maximum period of 20 years. Second, in the case of an outright purchase, an additional discount of 30 percent is provided. The previous owners are entitled to receive 80 percent of the purchase money, the remaining 20 percent being paid into the National Housing Fund.

Tenants are given another option: if they give up the tenancy, they are entitled to compensation equivalent to 30 percent of the original book value of the unit. In cases where the unit is restituted to the original owner, the owner is entitled to compensation of 30 percent of its value upon the sale of the unit to the tenant.

In cases where the unit is restituted to the original owner, the owner is entitled to a 30 percent compensation upon sale of the unit to the tenant on these terms.

In the cases where the tenant does not want to buy the unit, he or she is entitled to a tenancy agreement on a permanent basis and a guaranteed nonprofit rent. If a tenant who chooses to buy the dwelling in monthly installments, which later on exceed one-third of the household income, he or she may request the transfer of property back to the original owner, allowing the purchaser to become a tenant again.

The remaining part of the socially owned rented housing stock for which no claims are received from either tenants or expropriated previous owners, remains the property of the present owners—that is, the enterprises and municipal authorities.

THE IMPACT OF PRIVATIZATION

Even if accurate information were available, it would still be a very difficult task to examine the impact of housing privatization on a society like modern Slovenia. Here, all the social spheres are simultaneously changing: the monetary, fiscal, and banking systems, the welfare system, labor legislation, public administration, and even the regional administrative units. There is a high unemploy-ment rate, rising from 5 percent in 1990, to 8 percent in 1991, and to 13 percent in mid-1992. The level of real wages is decreasing, and many enterprises are suffering heavy losses and are closing down.

Housing is affected by these changes, and there are also many changes in the housing system which are not related to the privatization measures. Under these circumstances, an effort to isolate analytically the precise impact of housing pri-vatization incurs many risks. The specific goals of privatization were not clearly articulated by policymakers. Thus a very wide space is available for "handy" interpretations in which all recent improvements—or, alternatively, any deteri-oration—in housing may be attributed to privatization. With this in mind, I will mostly concentrate on a description of the most obvious effects of privatization, notably on the progress of the private sector in housing. However, a few develop-ments that are probable outcomes of privatization are also discussed.

Conversion and Its Impacts

The sale of social rented housing to sitting tenants became one of the important issues in the media, as well as in everyday conversations following the 1991 Housing Act. The outright purchase, with its 60 percent discount, was considered the "deal of the century." Let us illustrate it with an example of an average social rented apartment of 56 square meters of floor space and modern equipment. Its purchase price is approximately 20 percent of the price if it were bought on the free market.

By the middle of 1992, 76,000 units were sold, representing approximately one-third of the rented stock. Official data is not yet available, but it is estimated that the method of outright purchase was more popular. The majority of the sale contracts were signed in the two months following the implementation of the Act. Later, the rate of sales substantially decreased. At the present rate, the sales tar-get—namely, one-half of social property—will hardly be reached. The "conver-sion euphoria" seems to be over.

What are the effects of conversion of housing in the social rented sector in terms of social equality? As there are no empirical data available, only a general conclusion can be made. The better-off households who were overrepresented among the tenants were also overrepresented among those who profited from "the deal of the century." However, the relatively low price of housing units, especially for those lacking modern equipment, together with the possibility of paying by installments equal to a nonprofit rent, leads to the hypothesis that those tenants with medium and low levels of income were not necessarily excluded from the conversion process.

Moreover the purchasing power of tenants did not depend only on their current registered incomes, but also on savings, much of it earned in informal activities, as well as on savings from family who were very eager to participate in such a fabulous investment. The analysis is further complicated by the general instability in income levels. Many of the previously affluent households are facing a drastic decrease in their incomes, while at the same time a new rich elite is emerging. However, one identifiable impact of the conversion seems to be the change in the meaning of tenure. Renting is changing from a desirable and positive status to a neutral or even marginal tenure.

Has the maintenance of property improved after the tenure conversion? Of course, more time is needed for such effects to appear. However, the question is likely to remain, to what extent would such an improvement be a direct result of the conversion itself—or, alternatively, of the newly specified duties of repair or, indeed, as a result of the improved supply of maintenance services?

There were also important side effects from the tenure conversion. First, it influenced the monetary system, since the sales managed to "pull people's savings out of their socks" and bring a substantial amount of foreign hard currency into circulation. The resultant high supply of foreign currency affected the currency rate and enabled the National Reserve Fund to improve its foreign currency reserves. However, this led to an internal liquidity problem, causing a "monetary shock." The second side effect was that the prices of real estate decreased substantially. This spill-over effect was experienced in the market for second-hand cars, where prices also decreased.

A criticism was made later that some of these harmful impacts on the economy could have been avoided. It was argued that the purchasing power of tenants had been underestimated and the price of homes was set unreasonably low. It was suggested that the monetary shock could have been avoided if a gradual rather than an outright purchase had been encouraged (Bajt, 1992).

However, the possible monetary side effects of the conversion were not examined during the preparation of the conversion legislation. The importance of the effects of these developments in the housing sector on other sectors was seriously underestimated.

Privatization in Different Segments of Housing

In the construction industry, no special privatization guidelines were given, as construction firms were subject to the same models as other companies. The introduction of market competition was expected to lead to the creation of new small venture networks, but no particular initiative was made to encourage their development.

In the last few years, many of the large building firms in social ownership who were facing threats of bankruptcy made efforts to adjust to a strongly diminishing and highly selective demand for their products. They also substantially reduced the number of employees, many of whom were immigrants.

The drastic change in the demand for housing initiated changes in the housing construction industry. There was a general decline in the purchasing power of private individuals as general income levels decreased and the supply of cheap housing loans from enterprise housing funds dried up. The Self-managing Interest Communities for Housing were abolished. These organizations, together with enterprise housing funds, had provided the finance that had sustained the stable, almost guaranteed, demand. These changes coincided with a general decline in prices of real estate caused by the tenure conversion. However, the smaller private firms, most of whom had been engaged in private construction for future home owners, were not badly affected, as demand in that sector was substantially unaffected during the period of privatization.

Many small private firms emerged in the field of housing maintenance after the introduction of the Housing Act 1991. They are competing with the social sector municipal maintenance agencies to take over the maintenance of multifamily housing blocks.

No substantial progress is yet visible in the provision of rented housing in the private sector. Such change would require a longer period of time to materialize. The process of denationalization—that is, the restitution of property to private prewar owners—is far from being completed, and its effect on the future structure of housing provision is not predictable. There are no parameters available that could predict the future uses of the restituted property. It is not known how much of it will be used as a home—perhaps as a second or third home for the owner—or alternatively how much will be used on a commercial basis, available for rent in the private or nonprofit sector.

No greater progress has been made in the provision of rented property in the nonprofit sector. In the existing housing stock, nonprofit arrangements will be made for rented units that have remained unsold, and in these situations the tenants are legally protected. However, the new unoccupied units for nonprofit rent are of crucial importance, since they will provide the only means of entry to this sector for new cohorts of the population who are unable to qualify for social renting or to enter home ownership. The younger urban cohorts with medium-level incomes will be the group most likely to be victimized by the failure of this sector. Yet in the face of unstable prices and insufficient sources of loan capital and dependent on untested schemes, the new organizations offering housing at nonprofit rents are likely to be a high-risk investment (for further comparison of the risks between different housing sectors, see Mandič, 1993).

The development of housing finance in the private sector, which is crucial for the future development of housing, has made little progress. The private sector has not made any effort to provide low-cost capital in a way that would displace the former social sector—that is, the enterprises and self-managing "mutuality" housing funders who used to provide cheap home loans. During this period, when the commercial banks were providing loans on a very high interest rate, no other private low-cost financial institution emerged, despite an interest rate of 17 percent being charged by most lenders in mid-1992. There are no home-savings banks, building societies, or cooperative savings banks in Slovenia.

Although the supplementary role of the state in housing finance has been established, there are no parallel institutions providing private financial services that could supplement income and personal savings.

CONCLUSIONS

This chapter has described how the Slovenian housing system was crucially affected by the concepts and organizational schemes of social ownership, which aimed to replace both state and private responsibility for housing. With the general shift in thinking toward privatization and the promotion of the private sector, the previous organizational structure, with the social sector as its centerpiece, is being dissolved and replaced by new structures in which the private sector is expected to replace the social sector (see Table 9.1).

The most noticeable change for housing policy is the omission of the previous general model for rented housing in which an enterprise in social ownership— that is, an employer—had a key role. It was formerly the enterprise that invested in housing for rent and allocated accommodation. It also provided most low-cost home loans to individuals. Moreover, enterprises played an important role in other spheres of housing construction, development, and management.

Recently the socialist system of self-management has been abolished and the concept of social ownership rejected. Social ownership was generally recognized as being unable to provide economic efficiency, due to a lack of motivation, which could be provided by private owners. Emancipation and development of the private sector is perceived as the general solution. This axiom, which was established in the general economic debates, has diffused into housing. However, it must be remembered that even under the previous arrangements, the private sector was far from being ruled out. Private housing construction, especially self-help, was widespread, and home ownership covered two-thirds of the total housing stock.

New ideological and organizational schemes are being applied to housing following from the Housing Act 1991 and other legislative innovations. Under the new schemes, the social sector is replaced by the private sector, and the state retains a supplementary role. New instruments of housing policy have required implementation so that the state may carry out its supportive function.

The private sector has made some progress, but its performance varies across the different sectors within housing. It seems to have been successful in competing with the social sector in housing maintenance. In construction, it seems to have already won the race, as its output substantially exceeds that of the social sector. However, it has not made any progress yet in the provision of housing for rent or in the provision of low-cost housing capital.

It is an open question as to what extent the private sector will be able to perform these roles, which have been left vacant by the retreat of the social sector. These sectors appear to be exposed to a transitional vacuum created by the dissolution of the previous schemes, while the new schemes based on expectations of private sector activity are not yet in operation. Of course it remains to be seen whether this vacuum is only a transitional phase and to what extent it might be structural and based on an unrealistic expectation of the private sector's performance.

The impact of privatization is a very challenging issue. As the goals of privatization and its outcome measures were not well articulated by the policymakers and since all social spheres are simultaneously changing, it is difficult to isolate those changes that are the direct outcome of housing privatization.

One of these issues centers on the transitional vacuum in the housing finance system. The source of low-cost capital for housing investment has changed. Money will no longer be raised from the net income of employer enterprises. Rather, it will be raised by local taxation on personal income and private property. The previous source, which represented one-half of all housing investment, has been relieved of that responsibility, while the new system of municipal taxation is not yet functioning. As it is likely to be very unpopular, it might take years to implement the new tax system. This situation means a substantial loss to housing finance but a gain to household budgets. Yet at a time of general decline in wage levels, this "gain" is not visible, since wages are still lower than they used to be. This redistribution of resources in favor of personal incomes appears to be a "silent and invisible privatization"; it is up to the people to raise the issue in the local political arena.

REFERENCES

Bajt, A. 1992. Gospodarski vidiki zasebljenja stanovanj. *Gospodarska Gibanja* 224, 25–42.

Housing Act, The. 1991. *Stanovanjski Zakon.* Uradni list Rupublika Slovenje (October 11).

Kos, D. 1992. A case study of conflicting housing pluralism in Yugoslavia: Informal (self-help) activities in the formal housing system. In B. Turner, J. Hegedüs, and I. Tosics (eds.), *The Reform of Housing in Eastern Europe and the Soviet Union.* London: Routledge.

Kovac, B. 1991. Entrepreneurship and privatisation of social ownership in economic reforms. In J. Simmis and J. Dekleva (eds.), *Yugoslavia in Turmoil: After Self-management?* (pp. 87–100). London and New York: Pinter Publishers.

Mandic, S. 1991. *Analiza Obstojecega Stanja Stanovanjske Preskrbe Prebivalstva.* Ljubljana: University of Ljubljana, Institute of Social Sciences.

Mandic, S. 1992. Reformism in Yugoslavia. In B. Turner, J. Hegedüs, and I. Tosics (eds.), *The Reform of Housing in Eastern Europe and the Soviet Union* (pp. 296–307). London and New York: Routledge.

Mandic, S. 1993. Restructuring of the housing policy system in Slovenia: Its logic and anticipated effects. In I. Svetlik (ed.), *Social Policy in Slovenia: Between Tradition and Innovation* (pp. 66–83). Avebury: Gower.

Mandic, S., and Rop, T. 1993. New housing challenges in Slovenia. *Cities* 10 (3), 237–245.

Mencinger, J. 1991. From self-management to a capitalist economy? In J. Simmis and J. Dekleva (eds.), *Yugoslavia in Turmoil: After Self-management?* (pp. 71–86). London and New York: Pinter Publishers.

Ministry of Environmental Protection and Regional Planning. 1991. *Izhodisca za Nacionalni Stanovanjski Program* [Starting-points for the national housing program]. Ljubljana: Ministry of Environmental Protection and Regional Planning.

Szelényi, I. 1983. *Urban Inequalities under State Socialism.* New York: Oxford University Press.

10

The Patterns of Housing Privatization in Eastern Europe

David Clapham and Keith Kintrea

The aim of this chapter is to review the experience of housing privatization in East European countries with a view to drawing out similarities and differences and establishing patterns. In particular the focus is on two issues that were raised in chapter 1, namely the objectives of privatization and the forms or mechanisms used. The rather scant evidence on the short-term impact of privatization policies is then assessed and the possible long-term impact examined. Finally, the future trajectory of East European housing systems is discussed.

THE AIMS OF PRIVATIZATION

In chapter 1, the aims of privatization in housing were outlined. The three major ones were seen as reducing public expenditure, providing a political symbol, and creating a more efficient housing system. Each of these is now reviewed in the light of the experience recounted in the previous chapters. The intention is to evaluate the importance of the objective in driving privatization and to assess how far the aim has been achieved in practice.

Reducing Public Expenditure

It is clear that in all the East European countries, with the possible exception of the former East Germany, public finances are under considerable pressure. Therefore, there is perceived to be little or no public money available for investment in housing, whether in new building, renovation of older properties, or even in ongoing repairs to existing public stock.

In the new *Länder* of Germany, public funds have been provided by the German Federal government. These have allowed the pilot projects described in chapter 4 to include the renovation of properties with public money as a prelude and an aid to sale into the private sector. In other countries, sales have generally been of unimproved stock, and one of the objectives of sales has been for the state to avoid the costs of renovation and future repair. This second approach has a number of implications.

The lack of state renovation and repair, coupled with the poor condition of much of the stock, is likely to limit sales to some degree. Buyers will need to find money for renovation and repair as well as the cost of purchase, and, in a situation where personal incomes are low, this could severely affect demand. This issue was acknowledged in Germany and was the major reason why pilot projects were introduced to stimulate demand. However, the poor condition of the stock may be reflected in a low sales price, thus ensuring high demand but leading to low sales revenue overall. Therefore, whatever the price, it seems unlikely that sales of stock in poor condition will result in large state revenues, a point that is accepted by most East European governments. Nevertheless, any income is considered to be welcome, and the avoidance of state expenditure on renovation and repair is considered to be important.

The transfer of responsibility for future repairs from the state will only reduce state expenditures in the long run if the new owners are able and willing to shoulder the responsibility. Much state expenditure on housing in Western countries is devoted to the payment of grants and to other mechanisms designed to improve the condition of private sector stock. The issue of future repair responsibility is one to which we return later in the chapter.

East European countries have varied considerably in their concern with generating revenue from sales. For example, in Bulgaria sale prices have been low, and there has been little attempt to use the proceeds other than for meeting current government expenditures. However, sales in Bulgaria have been fast, with approximately half the stock being sold before prices were increased. In Slovenia, also, sales were rapid, with a third of the stock being sold in the nine months following legislation in 1991, with the majority of sales at 20 percent of market value (see chapter 9). The success of the sell-off released a considerable volume of personal savings (often in foreign hard currency) into the country's economy; 20 percent of the sale proceeds have been devoted to a National Housing Fund, which has been given responsibility for the provision of low-cost housing loans for home owners and for investment into nonprofit housing.

In the Czech and Slovak Republics, control over the speed of sales of public stock and the price charged has been devolved to local authorities, who are adopting a variety of practices. In some areas, the proceeds of sales are being collected in development funds, with the intention of reinvesting in housing and other kinds of urban renewal projects. However, in some countries such as

Slovenia or to a lesser extent Poland, an important proportion of the stock is owned by state enterprises rather than municipal government. In some cases, enterprises hand over the stock to local authorities to avoid management and maintenance costs, but where they have privatized the stock themselves, they can use the proceeds to invest in enterprise production rather than reinvesting in housing.

Therefore, in some countries at least, there is a desire to use the proceeds from sales to invest in housing and the urban infrastructure. However, there is little evidence that the desire for income is itself an important issue in the decision to adopt a privatization policy or in the choice between different mechanisms of privatization. For example, Russia and Poland—two countries that have severe economic problems and extreme pressure on public finances—are among the slowest in adopting programs for the sale of housing. Several years after the political changes, the adoption of a sales program was still being debated in both countries and the options reviewed, but little action had been taken.

In countries such as Slovenia, Hungary, and Bulgaria, where sales programs have been instituted, relatively low selling prices have been adopted. Indeed, in almost all countries (Russia and Hungary being the exceptions), restitution (the return of property to the original owners before nationalization) has taken precedence over sales. Restitution offers no financial revenue to the state and can cost substantial sums in compensation where the return of property is not possible.

Not surprisingly, given the continuing political instability in most of Eastern Europe and the pressing economic problems, it is the short-term view of financial issues that predominates. Decisions about the sale price seem to be made by reference to the size of the revenue in the short rather than long-term. In most cases, sale prices have been low, resulting in a high volume of sales. Even if this is the most appropriate strategy for maximizing short-term revenue and is the way to maximize the short-term savings to be made by the state in maintenance and repair, the long-term consequences for public expenditure may be grave if the state is forced to intervene later if property is not repaired.

The privatization of housing, particularly through the sale of state-owned stock, can potentially make a large impact on state finances, as the British experience shows. However, the desire to generate income does not seem to be the major objective of the privatization program, although it is clearly an issue that is taken into account along with others.

Promoting a More Efficient Housing System

In many East European countries, there has been little debate about the merits of housing privatization. There is a widespread political consensus that privatization is necessary in order to create a functioning housing market. In turn, a market is considered necessary for an efficient and well-functioning housing system. However, in countries such as Slovenia, the creation of a market in housing was perceived as following directly from the creation of markets in other commodities. Also, the mechanisms of privatization that were employed were based on those used elsewhere. In other words, housing was viewed as just another commodity, which did not demand any form of special consideration or treatment. The general case for markets is held to apply in housing, which is viewed as a commodity like any other. This view was held to a greater or lesser extent in most of the countries considered in the book.

There has been some consideration of the specific impacts of markets in housing. In particular, there is a widespread belief that the introduction of a market will lead to more housing being produced and more renovation and maintenance work. It was mentioned in chapter 2 that a severe housing shortage exists in most East European countries. Housing construction has been held back by a shortage of public funds, especially during the 1980s, and by the lack of an effective mechanism for private construction (self-build housing had only a limited impact in most countries because of the difficulties of acquiring land and materials). The belief is that a market will encourage private companies to construct new housing to meet the demand and reduce the housing shortage. However, demand is not the same as need, and it remains to be seen whether needs will be translated into effective demand and households will be able or willing to pay the prices charged by private developers. This must particularly be the case in the short term, when sales of public sector housing are taking place at heavily discounted prices and where rents in many countries are still low. For example, rents in the Czech Republic had increased by 180 percent over two years, but were still closely controlled in 1993 in an attempt to restrain inflation. Low rents are a disincentive to buy as well as placing a question mark over the profitability of private renting and of new construction for owner-occupation.

The other area where a market system was thought to offer benefits was in the maintenance of existing stock. It was felt that private owners (whether owner–occupiers or private landlords) would have an incentive to maintain their property and would be able to devote more resources to maintenance than the state had been able to do. The ability of owners to pay repair costs had been questioned earlier. It is worth noting here the implicit faith that is placed in the importance of ownership in bringing about personal responsibility for housing. Kintrea and Köhli note in chapter 4 the German belief that private ownership is a prerequisite for personal responsibility, because people bear the consequences of their own actions. A similar belief was highlighted by Mandič in chapter 9, where she outlines the very general view held by all political parties that private ownership will lead to "social and economic efficiency." There are parallels here with the political belief in home ownership in Britain (Saunders, 1990).

One area where benefits are expected from a market system is in the efficiency of state maintenance and management enterprises. In chapter 1, it was stated that these organizations were universally considered to be inefficient and unresponsive. A market system would open the enterprises to competition and force them to look for custom. It is believed that this will force them to become more efficient by adopting more commercially oriented working practices and to provide a better service to their customers. There is some evidence from Hungary that the service provided by privatized management and maintenance companies is rated highly by tenants (Hegedüs, Mark, Struyk, and Tosics, 1994). Therefore, it may be that the envisaged efficiency gains from privatization may be forthcoming. Evidence at present is very slight.

In practice, the privatization of construction and maintenance enterprises has been slow in most countries (the exception here being Hungary). Most often, they have simply been closed down or heavily cut back, and they have not been replaced by significant private sector enterprise. Western-owned private developers have been active in areas such as the north of the Czech Republic, and small private construction companies are being set up in many countries, so some competition is emerging. In general, there has been little thought from governments about the particular impact of the creation of a market-oriented housing system. Instead, the general case for markets as leading to greater efficiency has been applied in housing as in other commodities.

Privatization as a Symbol

The lack of differentiation between housing and other goods and services and the transfer of industrial models of privatization to housing would seem to show that there is little symbolic importance attached to the privatization of housing per se. The primary symbolic importance seems to be attached to the concept of markets. The privatization of housing is seen as one step toward the creation of a market economy and a society based on a new set of norms.

However, housing clearly has an importance beyond this. Kozlowski mentions in chapter 8 the importance attached to the ownership of housing in Poland as a means of "buying social calm" at a time of substantial change and stress. Perhaps not surprisingly, the objective is rarely explicitly stated. Although this does not necessarily mean that it is not important, it does make its importance difficult to estimate. On the one hand, it may be argued that it cannot be very important, as some countries such as Poland and the former Czechoslovakia have acted very slowly. However, this is mainly because privatization proposals for housing have been the source of long-standing political debate and deadlock, with little action resulting. On the other hand, there is clearly a desire by many people in most East European countries to buy their house as a way of ensuring that they can play a role in the new market system. In Budapest, 70 percent of tenants are considering buying their dwelling. The large discounts available mean that most people are able to view the acquisition of a house as an investment, even though in some countries there are controls designed to prevent "profiteering" by stipulating that discounts have to be repaid if dwellings are sold within a particular time period. Of course, it is unclear what the level of house prices will be in the medium term, although current purchase prices are often a long way below the current cost of new construction. Therefore, as an investment, the purchase of a state-owned apartment or house seems to be a reasonably secure investment in most cases, although this is obviously dependent on factors in individual cases such as the size of the discount achieved, the physical condition, the location and type of dwelling, and so on.

Aside from investment issues, it is evident that property ownership has an important meaning as a symbol of a democratic market society. The British idea of a property-owning democracy seems to describe the vision of politicians and many voters in Eastern Europe. This fits well in many countries with the revival of traditional cultural values, as epitomized by the growing political and cultural importance of the Catholic Church. There has been a resurgence in the past few years in traditional "family values," with importance attached to the family unit and the duty of the family to look after its own members. In political terms, this has shown itself in campaigns against abortion. The impact of these cultural values in housing has been to strengthen the move toward private ownership as a means of encouraging families to take responsibility for themselves. It has also led to some moralistic practices in housing. For example, in one town in the north of the Czech Republic, all divorced people were taken off the waiting list for state housing.

Restitution (the return of nationalized property to the original owners) also represents symbolically a return to traditional forms of social organization and a desire to set aside the intervening 40 years and expunge their memory. This is over and above its importance in restoring private ownership and helping to create a private market.

Therefore, the privatization of housing has had a symbolic importance in all of the countries examined here. It has represented a government commitment to a market society and has given tenants an opportunity to acquire a stake in the society through the ownership of their home.

Conclusion: The Aims of Privatization

Privatization of housing has primarily been seen as a way of creating a more efficient housing system that would deal with housing shortages and would lead to higher levels of maintenance. Pragmatically, privatization was also an answer to the state's problem of a shortage of resources. Although little importance seems to have been given to the capital receipts generated by the sale of housing assets, the motive of avoiding future expenditure on maintenance and new construction was very important. In practical terms, if the private sector is not encouraged to build new houses or renew older ones, these activities will not be carried out by the state, because of financial constraints.

At the same time, privatization of housing is congruent with the reemergence of traditional family values and is symbolically important in giving households a stake in the new market society and in buying "social calm." It is also seen by many political parties as a good way of winning votes.

All of these motives are important in the general support for privatization in housing, but they may conflict when individual mechanisms are considered. This explains why legislation on the sale of the state housing was so hotly disputed in Poland and was delayed in its implementation in the former Czechoslovakia. The most controversial factor is the price at which dwellings are sold, because many other factors stem directly from this one. A low selling price (all other things being equal) will result in a higher level of sales, thus demonstrating a symbolic political resolve to create a market society and giving a larger number of people a symbolic stake in that society. It also reduces more quickly state responsibility for maintenance. However, for sales to be high, rents have to be increased to provide an incentive to buy. Large rent increases have been implemented in most countries, but further increases are limited by the need to restrain inflation and to assuage public outcry over falling living standards. Although many countries have discussed them, only the former East Germany had introduced a housing allowance scheme by the end of 1993 which protects the lowest-income families from large rent increases. As a consequence, rents have been increased fivefold since reunification. Although allowance schemes have been discussed in the Czech Republic and Slovakia, they had not been implemented.

Also, low prices also have a depressing effect on the private housing market, reducing the incentive for private builders. As one measure of the efficiency of the housing market over the state-dominated system is held to be its ability to ensure a high rate of new production, this effect is particularly important. Also, Mandič in her chapter mentions the "monetary shock" that a high volume of sales in a short period of time caused in the Slovenian economy.

Restitution also highlights some of the dilemmas over the aims of privatization. It achieves the symbolic importance of achieving private ownership and banishing the old system of state ownership. However, it brings no revenue and can cost the state considerable sums of money in compensation.

The balance of advantage, at least in the short term, is probably in favor of low-price sales, which is why all the countries except the former East Germany have taken this option. However, there are pressures in some countries such as Bulgaria and Hungary for a steadier approach. In Slovenia, low-price sales were restricted at the outset to a two-year period, after which prices can be increased.

FORMS OF PRIVATIZATION

In chapter 1, privatization in Britain was said to have taken three main forms (see Stoker, 1991):

1. the sale of public (local authority) assets;
2. initiatives aimed at introducing "market discipline" into service delivery;
3. encouragement of private sector provision and investment.

All of these elements have been present in East European countries. In particular, the sale and restitution of formerly state-owned housing has been widespread. Market discipline has been introduced through the restructuring of state-owned management and maintenance enterprises, although it is unclear whether this is merely a stepping-stone to a move fully into the private sector. Also, this form of privatization has been less fully developed than the other two. There has been a widespread encouragement of the private sector, primarily through attempts to create market structures such as a legal basis for ownership and a finance system. The precise forms that privatization has taken are now reviewed.

Restitution

The existence of restitution is a unique feature of housing privatization in East European countries compared to experience in the West. The only country where restitution has not been an issue is in Russia, because nationalization took place there much earlier than in most other countries, where it usually occurred in the late 1940s or 1950s. Restitution consists of the return of property taken over by the communist regimes to the previous owners or their successors. Obviously this may not always be possible, as properties may have been demolished or redeveloped in the intervening 50 years. In these instances, compensation is usually payable. In most countries, people have to register claims within a time limit, which has usually been two or three years. However, it is clearly going to take many years for all the claims to be processed and for titles to be settled.

Restitution applies to housing, and so privately owned property built before nationalization can be subject to restitution claims. Usually this involves the older tenemental stock in the center of cities and large towns, which was previously owned by private landlords. Through restitution existing state tenants could find themselves becoming the tenants of a private landlord. Usually existing tenants have some security of occupation, and in some countries such as Slovenia they can still exercise the right to buy their apartment. However, in the Czech Republic there was no control over the rents of new tenancies. This system of decontrol on vacant possession was the same as the one that led to widespread harassment of tenants by landlords in Britain in the 1960s in order to gain vacant possession.

There could also be problems of renovation and maintenance. With rents in most countries still controlled at below-cost levels, landlords will not be able, in the short term at least, to use rental income to carry out renovation and maintenance where this is needed. Therefore, for landlords, their new responsibilities would seem to be unprofitable until rents can be raised, and for tenants there is no guarantee that the service they will receive from their landlord will be improved.

Restitution also influences other aspects of privatization policy. Thus sales of older state housing cannot take place until claims for restitution have been settled. Therefore, restitution has slowed down the implementation of other disposal policies. Also, unlike disposal mechanisms, restitution does not result in a capital receipt for the state.

The extent of restitution in housing is difficult to establish at present in all the countries. It is an uncertain factor that makes it difficult for governments and local authorities to plan rationally for the future, even if they wish to. Until restitution processes are finalized, it will be very difficult to judge what the future housing systems of these countries will look like.

Cooperatives to Condominiums

In some countries, noticeably the former Czechoslovakia, Hungary, Poland, and Russia, a relatively large cooperative sector has been developed. For the state, cooperatives were mainly a way of reducing state expenditure by encouraging households to invest in their own housing by paying to join the cooperative. Because of the higher costs, cooperative apartments were usually less desirable than state-owned apartments, and they were generally inhabited by middle-income groups. The higher-income groups, as part of the political elite, secured a state-owned apartment, whereas lower-income groups could not afford to pay. One face of the privatization program has been the transformation of cooperatives into a form of condominium ownership.

In the former Czechoslovakia, legislation was passed in 1992 to allow occupiers of cooperative apartments to apply for ownership of the apartment and to repay to the cooperative a proportion of the outstanding debt. A household also becomes a joint owner of the common areas of the house, where their stake is in proportion to the floor space of their apartment. The opportunity was open for only six months, and it is unclear how many occupiers took advantage of it.

In Poland, legislation was proposed in 1993 to allow cooperative occupiers to purchase their apartments at a price also based on the outstanding debt, as in Czechoslovakia. The proposed arrangements for management and maintenance were vague and were criticized by Kozlowski in chapter 7.

Cooperatives are an obvious candidate for privatization, as households have already contributed toward their housing and the sums of money needed to "complete" the purchase can be small for households who have been members for some time and will already have paid off a high proportion of debt.

Sale of State Housing Stock

In all of the countries covered in this book, there have been programs designed to sell state housing. Sales may be to existing tenants or to other private individuals or companies. The extent of the latter has not been extensive, for a number of reasons. First, the majority (although not all) of sales to other than the occupier have been of vacant property that is in poor condition. The incidence of this kind of property varies considerably between different areas and countries. Vacant property has been the most straightforward to sell and has usually been auctioned off. Already in some towns the impact of these sales is evident as some new

178 • Housing Privatization in Eastern Europe

owners carry out renovation work. However, as outlined earlier, some of the housing stock has been converted into offices and retail premises and been lost for housing purposes (Kovacs, 1994).

The sale of tenanted property to people other than the occupiers is clearly fraught with problems. In countries such as Slovenia, tenants can still exercise their right-to-buy at a discount that could damage private landlords. Also, in most countries rents are still set at below market levels, and so there is little incentive to set up in business as a private landlord, at least in the short term. For these reasons, the sale of housing to people other than the owners has distinct limitations and is unlikely to be a major constituent of the privatization program unless rent controls are removed.

The most potential for sales is undoubtedly to existing occupiers, and this issue has caused considerable political debate in most of the countries, as outlined earlier, mainly on the question of price. The low-price strategy adopted by most countries has been justified on the basis of an analogy of a car needing a push start so that it can spring into life itself.

In Hungary, initial sales have been extensive, reflecting the low prices charged. There has been some political controversy over the continuation of the policy, but it has proved to be politically difficult to turn off the tap, as those who have not taken advantage of the option to purchase for one reason or another do not want to have that option removed. The social justice argument used is that the advantages that have been given to some should be available to all. In both Hungary and Russia, the sale of property to the occupiers first took place before political democracy was established. Sales at this time mostly took place to influential people in the communist regimes—the *nomenclatura*, as they have been called. There is widespread pressure for others to enjoy the same opportunities. The force of this argument is strengthened by the evidence from Hungary, which shows that it is the more affluent families, those who profited most from the old political regime, who are more likely to have taken advantage of the opportunity. Therefore, to prolong the analogy—the car that has been push-started can soon be careering along at top speed, with no one able to stop it.

As outlined earlier, the disadvantages of the low-price/quick-sell approach are the lack of any appreciable receipts and the quick loss of rental stock. The main advantage is the fast spread of ownership and the political, social, and economic benefits, which, it is believed by many politicians and voters, it will bring. Also, the state can quickly absolve itself from responsibility for the stock.

The alternative option is to set prices relatively high, with the result that sales will be slower. This is the approach being taken in the new *Länder* of Germany and is being considered in Poland. The higher price does not necessarily mean that income to the state will be greater than under the low-price option because the level of sales may be much less in the short run and possibly also in the long run, with many households not being able to afford to purchase. Nevertheless, it could be argued that the high price conserves rented housing and makes more effective use of the housing stock. However, this is subject to substantial argument and debate. There are also redistributive issues involved, as the British experience would indicate that the households most likely to take up the option to purchase are more affluent households who are relatively well advantaged in the housing system. There is some evidence to support this proposition in Hungary (Hegedüs and Tosics, 1994). In the case of Moscow, Daniell and Struyk (1994) have argued that households face conflicting economic pressures, with the value of the house being counterbalanced by the responsibilities for maintenance. As a consequence, the incentive for residents to buy is greater where the value of the property is greater and repair costs are lower. There is little empirical evidence to judge experience in other East European countries, but it seems probable that a low-price policy effectively means large subsidies being given to relatively afflu-ent households. In response, it can be argued that the low-price approach extends subsidy to lower-income groups, who would not be able to buy under the high price option. Also, under the high-price option, owners will have less money to carry out renovation and meet continuing repair commitments.

The debates over which option to pursue have been long and bitter in many countries, with some such as Poland still needing to resolve the issue in 1993. Russia, the Czech Republic, and Hungary have either not adopted a national policy or have left considerable leeway for local authorities to decide sale prices and, therefore, the pace of privatization. The freedom has led to substantial varia-tions in practice. Thus, in Russia as a whole, there have been only a small number of sales, but in Moscow 45 percent of the municipal stock has been sold.

Slovenia and Bulgaria have both adopted a national low-price privatization program resulting in very high levels of sales across the country. However, in Slovenia this policy has initially been limited to three years.

The former East Germany is the only country considered here to have adopted a high-price sales strategy. It has been able to do this because of the investment from the Federal German government, which has allowed maintenance of exist-ing stock to be increased and has reduced the need for short-term receipts. The sale of stock has been undertaken on a planned and long-term basis without the short-term rush in sales brought about by low prices. Sales amounted to 20,000 units in 1992 out of a stock of 2.8 million, despite a fivefold increase in rents since reunification.

Construction and Maintenance Enterprises

Privatization and construction of maintenance enterprises has been undertaken or is planned to be undertaken in all of the countries examined here. However, this form of privatization has not been regarded primarily as a housing measure. Rather, it has been considered as one part of the privatization of industry. As a consequence, the form that privatization has taken in different countries has largely been influenced by the general approach to other industries. An example of this is in Slovenia, where the privatization of the construction enterprises was awaiting the result of a long-standing political debate over the best way of priva-

tizing the self-management enterprise system, which was the usual pattern in the
former Yugoslavia. The options considered in Slovenia are instructive. On the
one hand, it has been suggested that there should be gradual privatization, with
the existing employees and managers being the major shareholders. An alternative view gives the major role to investment funds supported by the government
and pushes for much faster privatization. As Mandič reports in chapter 9, a compromise between these two positions was being worked out in 1993. A third
option of sale to Western interests does not seem to have been considered in this
sphere, although it has been implemented in other sectors. Similarly, in the
former Czechoslovakia, two forms of privatization have taken place: the outright
privatization of enterprises and coupon privatization, where citizens are given
vouchers that can be exchanged for shares in privatized enterprises.

In practice, even in countries such as Russia, where there has been only slow
reform, existing construction enterprises have had to restructure themselves
and shed labor as their traditional function has changed. New construction by
the state decreased considerably in all countries. There is now very little state-
financed and -controlled construction, and local authorities have become the
major players, although they do not have the resources for much new construction work. Building for the private sector involves very different ways of working and organizational structures from those traditionally employed. Also, new
production has been hindered by delays in implementing a financial and legal
structure for home ownership, which will be considered later.

In addition, the new structure of housing provision has resulted in competition
arising for the state enterprises from new directions. For example, the growth in
renovation of individual properties caused by sales of formerly state-owned
property has led to an increase in the number of small building contractors who
are also well placed to compete with the old state enterprises for housing repair
work if the volume of this kind of work increases, as it needs to do. The new
companies, usually set up by one or two craftsmen, have the advantages of small
scale and a local base. They are also helped by the return to traditional construction techniques, which require traditional craft skills, whereas the former state
enterprises had concentrated on prefabricated construction.

Competition has also arisen to some degree in the new activity of construction
for home ownership. In some areas, such as the north of the Czech Republic,
foreign companies (in this area mostly German) have developed new housing
schemes, building traditional villas. However, such developments are not common in all areas, and the prices are high relative to the discounted sales in the
public sector and when compared to average earnings. Therefore, although important, foreign private developments are likely to play only a minor role in the
near future.

It is a matter of conjecture whether the privatized state enterprises can meet the
new competition and survive. One likely scenario is that they will concentrate on
industrial and commercial development and will leave the housing sector to

smaller companies. The management and maintenance enterprises have also been under competition. For example, in the former Czechoslovakia they have been forced to restructure and to reduce in scale, both by decentralizing their operations and by reducing their overall staff numbers. These changes have occurred both as a prelude to and as a result of privatization, with the majority of enterprises being privatized by early 1993. In Hungary, there was a substantial reduction in demand for housing built by the large construction companies, and many were privatized and split into smaller private companies. The number of small companies increased from 74 in 1985 to 4,575 by 1992.

The future of maintenance and management companies depends on many factors, including the future size of the rental sector—both public and private—and the arrangements for maintenance and management of private sector dwellings, particularly those in multiapartment buildings. These are issues to which we shall return.

Finance and Exchange Systems

Although all East European countries retained a private sector throughout the postwar years, it was very different from the private sector in Western Europe. For example, occupiers generally held a "right-to-reside" in a dwelling rather than ownership, which was formally vested in the state. In general, although it was possible to buy and sell a house, transactions were controlled by the state, which could set the price and could determine who the buyer would be. Of course, controls were not always effective, and informal transactions took place on a large scale in countries such as Hungary. An important aspect of privatization has been the need to clarify the right of ownership and to create a framework for the private system to operate as a market.

The creation of a legal framework that allows for ownership is unproblematic for single-dwelling buildings, but is more complex for multidwelling buildings such as tenement blocks, or multistory apartment houses. In the West, all countries have developed over the centuries their own systems for apportioning rights and responsibilities between the different interests involved. For example, in the United States there is the condominium form, which has been influential in other countries.

East European countries have been faced with the task of creating a workable system in a short period of time, and not all had completed the task by 1993. There are a large number of legal issues involved, but for our present purpose the key issue is responsibility for repair. If the housing stock is to be renovated and kept in good repair, there needs to be a mechanism for the upkeep of the structure and communal parts of multidwelling properties.

The former East Germany had the advantage over other countries of being able to incorporate West German law, which included an extensive body of condominium law, as a whole.

Kozlowski outlines in chapter 8 how existing Polish law did not define precisely the rights and obligations of owners. In early 1993, a law was proposed to clarify ownership by establishing a condominium form of organization to be responsible for the maintenance and management of the building as a whole. The discharge of its responsibilities may be undertaken by the individual owners themselves or by another agency, such as a management and maintenance company.

In the new *Länder* of Germany and in Slovenia, a revised ownership framework has been complemented by clearer duties of repair by owners. The result is hoped to be an arrest of the physical decline of multidwelling buildings and a greater demand for maintenance.

The other major issue is the creation of a financial system that allows households access to credit for house purchase. In Slovenia, a national housing bank has been created, with the granting of loans for purchase as one of its primary functions. Funds for the bank have been created from the sale of state properties. However, existing state loans for home ownership have been curtailed, the housing bank has not yet made a major impact, and the private sector has not yet moved to fill the finance gap. Loans from private banks are expensive, and there are no financial institutions such as British building societies specializing in lending for home ownership.

In Slovakia, Michalovic notes that the first savings and loan institution was started in November 1992. This was the first institution to implement a system of personal savings, leading to preferential loans for house purchase. The state also makes a contribution.

In all countries, it appears that loans for house purchase have not been easily available. The sale of state housing is paid for from savings or by installments. The practice of house purchase by using long-term loans is not a usual one in any of the countries.

As a result of increasing private transactions, private sales agents, which did not exist before, have emerged to make transactions easier. For example, in Moscow a diverse and relatively rudimentary real estate brokerage service has emerged (Khaddari and Pusanov, 1993), although such a system has not evolved in St. Petersburg (Boyce, 1993).

THE IMPACT OF PRIVATIZATION

One of the aims of the book has been to assess the impact of privatization measures. However, this is not an easy task, as many of the changes are very recent and their full impact has yet to be made. Also, there is a lack of detailed empirical research on the East European countries, which would provide information on which an evaluation could be based. Therefore, at this stage it is only possible to make an assessment of the short-term impact of privatization and to offer some thoughts on what the possible long-term effect will be.

Transition Period

In the short term, most East European countries are facing a very difficult transition into market economies. In countries such as Poland and Russia, the transition period seems to have compounded existing economic problems rather than mitigating them, creating political and social problems. In Poland, the large number of political parties represented in Parliament is making decisive political action difficult. In Russia, political pressure and growing social dissatisfaction has forced a slow-down in the pace of market reforms.

In the former East Germany, integration has brought the closure of many of the state-owned industries and substantial unemployment. The countries with the stronger economies, such as Hungary and the Czech Republic, have suffered less in the short term, but even here living standards have not risen for the majority of people and have fallen for many.

Undoubtedly, public expectations of a market economy and democracy were very high at the outset of reform, but subsequent problems have led to examples of social unrest. The rise of fascism in the former East Germany and the growth of racism in the Czech Republic are examples of social tensions. Uncertainty and insecurity has led in some countries to a political reaction to slow down the pace of reform and to keep some of the key socialist mechanisms of social security. Therefore, reformed Communist parties have been elected into power in a number of countries. In all countries, the extent of criminal behavior has increased. All of these pressures have had an impact on the housing sphere.

Economic problems have resulted in the move toward market rents in most countries taking many years. After massive rent rises in the first year or two, increases have been moderated or even stopped completely in the fight against inflation and the need to retain political support. Nevertheless, for most households, housing costs have increased considerably at a time of constant, if not falling, incomes.

Problems in industry as a whole have been mirrored by difficulties faced by the construction industry. The result is a collapse of new construction in all countries, despite the acute shortages that exist. In the short term, the demise of the old state system of production has not been accompanied by an equivalent level of activity from the new market system. Clearly, the sale of existing state housing has diverted demand from new construction in the short term. Where sales have been rapid, such as in Slovenia, the large discounts available have had the effect of lowering market prices in the private sector, which reduces the incentive for new development.

The sales of state housing to the private sector have resulted in some renovation activity in the short term. No statistics are available to establish the extent of this activity, but it is evident in many towns as vacant dwellings in a poor condition are being renovated. Nevertheless, the degree of activity seems to vary considerably between different countries and different areas and is most evident in older villas built before the socialist regime. Sales of newer system-built apartments have been slower, and investment in them has been lacking. Funds generated from sales have not been large enough to allow much-needed investment in the remaining stock. Two important steps have been taken in most countries, which should help the stock condition problem in the medium term. One is the restructuring and privatization of management and maintenance enterprises. The second is the clarification of legal rights and responsibilities in relation to repair of the private sector stock.

In the short term, then, there has been little improvement in the condition of the housing stock or alleviation of severe housing shortages. The exception to this general picture is in the former East Germany, where legal obligations to keep housing in good repair have been introduced and public grants have been made available for the renovation of existing property.

Perhaps the major impact of privatization measures in the short term has been rapid tenure change in most countries because of restitution and, in particular, the sale of public dwellings to the tenants through the right to buy. Whether rapid tenure change is desirable or not in the longer term is discussed later. However, the transfer of public sector stock into private ownership is the most immediate impact of privatization.

A degree of progress has been made in creating the legal and institutional framework for a private market, but some countries have yet to implement a legal framework for the joint management and maintenance of multidwelling buildings, and finance mechanisms have also been slow to develop.

From the consumer's point of view, the transition period has offered only one advantage, which is the opportunity to buy their public sector dwelling at a cheap price. Along with the ownership of their dwelling, households have also taken responsibility for the physical upkeep of the house. The implications of this will vary considerably between families, but in general households seem to have got a bargain.

However, not all households have been able to buy their house or apartment, and those left in the public sector have faced substantially increased rents, with little, if any, improvement in the repair service they receive. Overcrowding is still common, with little prospect of new state building to ease the situation.

The Longer-Term Impacts

In chapter 1, a number of areas were highlighted that could form the focus of an evaluation of the privatization experience. Some of these factors, which related to the objectives of privatization, were considered earlier. The aim here is to focus on the longer-term changes in the housing system which could occur and their impact on housing consumers. Clearly, any rigorous evaluation cannot yet take place, as the reforms are in their infancy and there is, as yet, little information on which to base an evaluation. What follows, therefore, is intended as an outline of factors to explore in the future and some conjecture on what may happen. The discussion is divided into four sections: (1) the tenure structure, (2) the public rented sector, (3) maintenance and stock condition, and (4) social equality. Each of these are now explored in turn.

Tenure Structure. As outlined earlier, governments in the East European countries have not had a clear idea of a future ideal tenure structure but have, instead, sought to privatize the public rented stock. Even Bulgaria, which has a much lower proportion of public rented stock (9%) than is common in West European countries (although higher than in the United States), has sought to privatize. The exception to the generalization is Slovenia, where the government has laid out its anticipated tenure structure in the year 2000. In this projection, owner-occupation is expected to rise to 75 percent of the stock (from 67%), municipal rental to remain steady at 4 percent, and nonprofit rental to increase to 15 percent (no such sector exists at present). The projection foresees only a marginal increase in owner-occupation, but a change in enterprise rental housing to private landlords (5%) and nonprofit rental.

Other countries have not been as explicit in their future projections, but most do not appear to envisage such a marginal increase in owner-occupation. As outlined earlier, sales of public rented stock have been extensive in all countries (except East Germany), resulting in significant reductions of public sectors over a short period of time. The result could be rental sectors of between 10 and 15 percent of the total stock in a few years' time and owner-occupation rates at around 80 percent.

Clearly, this is conjecture, as it is unclear whether current low price sales programs will be maintained (or implemented on a widespread basis in Poland or Russia). Also, it is unclear what the long-term demand for owner-occupation will be, as it will be influenced by economic factors such as the level of unemployment, the rate of inflation, and general living standards. The experience in Britain was that a high level of initial sales decreased after the first few years, but sales continued at a steady rate as households moved into the position in the life cycle (at the earning peak in the 40s) when they were able to buy. Therefore, it seems likely that sales will continue, albeit at a reduced rate, even if sales prices are increased. The trend toward a larger owner-occupied sector and a smaller public rented sector is a major achievement of the privatization policy. However, the rapid tenure change raises two important long-term issues—namely, the future of the public rented sector and the ongoing maintenance of private stock.

The Public Sector. There are no plans in any of the countries at present to build any more public rented housing or to promote a "social rented sector" along Western lines. In all countries, it is envisaged that the sector will shrink in size and will be largely restricted to marginal households who are not able to buy. There is a clear danger that the public rented sector could deteriorate into a residualized tenure, with deteriorating physical conditions and increasing stigma, such as exists in the United States, and which, many argue, is currently emerging in Britain.

The chances of this happening seem to be very real. The public rented stock is already generally in poor condition and, from evidence in Hungary and Moscow, it is the better stock that is being sold, with the stock in worst condition remaining. At present it is difficult to see where funds for the renovation of the stock will come from. Proceeds from sales will be relatively small because of the low-price policies, and they may be spent on other things such as basic infrastructure (roads, public transport, and so on) or on industrial development. Rents will almost certainly continue to rise to a level that will cover a realistic level of management and ongoing repair costs. Renovation costs could then be funded from borrowing, with repayments and interest being charged to rents over a long period (say, 30 years). However, without the introduction of a housing allowance scheme to provide financial help, the substantial increases in rents necessary would be out of reach of the poorest of the population who will be concentrated in the sector. In Britain, one-third of tenants have all of their rent paid from an allowance scheme, and a further third receive some help with their rent.

The importance of finding the money is emphasized by the key role that housing plays in reinforcing economic disadvantage (Clapham, Kemp, and Smith, 1990). The danger is of creating an underclass of people cut off from the mainstream of society and alienated from it.

The creation of a larger owner-occupied sector in East European countries through low-price sales inevitably means that many owners will have low incomes. A key question for the future is whether low-income owners will be willing or able to keep their houses in good repair. One of the main beliefs behind the reforms is that owners will look after their own housing better than the state. But even assuming that ownership gives households a greater incentive to improve their housing and keep it in good repair, they need financial resources to do this. In Western countries, much state financial help is given to owner–occupiers living in poor housing conditions. Institutional structures, such as community-based housing associations in Scotland, have been created to deal with the particularly acute renovation problems of multidwelling buildings.

It seems inevitable that the changing tenure structure will not obviate the need for state expenditure on housing repair in the longer term. Privatization may encourage households to use their own resources on their housing in contrast to the previous state-dominated system, but it seems unlikely that this will be enough by itself to deal with stock condition problems.

Social Equality. The low-price sales policy has had the effect of making home ownership possible for relatively low-income households. However, it must be remembered that many tenants of local authorities and enterprises were relatively well off. In contrast to the position in most Western countries, public rented apartments were considered to be a desirable commodity and were allocated to the elite in the society, such as party members and skilled workers. In general, the favored groups lived in the most popular housing, which after privatization has the highest market value. A consequence of low-price sales is that the higher-income groups receive a relatively large one-off subsidy, which could amount to 70 percent of the market value of the house. It is estimated that in Budapest, upper-income groups have received 40 percent of the total of this windfall subsidy, while lower-income groups have received 17 percent (Hegedüs, Mark, Struyk, and Tosics, 1993).

In the past, high-income groups have received subsidy, as rents have been well below market levels. Therefore, it can be argued that the windfall subsidy is merely continuing the previous unequal system. Nevertheless, it is possible to conceive of an alternative system of market price privatization and market rents in the remaining sector, with poorer households protected by a targeted housing allowance. In this scenario, subsidy would be closely targeted on low-income households rather than on higher-income households, as at present.

It may be argued that privatization has strengthened the right of ownership, and this has improved the assets held by existing private sector households. Although sales were usually possible in the past, they were restricted. The new reforms have meant that relatively low-income households who have pre-dominated in the private sector have been given control over a more marketable asset.

At present it is impossible to quantify the impact of privatization on social inequalities, but clearly the impact could potentially be large and could be re-flected in spatial differences. There is an increasing interest in the urban impact of the privatization of economic and housing systems. It is argued that there has been a substantial change in the inner city, with commercial development and luxury housing displacing many poorer residents (Pichler-Milanovitch, 1994). Restitution has brought private ownership to many inner-city areas. Sykora (1994) shows that 70 to 75 percent of the stock in the central city districts of Prague has been restituted, thus reducing substantially the availability of public rented housing in these neighborhoods.

EAST EUROPEAN HOUSING SYSTEMS

In chapter 2, Hegedüs and Tosics described what they characterized as an East European housing model. This has been further refined by Clapham (1995). The basic idea is that there was a set of common processes at work in these societies, linked to their social, economic, and political structure—namely, state ownership and distribution; centrally planned production; provision free at the point of use; and exclusion of market mechanisms. However, it was argued that these pro-cesses represented an ideal that was never fully implemented because of a short-age of finance for investment and the financial and political costs of controlling private transactions. Both the extent of attachment to the ideals and the force of the constraints varied considerably over time and between different countries. Therefore, housing systems were quite different in their institutions and their tenure structures. However, it is argued that despite these superficial differences, the common fundamentals of the housing systems are similar enough for the concept of an East European housing model to be a meaningful and useful analytical tool.

Furthermore, the chapters in this book have shown that there are similarities in the actions that different countries have taken during the transitional period. The common set of problems encountered and the similar mechanisms used to privatize the system mean that it is also meaningful to use the concept of a transitional housing system. Again, this does not imply that there are no important variations between countries. The preceding chapters show clearly that, for example, the speed of privatization in Poland or Russia is very different from that in Hungary.

The question to be addressed here is what the housing systems will look like in the medium term. Will the similarities still make the use of a typology of an East European housing system useful? The answer to this question is clearly negative. Although the legacy of the socialist system will remain for a long time, all East European countries have rejected the old structures and institutions and have attempted to rebuild almost completely their housing systems as part of a radical reconstruction of the economic, social, and political structures of the society. Therefore, it is unlikely that the legacy of housing institutions will be significant or prolonged enough to differentiate the housing systems from those in other countries. This is partly because many East European countries have explicitly looked to the West for advice and for structures that are appropriate for market systems. For example, the legal structure of ownership in multidwelling buildings adopted in most countries leans heavily on U.S. condominium law.

For these reasons it is unlikely that, after a period of transition, there will be a unique East European model. This seems to lead to the conclusion that there is a convergence of the fundamental imperatives of housing systems in Europe, though this does not mean that the differences between East European systems in, for example, tenure structures will disappear or that they will resemble existing West European systems in all respects. On the contrary, the challenges of the transition process will undoubtedly lead to substantially different policies and institutions developed through state action—a process that will be given impetus by the different political choices made by electorates in the new democratic systems. A number of countries have recently elected reformed Communist parties into power in what may be seen as a reaction to the insecurities of the transition process.

Therefore, the housing system in each of the East European countries will be unique in many respects, but they are sure to be market-driven systems that are fundamentally different from the East European model outlined earlier.

REFERENCES

Boyce, N. 1993. Russia on the way to a housing market: A case study of St. Petersburg. *Environment and Planning A* 25 (7), 975–986.

Clapham, D. (1995). Privatisation and the East European Housing Model. *Urban Studies* 32 (415), 679–694.

Clapham, D., Kemp, P., and Smith, S. J. 1990. *Housing and Social Policy.* Basingstoke: Macmillan.

Daniell, J., and Struyk, R. 1994. Housing privatization in Moscow: Who privatizes and why? *International Journal of Urban and Regional Research* 18 (3), 510–525.

Hegedüs, J., Mark, K., Struyk, R., and Tosics, I. 1993. Local options for the transformation of the public rental sector: Empirical results from two cities in Hungary. *Cities* 10 (3), 257–271.

Hegedüs, J., Mark, K., Struyk, R., and Tosics, I. 1994. Tenant satisfaction with public housing management: Budapest in transition. *Housing Studies* 9 (3), 315–328.

Hegedüs, J., and Tosics, I. 1994. Privatisation and rehabilitation in the Budapest Inner Districts. *Housing Studies* 9 (1), 39–54.

Khaddari, J., and Pusanov, A. 1993. Beginnings of real estate brokerage in Moscow. *Housing Policy Debate* 4 (4), 627–645.

Kovacs, Z. (1994). A city at the crossroads: Social and economic transformation in Budapest. *Urban Studies* 31, 1081–1096.

Pichler-Milanovitch, N. 1994. The role of housing policy in the transformation process of Central–East European cities. *Urban Studies* 31 (7), 1097–1116.

Saunders, P. 1990. *A Nation of Home Owners.* London: Unwin Hyman.

Stoker, G. 1991. *The Politics of Local Government.* Basingstoke: Macmillan.

Sykora, L. 1994. Local urban restructuring as a mirror of globalisation processes: Prague in the 1990s. *Urban Studies* 31 (7), 1149–1166.

Selected Bibliography

East European Housing in General

Sillence (1990) provides a picture of East European housing on the eve of the political and economic changes that overturned the communist era, while the Turner, Hegedüs, and Tosics (1992) volume captures some of the early thinking about housing reform.

J. A. A. Sillence (ed.), *Housing Policies in Eastern Europe and the Soviet Union.* London and New York: Routledge, 1990.

Bengt Turner, József Hegedüs, and Iván Tosics (eds.), *The Reform of Housing in Eastern Europe and the Soviet Union.* London and New York: Routledge, 1992.

A large volume of material on housing reform has been produced by Western institutions with a strong free-market perspective:

B. Renaud, "Housing reform in socialist economies." *Discussion Paper 125.* Washington, DC: The World Bank, 1991.

J. Telgarsky and R. Struyk, "Toward a market–oriented housing sector in Eastern Europe." *Urban Institute Report 90–10.* Washington, DC: The Urban Institute, 1990.

Cities 10 (1993), Part 3, is a special issue devoted to housing in Eastern Europe.

Housing Privatization

R. Forrest and A. Murie, *Selling the Welfare State.* London and New York: Routledge, 1988.

D. Clapham, "Privatisation and the East European Model." *Urban Studies* 32 (1995), Nos 4/5, 679–694.

The East European Model

I. Szelényi, *Urban Inequalities under State Socialism.* Oxford: Oxford University Press, 1983.

Germany

O. Dienemann, "Housing problems in the former German Democratic Republic and the 'New German States'" In G. Hallett (ed.), *The New Housing Shortage.* London and New York: Routledge, 1993.

P. Marcuse and W. Schumann, "Housing in the colours of the GDR." In B. Turner, J. Hegedüs, and I. Tosics (eds.), *The Reform of Housing in Eastern Europe and the Soviet Union.* London and New York: Routledge, 1992.

Hungary

J. Hegedüs, K. Mark, R. Struyk, and I. Tosics, "Local options for the transformation of the public rental sector: Empirical results from two cities in Hungary." *Cities* 10 (1993), No. 3, 257–271.

The Russian Federation

R. Struyk and J. Telgarsky, *The Puzzle of Housing Privatization in Eastern Europe.* Washington, DC: The Urban Institute, 1991.

N. Boyce, "Russia on the way to housing market: A case study of St Petersburg." *Environment and Planning A* 25 (1993), No. 7, 975–986.

Bulgaria

M. Hoffman, M. Koleva, M. Ravicz, and M. Mikelsons, "The Bulgarian housing sector. An assessment." *Bulgaria Paper No. 1C.* Washington, DC: The Urban Institute, 1992.

Poland

E. Kozlowski, "The housing system in Poland: Changes and directions." In B. Turner, J. Hegedüs, and I. Tosics (eds.), *The Reform of Housing in Eastern Europe and the Soviet Union.* London and New York: Routledge, 1992.

Czechoslovakia (now the Czech and Slovak Republics)

J. Musil, "Recent changes in the housing system and policy in Czechoslovakia." In B. Turner, J. Hegedüs, and I. Tosics (eds.), *The Reform of Housing in Eastern Europe and the Soviet Union.* London and New York: Routledge, 1992.

J. Musil, "The Czech housing system in the middle of transition." *Urban Studies* 32 (1995), No. 10, 1679–1684.

Slovenia

S. Mandič and D. Clapham, "The meaning of home ownership in the transition from socialism." *Urban Studies* 33 (1996), No. 1, 83–97.
S. Mandič and T. Rop, "New housing challenges in Slovenia." *Cities* 10 (1993), No. 3, 237–245.

Index

Act of Denationalization (1991), Slovenia, 153, 154
Act of Economic Enterprises (1992), Hungary, 68
Act on Local Governments, Hungary 58
Afanasiev, Y., 79
Albania, xi, 15
Alliance for the Democratic Left, Poland, 126, 133
Alliance of Free Democrats, Hungary, 58
Alliance of Young Democrats, Hungary, 58
Allocation: housing, 21, 28, 38, 108, 114, 129, 131, 141 (in Bulgaria, 97, 100, 103, 105–106; in Eastern bloc, 17, 21; market, 38; nonmarket, 19; political control of, 18, 29, 38; in Slovenia, 154, 155, 158; in socialist housing model, 34; state, 21); of living space, in Russian Federation, 86; of state grants, 18, 36; of subsidies, in Eastern bloc, 18
Allowance, housing, 175, 186, 187; in Czechoslovakia, 148; in Germany, 41, 42, 47, 53; in Hungary, 63, 64, 65; in Slovenia, 155
Amendments to the Constitution of the Republic of Slovenia (1989), 151
"Anglo-Saxon" housing model, 9

Associations, housing, 138; commercial orientation of, 5; community-based, in Scotland, 186; funding of, 5; rent setting by, 5
Australia, "Anglo-Saxon" housing model in, 9

Baar, T., 67
Bajt, A., 163
Ball, M., 24, 27
Basic Organization of Associated Labor, Slovenia, 154
Bater, J., 20
Bauer, T., 16, 21
Berezin, M., 79–95
Berlin, housing conditions in, 44
Bessonova, O., 23
Bidding for Public Construction Work Act, Hungary, 68
Bohemia, 139
Boldyrev, Y., 79
Boyce, N., 182
Bratislava, 141, 144
Britain, xi, 5, 12, 172, 176, 185, 186; "Anglo-Saxon" housing model, 9; council housing in, sale of, 3; GDP of, 41; housing finance in, 2;

Britain (*continued*), National Health
Service, 6; privatization in, forms of,
175; privatization of housing in, 1, 2, 4,
6–7, 13 (aims of, 7, 9; for labor mobility,
10); provision of social rented housing
in, 8; reduction of public expenditure as
aim of privatization in, 7; Right to Buy
policy, 63; tax relief on mortgage interest
payments in, 3
Bucholz, H., 43, 44, 45
Buckley, R., 62
Budapest, 38, 59, 61, 62, 65, 66, 67, 70, 72,
73, 173, 187; housing authority for, 58,
63; political change in, 58; Public Rental
Sector (BRPS), 59, 62, 71–75
Budget Act (1992), Poland, 125
Bulgaria, xiii, 28, 34, 97–116, 170, 171, 175,
179, 185; housing (allocation, 105–106;
construction, 32, 33, 113; cooperative,
27; costs and subsidies, 103–105; finance
in, 108–109; and land prices in, 110;
management and maintenance, 105;
market, 109–110; provision, 99–100,
100–102; stock in, 99–100; tenure in,
103); impact of privatization: (on
housing demand, 114–115; on housing
supply, 113–115); National Agency of
Privatization, Bulgaria, 107; political
reform in, 98–99; prefabricated
construction in, 33; price of public
housing in, 111; price reform in, 108;
privatization measures in, 107–113 (of
public housing, 111–112); property rights
in, 25, 102–103; reaction to economic
crisis, 31; reform in, 98–99 (of socialist
housing model, 34); restitution of prewar
property in, 112–113; restructuring of
state enterprises in, 107; tenure structure
in, 102–103
Bulgarian Socialist Party, 106
Bunchak, J., 23, 30, 39

Canada, "Anglo-Saxon" housing model of, 9
Capital City Act (1992), Hungary, 58
Carter, F., 101
Cegielski, J., 26
Centralization: in Eastern Europe, 29–30; of
investment decisions, in Eastern bloc, 17;
of housing, in Russian Federation, 85;
policy, 30

Centrally planned economy, 16, 100; of
Eastern Bloc, 16; failure of, and socialist
housing model, 35; in GDR, transition to
market economy, 54
Christian Democracy and Labor Solidarity
Party, Poland, 126
Christian Democratic Party (CDU),
Germany, 41, 42
Christian Democratic Party, Hungary, 58
Christian Democratic Party, Slovenia, 153
Christian–National Union, Poland, 126
Citizens' Association Centrum, Poland, 126
Clapham, D., 1–13, 169–189, 186, 187
Communist Party, xii, xiii, 28, 42, 98, 152,
176, 178, 183, 188; abolition of role of,
80; Czechoslovakian, housing
construction under, 26; economic system
under, 16, 18
Competitive tendering, for public services,
4, 5
Complex Housing Construction System,
Czechoslovakia, 146
Condominium law, 182; in Germany, 48, 50,
51; in Poland, 133; in United States, 188
Confederacy of Sovereign Poland, 126
Conservative Christian Democratic
Coalition, Hungary, 58
Conservative–Liberal Party, Poland, 126
Construction, housing: in Bulgaria, 99, 109;
cooperatives, 33, 84, 88 (in
Czechoslovakia, 28; in Russian
Federation, 87); in Czechoslovakia, 146,
149; decentralization of, Hungary,
68–70; in German Democratic Republic
(GDR), 43–45; in Hungary; individual,
21–22, 22 (administrative control of, 22;
in GDR, 44; suppression of, 30);
minimum space standards for, 25; in
Poland, 120, 122, 123, 124, 126, 132;
and political pressure, 18, 26; and
population mobility, 25; prefabricated
panel, 29, 32, 33, 44, 68, 94, 100, 107,
125, 156, 180; public and private,
characteristics of, 4; regulation of, 17,
26; in Russian Federation, 81, 82, 83, 85,
86, 87, 88, 91, 93; in Slovenia, 156, 164,
165; social, in FRG, 42; speculative
building, 21; state, 30, 32, 33 (monopoly
in, 17; subsidized, 25, 32)

Cooperatives, housing 3, 26, 27, 28, 32, 33, 177; allocation of under state control, 28; in Bulgaria, 101, 102, 103, 104, 115; in Czechoslovakia, 138, 140, 142, 145, 146, 148; in GDR, 43, 45, 48, 53; in Hungary, 67; in Poland, 121, 122, 123, 128, 133; revival of, 27; in Russian Federation, 84, 87, 88; in Slovenia, 156; types of, 28

Cotenancies, 25

Council house sales, in Britain, 7

Czechoslovakia, xiii, 24, 28, 29, 135–149, 173–183; changes in housing management, 143–144; changes in housing sector in, 141–143; cooperative housing in, 28; dwellings completed by KBV system in, 146; housing construction in, 26, 32, 33; housing privatization in, 141–145; housing situation in, 26, 137–141; housing stock in, 139, 143; outlook for housing sector in, 146–148; political reform in, 135–137; prefabricated construction in, 33; Principles of Housing Policy Reform, 141; privatization of apartments in, 144–145; property rights in, 25; reaction to economic crisis, 31; real estate market in, 144; reform of socialist housing model in, 34; regulated housing market in, 21; separation of, 135

Daniell, J., 179

Dawson, A., 19

Decentralization, 23, 26, 98, 107, 116; and economic crisis, 31–35; of housing construction, in Hungary, 68–70

Democratic Renewal Party, Slovenia, 152

Denationalization, in Slovenia, 153, 161, 164

Dienemann, O., 43, 44, 46, 49

Dimitrov, D., 97–116, 110, 111, 112, 113

Eastern Bloc, xi, 135; disintegration of, 15; housing model of, 15

East European housing model, xii, 169, 187, 188; collapse of, 57; development of, 15–38; failure of, 15–38; outlook for, 187–189; social effects of, 35–37; structural tensions of, 16–19; theory of, 16–17

East European Working Group of the European Network, xi

East Germany; see Germany: German Democratic Republic (GDR)

Economic and Social Research Council, Britain, xi

Economic crisis, Eastern Europe, 31–35

Economic model, communist, 16, 26

Economic restructuring, 10

Economy: centrally planned, 16, 100; in Hungary, 31, 58–59; institutional system of, 26

Ekaterinburg, 90, 94

"European" housing model, 9

"Exit" option, for achieving housing goals, 20, 21–22, 37

Faltan, L., 22

Federal Republic of Germany; see Germany

Feedback, economic and political, 17–18

Fehér, H., 16

Finance, housing, 182, 184, 187; in Britain, 3; in Bulgaria, 97, 100, 102, 104, 107, 108, 109, 114, 115, 116; in Czechoslovakia, 138, 140, 146, 147, 149; Eastern Europe, 27, 28, 176, 181–182; in Germany, xii, 45; in Hungary, 31, 68, 70; in Poland, 119, 123, 125, 126, 133; in Russian Federation, 83, 85, 86, 94; in Slovenia, 160, 164, 165, 166

Forrest, R., 7

France, provision of social rented housing in, 8

Franek, J., 28, 29

FRG; see Germany, Federal Republic of, 41

Gaidar, 80

Gallagher, P., 25

GDR; see Germany, German Democratic Republic

Georgiev, G., 97–116

Germany, xii, 41–55, 169, 170, 178, 182; Federal Republic of (FRG) (decentralized government in, 53; housing system of, 42–43; social housing in, 2; Wohngeld [housing allowances], in FRG, 42, 47); German Democratic Republic (GDR), 24, 28, 175, 179, 182, 183, 184, 185 (centralization policy in, 30; failure of industry of, 42;

Germany: GDR (*continued*), housing
construction in, 32, 33; housing in,
43–45; land ownership in, 23;
prefabricated construction in, 33;
privatization of housing in, 45–55;
reaction to economic crisis, 31; rents in,
47; uprisings in, 26); provision of social
rented housing in, 8; reduction of public
expenditure as aim of privatization in, 7;
Reunification Treaty, Germany, 41;
Treuhandstalt, 42, 46; Unification
Treaty, 46, 47, 53
Gorbachev, M., 82
Grigorov, G., 104

Handiakova, A., 140
Harloe, M., 24, 27, 39
Heald, D., 6
Hegedüs, J., 15–38, 57–77, 115, 173, 179,
187
Heller, A., 16, 78
Hoffman, M., 23, 24, 103, 104, 107, 111,
112
Homeless Association, Poland, 126
Honecker, E., 44
Housing: associations, *see* Associations,
housing; cooperatives, *see* Cooperatives,
housing; costs and subsidies, Bulgaria,
103–105; demand, impact of
privatization on, Bulgaria, 114–115;
management, *see* Management, housing;
market, *see* Market, housing; models, *see*
Models, housing; organizations, in FRG,
tax status of, 42; ownership and tenure,
in Slovenia, 155–156; production,
efficiency gains from, 11–12; program,
"reduced-quality," in Hungary, 26;
property structure, in Russia, 83–87;
reform, 32; situation (in Bulgaria,
100–102; in Czechoslovakia, 137–143,
146–148; effect of privatization on, 12;
in Poland, 120–126; in Slovenia,
154–158); stock, 120, 121 (and
ownership, in Hungary, 59–61);
subsidies, as indirect wage, 18; supply,
impact of privatization on, in Bulgaria,
113–114; systems, *see* Systems, housing;
see also Allocation
Housing Act (1983), Hungary, 60; (1991)

Slovenia, 154, 158, 159, 160, 161, 162,
164, 165
Housing Councils, Slovenia, 154
Housing Reform (1983), Hungary, 68
Hungarian Democratic Forum, 58
Hungary, xii, 21, 24, 26, 28, 29, 30, 31, 36,
37, 57–77, 136, 171, 173, 175, 177, 178,
179, 181, 183, 186, 188; cooperative
apartments in, 27; decentralization of
housing construction in, 68–70;
economic situation in, 58–59; housing
construction in, 26, 33, 69 (and political
pressure, 26, 27; reduction of, 32);
housing privatization, local options for,
64–66; housing stock and ownership,
59–61; housing subsidies in, 35; housing
system of, 36–37; legal environment, and
housing, 58; National Housing Strategy,
63; nationalization of housing in, 24;
New Economic Mechanism in, 30; plan
bargaining in, 16; political environment,
and housing, 58; prefabricated
construction in, 33; privatization of
housing management in, 66–68; reaction
to economic crisis, 31; social impact, of
housing privatization in, 70–77; state-
owned housing in, private-sector
characteristics of, 3; uprisings in, 26

Income: in Bulgaria, 98, 104, 114, 115; in
Czechoslovakia, 147, 148; in Germany,
42; in Hungary, 76; regulation, 16; in
Russian Federation, 81, 87; in Slovenia,
163, 164
Inflation: in Britain, control of, 7; in
Bulgaria, 98, 108, 109, 113, 116; in
Czech Republic, 172, 175; in Eastern
Europe, 10, 32, 183, 185; in Hungary, 59,
60, 62, 136; in Poland, 125, 131, 132,
136; in Russian Federation, 80, 91, 93; in
Slovenia, 157
International Monetary Fund, 34

Jarzabek, Z., 126

Kaganova, O., 79–95
Kansky, K., 21, 22, 24, 25, 26, 28, 30
Kemeny, J., 9
Kemp, P., 186

Khaddari, J., 182
Khrushchev, N., 26, 90, 94
Kintrea, K., 1–13, 41–55, 169–189
Köhli, J., 41–55, 172
Koleva, M., 34, 104
Konaktchiev, D., 99
Konrád, G., 19
Kornai, J., 16, 21
Kos, 156
Kosareva, N., 79–95
Kotacka, L., 22
Kovacs, Z., 178
Kozinska, D., 131
Kozlowski, E., 23, 25, 30, 119–134, 173, 177, 182
Krastev, L., 107

Labor mobility, as aim of housing privatization, 10
Labour Party, Britain, 9
Land ownership, 23
Land rights, in Russia, 83
Land-use planning system, 3
Law of Local Self-management, 1990, Russian Federation, 84
Law on Certain Property Injustice Mitigation, Czechoslovakia, 136
Law on Privatized Housing, 1991, Russian Federation, 89
Law on Property, 1991, Russian Federation, 84
Law on Property Rights Modification and Arrangement of Property Titles in Cooperatives, Czechoslovakia, 145
Law on Regulation of Credit Relationships, 1989, Poland, 124
Law on the Modification of Land and Other Agricultural Property Ownership Relations, 1991, Czechoslovakia, 136
League of Communists, Slovenia, 152
Legal environment, as framework for housing, in Hungary, 58
Le Grand, J., 6
Liberal–Democratic Congress, Poland, 126
Liberal Democratic Party, Slovenia, 152
Liberal Party, Slovenia, 153
Lundqvist, L., 43

Macroeconomic reform, in Bulgaria, 98–99

Maintenance, 108, 115, 185; enterprises, in Eastern Europe, 179–181; housing (in Britain, 4; in Bulgaria, 99, 105; in Czechoslovakia, 140, 143, 145, 149; in GDR, 43, 50; in Germany, 179; in Hungary, 60, 63, 66–68, 76; in Russia, 82; in U.S.S.R., 82, 83, 93; in Poland, 122, 129, 131)
Management, housing, xi, 189; in Bulgaria, 105; in Czechoslovakia, 141–144; in Hungary, 57, 64, 67, 77; in Slovenia, 157, 158, 160
Manchin, R., 36
Mandič, S., 151–166, 172, 175, 180
Marcuse, P., 43, 44, 45
Mark, K., 57–77, 173, 187
Market, housing 18, 19, 21, 36, 37, 38, 39, 171, 175, 188; in Bulgaria, 97, 99, 105, 106, 107, 109–110, 113, 115, 116; in Czechoslovakia, 141; in Germany, 46, 47; in Hungary, 63; lack of, 18; in Poland, 129, 131, 132; provision, growth of, 12; in Russian Federation, 83, 87, 88, 91, 92; as secondary distributing mechanism, inequalities caused by, 36; transition to (elements of, 83; in Russia, 87, 92–93)
Markovic, 153
Márkus, G., 16
Marmot, A., 28, 32
Matras, H., 33
Mencinger, J., 158
Metropolitan Research Institute, 70
Michalovic, P., 30, 39, 135–149, 182
Mikelsons, M., 104
"Military economy of housing," 23
Mitigation Law (1990), Czechoslovakia, 141
Models, housing, xii, 37; "Anglo-Saxon," 9; East European, 57, 187, 188 (failure of, 15–38; and private sector, 18); "European," 9; in Poland, 120; self-management, in Slovenia, 151; socialist, 1, 8 (decision-making structure of, 37; in Eastern Europe, 15–38; economic performance of, 38; equity of, 37; in GDR, 43); Soviet, 23; welfare, 37; Western, 37; see also Systems, housing
Morton, H., 21

Moscow, xiii, 84, 85, 89, 90, 91, 92, 93, 94, 95, 179, 182, 186; housing market in, 92–93
Moscow City Council, 80
Motev, S., 97–116
Murie, A., 7
Musil, J., 19, 21

National Agency of Privatization, Bulgaria, 107
National Health Service, Britain, 6
National Housing Fund, Slovenia, 160, 161, 170
National Housing Strategy, Hungary, 63
Neo-fascists, in new *Länder* of Germany, 42
Netherlands: "European" housing model, 9; provision of social rented housing in, 8; reduction of public expenditure as aim of privatization in, 7
New Economic Mechanism, in Hungary, 30
Nomenclatura privatization, 80, 178
Novosibirsk, 90

OECD, 47
Omsk, 90

Panel construction; *see* Prefabricated housing construction
Papanek, F., 140
Peasant Party, Poland, 133
Pichler-Milanovitch, N., 187
Pilot projects, for privatization, in Germany, 49
Plan bargaining, 16
Planned economy, competition within, 18
Planning system, 21, 104, 132; economic (central, 16, 21; Soviet, 16); land-use, in Western countries, 3
Poland, xiii, 24, 28, 30, 119–134, 136, 171, 173, 175, 177, 178, 179, 182, 183, 185, 188; cooperative apartments in, 27; cooperative housing in, 28; housing construction in, 32, 33; housing privatization in, 126–128; housing situation in, 26, 120; investors in housing construction, 123; limitation of private housing construction in, 29; maximum space standards in, 25; number of dwellings completed in, 122; prefabricated construction in, 32, 33;

privatization model in, 129–132; proportion of housing stock purchased by tenant, 127; reaction to economic crisis, 31; "shock strategy" in, 35; terms of construction credits in, 126
Polányi, K., 16
Political environment, as framework for housing, in Hungary, 58
Political reform; in Czechoslovakia, 135–137; in Poland, 120–126; in Slovenia, 151–154
Popov, G., 91, 92
Prague, 187
Prefabricated housing construction, 29, 32, 33, 44, 50, 68, 94, 100, 107, 125, 139, 156, 180
Price reform, in Bulgaria, 108
Principles of Housing Policy Reform, Czechoslovakia, 141
Pritkov, A., 79–95
Private sector; in Bulgaria, 107–108; concessions to, 26–29; in FRG, 42; in Hungary, 66; model, 3; in Slovenia, 160; suppression of, 30
Privatization, housing, *passim*; of apartments, Czechoslovakia, 144–145; "coupon technique," Czechoslovakia, 136; definition, xii, 1, 2–7; as end in itself, 8; evaluation of, 1, 2, 10–13; "give-away," in Hungary, 57–77; impact of, xiii, 169, 182–187 (in Hungary, 70–77; long-term, 184–187; in Russia, 93–95; short-term, 183–184; in Slovenia, 162–166); mechanisms for, 64–70, 169, 175–182 (in Bulgaria, 107–113; cooperatives, 177; finance and exchange systems, 181–182; privatization of maintenance enterprises, 179–181; sale of state housing stock, 177–179); model, in Poland, 129–132; objectives of, xii, xiii, 1, 2, 7–10, 169–175 (in Bulgaria, 106–107; efficiency of housing system, 158, 171–173; in Germany, 45; reduction of public expenditure, 169–171); in Slovenia, 159–161; symbolic importance of, xii, 7, 9–10, 11, 173–175 (in GDR, 46); in Western countries, 1; wider goals of, 2
Property Law (1990), in Bulgaria, 109
Property ownership, private vs. personal, 24

Property rights, 23, 24, 25, 83, 84, 98, 103, 105, 112; in Bulgaria, 102–103; in Eastern Europe, 23–26; in Hungary, 60; restriction on, 35; in Russia, 83

Property Transfer Act (1991), Hungary, 63

Public expenditure; in Germany, 54; reduction of, xii (as aim of privatization, 2, 7–8, 169–171; in Bulgaria, 106; measurement of, 11)

Pusanov, A., 182

Raban, P., 34

Rabenhorst, C. S., 67

Ravicz, M., 104, 108, 114

Real estate brokerage, Moscow, 182

Real estate market, 26, 31, 78, 141, 144, 157; in Czechoslovakia, 144; in Slovenia, 157–158

Recentralization, 29; in Hungary, 77

Refuse collection, privatization of, in Britain, 4

Renaud, B., 99, 104

Rental Housing Act (1993), Hungary, 63, 64, 65, 66

Rent control, 21, 178; in GDR, 43

Restitution Acts (1991, 1992), Bulgaria, 112

Restitution of prewar property, 171, 174, 175, 176, 177, 184, 187; in Bulgaria, 97, 98, 107, 112, 112–113; in Czechoslovakia, 136, 141, 148; in Germany, 47, 48, 53; in Hungary, 59; as means of privatization, 176–177; in Slovenia, 152, 153, 154, 155, 161, 164

Reunification Treaty, Germany, 41

Right to Buy policy, United Kingdom, 63

Romania, 28; centralization policy in, 30; housing construction in, reduction of, 32; prefabricated construction in, 33; reaction to economic crisis, 31

Rop, T., 156

Russian Federation (RSFSR), xiii, 20, 79–95, 171, 176, 177, 178, 179, 180, 183, 185, 188, disintegration of Soviet Union, 79–81; economic changes in, 80–81; housing construction in, 81, 85; housing policy in, 81–83; housing privatization in, 88–90 (options for, 90–92); housing property structure in, 83–87; per capita income in, 81; privatization in (outlook for, 93–95);

transition to a housing market in, 87–88; see also Soviet Union

Sakharov, A., 79

Sárkány, C., 57–77

Saunders, P., 172

Savings, role of in privatization, 22, 27, 31, 45, 104, 109, 119, 147, 156, 163, 170, 182

Sawicki, S., 19

Schumann, W., 43, 44, 45

Scotland, 186

Self-managing Interest Communities for Housing, Slovenia, 152, 154, 155, 156

"Self-reorganization," 22

Shatalin, 83

"Shock strategy," in Poland, 35

Simunek, I., 140

Slovakia, xiii, 135, 139, 140, 141, 144, 145, 147, 175, 182; dwellings completed by KBV system in, 146

Slovenia, xiii, 151–166, 170, 171, 175, 176, 178, 179, 180, 182, 183, 185; aims of privatization, 158–159; housing construction, 156–157; housing management, 157; housing ownership and tenure, 155–156; housing situation in, 154–158; impact of housing privatization, 162–165; National Housing Fund, 160, 161, 170; political reform in, 151–154; private sector in, 160–161; privatization (of socially rented housing, 161); privatization of housing, 159–161; real estate market, 157–158; Self-managing Interest Communities for Housing, 154, 155, 156

Slovenian Folk Party, 153

Slovenian National Party, 153, 154

Small Enterprises Act, Hungary, 68

Smallholders Party, Hungary, 58

Smith, S. J., 186, 189

Social Act (1993), Hungary, 63

Social Democratic Party, Germany, 42

Social Democratic Party, Slovenia, 152

Socialist Party, Hungary, 58

Social security, 41, 140, 183

Social stability, in Germany, 42

Socialist housing model, 1, 17, 37; decision-making structure of, 37; economic performance of, 38; equity of, 37;

Socialist housing model (*continued*), and housing cooperatives, 27; and population mobility, 25; private sector in, 18; private vs. personal property in, 24; reform of, 34; social effects of, 35–37

Socialist system, economic and political, transformation of, 35

Socioeconomic developmental model, 22

Sofia, 109, 110

Soós, K., 16

Soviet Union, xi, 19, 22, 23, 26, 59, 79, 80, 81, 82, 83, 87; area of influence of, 15, 16; disintegration of, 79–81; economic model of, 16; housing construction in, 32; political, economic, and housing policy principles, 37; *see also* Russian Federation

Starovoitova, G., 79

Stoker, G., 6, 7, 175

St. Petersburg, xiii, 80, 81, 84, 85, 89, 90, 92, 93, 94, 182

Street cleaning, privatization of, in Britain, 4

Struyk, R., 64, 71, 79–95, 173, 179, 187

Subsidies (*passim*): allocation of, 34 (control over, 18, 21, 28, 30; to private sector, 32); central state, in Hungary, 60; housing, 35 (in Bulgaria, 108–109; as indirect wage, 18; state, 34); reduction of, 31, 33

Subsidy system, housing, 33

Sullivan, D., 66

Sweden: "European" housing model of, 9; social expenditure in, 9

Sykora, L., 187

System building techniques; *see* Prefabricated panel construction

Systems, housing; in Bulgaria, 100; development of, xii; East European (impact of privatization on, xiii; outlook for, 169); Federal Republic of (FRG), 42–43; ideological pressure on, 35; market-oriented, movement toward, 2; promotion of efficient, xii, 7, 8–9; socialist, model of, xii; *see also* models, housing

Szelényi, I., 19, 35, 36, 37, 154

Szolnok, 67

Tax provisions, 3, 4, 6, 7, 42, 49, 68, 92, 105, 108, 109, 119, 133, 147, 166

Telgarsky, J., 94, 95

Tenure structure, in Bulgaria, 102–103

Thatcher, M., 63

Tosics, I., 15–38, 57–77, 115, 173, 179, 187

Trade Unions for the Protection of Society, Poland, 126

Transfer of State Property Act (1991), Hungary, 58

Treuhandstalt, 42, 46

Tsenkova, S., 97–116

Ulbrich, R., 42

Unemployment: benefit, 7 (in Germany, 41); in Bulgaria, 98, 114; in Czechoslovakia, 136; in Eastern Europe, 7, 10, 185; in Germany, 42, 183; in Hungary, 59; in new *Länder* of Germany, 42; in Slovenia, 162

Unification Treaty; in Germany, 46, 47, 53

Union of Democratic Forces, Bulgaria, 98, 106

Union of Real Policy, Poland, 126

United Nations, 103

United States, 181, 185, 186; "Anglo-Saxon" housing model of, 9; condominium law in, 188; GDP of, 41; loan subsidy programs in, 3; privatization of public housing agencies in, 5

Urban Institute, 70

USAID, xi, 67, 77; promotion of "Anglo-Saxon" housing model by, 9

Villani, K., 62

"Voice" option, for achieving housing goals, 20–21, 37

Von Beyme, K., 22

Voucher programs, 10

Warsaw, 133

Welfare redistribution, 36

Wohngeld [housing allowances], in FRG, 42, 47

World Bank, 34, 133; promotion of "Anglo-Saxon" housing model by, 9

Wullkopf, U., 42

Yavlinski, 83

Yeltsin, B., 79, 80

Young, S., 5

Yugoslavia, xi, xiii, 15, 59, 154, 180

Zaleska, E., 132

About the Editors and Contributors

EDITORS

DAVID CLAPHAM is Professor of Housing and Director of the Centre for Housing Management and Development at the University of Wales, Cardiff. Until 1994 he was a Reader at the Centre for Housing Research and Urban Studies at the University of Glasgow. David holds a PhD in Social Policy from the London School of Economics and is coauthor of *Housing Co-operatives in Britain* (1992), among many other books and articles.

JÓZSEF HEGEDÜS is Managing Director (with Iván Tosics) of the Metropolitan Research Institute in Budapest, Hungary, which they established in 1989. He holds a PhD in Sociology and previously held a post at the Hungarian Academy of Sciences. József has twice spent time as a visiting scholar at universities in the United States. He is coorganizer of the Eastern European Work Group of the European Network for Housing Research and has written widely in both Hungarian and English on housing and urban questions.

KEITH KINTREA is Lecturer in Housing and leader of the Urban Regeneration Research Group at the Centre for Housing Research and Urban Studies at the University of Glasgow, Scotland. Keith holds degrees in Geography and Urban Planning and has published widely in housing and urban regeneration. He is coauthor of the book *Housing Co-operatives in Britain* (1992).

IVÁN TOSICS is Managing Director (with József Hegedüs) of the Metropolitan Research Institute in Budapest, Hungary. Previously he worked as a researcher in the Institute for Building Economy and Organization in Budapest. He is a member of the Coordination Committee of the European Network for Housing Research and coorganizer of the Eastern European Working Group. Iván has carried out a wide range of research on housing policy and urban development on behalf of Hungarian and international institutions, including extensive work in USAID's Technical Assistance Program.

HELEN KAY is a Research Fellow at the University of Dundee, Scotland. Previously she worked as a researcher at the University of Glasgow, at the Scottish Office, and at the University of Exeter.

CONTRIBUTORS

MIKHAIL BEREZIN is General Director of AUREC Ltd., a private consultancy in St. Petersburg, Russia. He is an urban planner by training and his main interests are in urban modeling and urban development.

DIMITAR DIMITROV is a housing expert at the National Center for Regional Development and Housing Policy in Sofia, Bulgaria. He was educated in Geography and Philosophy and previously worked at the Complex Research Institute for Territorial and Urban Planning in Sofia.

GEORGE GEORGIEV is Manager of the Bulgarian Housing Association and also holds a post in housing policy at the National Center for Regional Development and Housing Policy in Sofia. He was educated in Sofia and in Moscow and holds a PhD in Urban Planning and Housing.

OLGA KAGANOVA is a Research Associate with the Urban Institute in Washington, DC. She holds a PhD in Mathematics and a qualification in Real Estate. Before moving to the United States, she founded a private consultancy firm in St. Petersburg, Russia, specializing in housing and urban research.

JÖRG KÖHLI was formerly with the Bundesministerium für Raumordnung, Bauwesen und Städtebau in Bonn, Germany. He has contributed to this book in a private capacity.

NODEZDHA KOSAREVA is Deputy Director of the USAID Shelter Cooperation Programme in Moscow, Russia. She has a PhD in Economics and formerly worked as a Senior Researcher in Housing Economics at the Institute of Economic Forecasting, U.S.S.R. Academy of Sciences.

EDWARD KOZLOWSKI currently works as a housing specialist and office manager of the Housing Finance Project of the Government of Poland and the World Bank in Warsaw. He is an economist and previously worked as a researcher and manager in institutes specializing in housing, physical planning, and the environment.

SRNA MANDIČ is a researcher at the Institute for Social Sciences at the University of Ljubljana, Slovenia. She is a Sociologist whose main interest is in housing, and she has written several papers for English-language journals and books, as well as being widely published in Slovenia.

KATHARINE MARK is a Research Associate with the Urban Institute in Washington, DC. She holds a Master's degree in Economics from the London School of Economics and specializes in housing finance and housing subsidies.

PETER MICHALOVIC is Director of VIP (Výskum Investície Poradenstvo), a private research institute in Bratislava, Slovakia. He was educated in Sociology and Business Studies in Prague and Bratislava and has written widely on housing and urban policy and housing finance.

STOICHO MOTEV is Deputy Head of the Housing Policy Division at the national Center for Regional Development and Housing Policy in Sofia, Bulgaria. He was educated at the Higher Institute of Architecture and Construction in Sofia. His main research interests are in the voluntary housing sector and affordable housing.

ANDREY PRITKOV is a Consultant with NEVA–VST, a private firm in St. Petersburg, Russia. His main interests are in real estate investments. He is a former St. Petersburg City Council representative.

CSILLA SÁRKÁNY is a Researcher at the Metropolitan Research Institute in Budapest. She was educated as an architect and urban planner and specializes in urban development and rehabilitation, and housing management.

RAYMOND STRUYK is a Senior Fellow at the Urban Institute in Washington, DC. His previous post was with the U.S. Department of Housing and Urban Development. He is an economist, holding a PhD from Washington University and has worked for considerable periods in East Europe and the former Soviet Union. His most recent publication is *Economic Restructuring in the Former Soviet Bloc: The Case of Housing*.

SASHA TSENKOVA is a researcher at the Department of Geography at the University of Toronto, Canada. She holds a Master's degree in Urban Studies from the University of Sussex, U.K., and a PhD in Architecture from the Technical University of Prague, Czech Republic.

ISBN 0-313-27214-X

90000>

EAN

9 780313 272141

HARDCOVER BAR CODE